VETERANS
VOICES

Personal accounts of wartime experiences

Compiled by

John Nixon

First published in 2020

© John Nixon

ISBN: 978-1-913898-03-8

Book interior Design by Russell Holden
www.pixeltweakspublications.com

Pixel Tweaks Publications
SELF-PUBLISHING MADE SIMPLE

www.johnnixonauthor.co.uk

Foreword

For some 28 years now I have been gathering the personal stories of airmen and women who were trained at or served at the three South Lakeland airfields, RAF Millom, RAF WALNEY and RAF Cark. Some of these stories appear in my previous books; however, this present compilation is comprised of new and unpublished material. Having reached the 75th anniversary of VE Day, it is timely surely that the voices of our RAF veterans are heard in their own words. Within these pages you will find accounts of service life which range from the humorous to the tragic, some short and some much more comprehensive but all given first hand. Like our first world war Tommies, their number is marching quietly into history having helped bring about that significant and hard-won victory over Hitlers Nazis in 1945.

Listen then as our veterans recount for you bombing raids over occupied territory, being shot down and evading the Germans, ditching in the Irish sea, surviving crashes in the mountains, breaking into the stations' mess bar and drinking the beer but also the horrors of Auschwitz and the death march.

Many of these stories will remain with you long after you put down this book, this material was placed in my hands by some of the most courageous, generous and kind-natured people it has ever been my good fortune to meet, and it is timely on this 75th anniversary of the end of WWII that their voices be heard.

For Bill and Ross,two of RAF Milloms finest!
also for John, Joanne, Jack, Avalon and Alfie.

MRS IRENE ASHLEY (NÉE DELANEY)

<u>Author's Note:</u>

Irene and her pal Jenny were among the first few members of the WAAF I was able to contact. It was with their stalwart enthusiasm and that of their comrades that I was able to establish a network of contacts between the RAF Millom Ladies, my thanks go out to them.

I joined the WAAF when I was twenty one years old. I was a very shy young girl and found my first posting to Millom very strange at first. When I first arrived there I spend a good while working in the Officers Mess and as a result I met a few more of the WAAF's and made a friend or two. Four of us were very friendly, myself and Jenny, Violet and a girl called Anne. My very first job before I started my official duties was to take the Group Captains dog for a good long walk around the station.

I became good pals with Jenny and although we were both really shy we began going to a few dances in Millom with a girl called Edie who actually lived in the town and it was fun, I loved dancing! I had a regular dancing partner who asked me to go to the pictures with him and I persuaded Jenny to come along and partner his pal Wilf. It was the start of a great friendship and they became married! Sadly my pal Jenny passed away a while ago but Wilf and I are still in touch. I was a drummer in the WAAF band and played at church parades and ceremonial occasions. I enjoyed it a great deal. I also got asked to fill in one night when someone dropped out of the pantomime which was being staged, what a laugh! Someone was whispering instructions from the wings and at one point the cast were all going one way and me another; I think they thought I was the comedian of the show! It has been great to be able to have re-lived some of those times through the RAF Millom reunions.

Irene Ashley (née Delaney) 2007

MR JIM ANDERSON – 1941

I was posted to RAF Millom as a fitter from February 1941 until, I think October 1941. Of my time there I have few clear memories save for the kindness of the local people and the atrocious weather! When I arrived we had nowhere to sleep and had to improvise a bed out of tables, benches etc. Also we had no proper toilet facilities and the station looked like a building site. I do recall remarking to a pal at the time that it did not seem to me to be a good idea to build an airfield right next to a mountain either!

The aircraft most in use at the unit were Blackburn Bothas, the engines of which would consume oil as fast as it could be poured into them. The Botha's were terribly underpowered and prone to engine seizures making them hugely unpopular with the crews. I believe that there were many crashes involving these aircraft whilst I was at the station but the two that stick in my mind were one which dived straight into the ground down in the south of England somewhere (all the crew killed) and one which landed on a sand bank out at sea, in this instance I think the crew all survived. I remember little else after than the fact that our station C/O was a man called Wray, a Group Captain I think, he was well liked by us all, a true gentleman.

Jim Anderson 2000

MR JIM ALLAM – 1941

I was stationed at RAF Millom, No.BGS then 2.AOS from 3rd February 1941 to 13th September 1941 as LAC Allam J. G77238.

During my time at Millom I was a Flight Rigger until I left to be retrained as a Fitter IIA at Innsworth Lane via a conversion course. I think my intake must have arrived in the stations very early days because I recall quite clearly that the place was barely complete and living conditions very basic. I also very well remember the Blackburn Botha which was the unit's main aircraft with Fairey Battles for target towing. The Botha was a most unstable and unpopular aircraft and I remember a Botha, (L6446) crashing near Dernarglar Loch. I had just left Millom that day to travel on leave to my home in Ayrshire in Scotland. My mates at Millom in those days were Ray Aldroyd of Ayrshire, Edgar Eustace of East Kilbride and Jimmy Adams who were all flight riggers like myself, Jimmy Adams went on to be a pilot but sadly did not survive the war.

I must say that my time at Millom was a pleasant one and I found the local people very hospitable. I have fond memories of expeditions into the Lake District and of weekends spent in Barrow-in-Furness. Myself and my three pals used to stay with a nice lady called Mrs Sexton at 14 Hall Street Barrow. On Saturday 10th May 1941 we discovered that her house had been completely destroyed in the bombing which had taken place that week. We never saw Mrs Sexton or her family again but were pleased to hear that they had been in a deep shelter at the time of the bombing and had survived uninjured.

Jim Allen 1998

MR BOB BRYANT – 1941

In early 1941 I transferred from the Royal Engineers following being evacuated from Dunkirk, to the RAF I was posted to No.2 A.O.S. RAF Millom around October 1941. I do remember clearly, however, that we were training in the infamous Blackburn Botha.

For my first flight I was astonished to find that the Bothas pilot was Sgt Sansom who had been a junior pupil when I was a prefect at Newport High School. I asked him "is this thing safe?", his reply was less than reassuring, he said "if we lose an engine don't wait for me!"

Training with us at the time was a chap called (I think) Ziggerman, we all knew him as Ziggy of course. Ziggy was a solicitor in civilian life and I recall he was from the Swansea area. One night in November poor Ziggy was aboard a Botha for a night navigational exercise when it suffered an engine failure on take-off and crashed into the sea. Luckily the aircraft came to rest in very shallow water. The Botha had a long corridor past the bomb bay to the escape hatch and it took poor Ziggy some time to get out. All crew escaped with minor knocks and scrapes, it could have been much worse. None of our flight lost anyone but I recall a crew from Walney being killed whilst I was at Millom. I saw Ziggy a few days afterwards and asked him if he was any worse. He said that things were not too bad but during his escape his fluorescence dye pack had activated and that he had swallowed large quantities of the bright green dye with the result that his urine remained an alarming colour for some time!! As you will have gathered, the Botha was not popular.

Bob Bryant 1996

MR NEVILLE BEALE – 1944

I trained at RAF Millom in November 1944. I was part of Meteorological Air Observers Course no.16. The course was a month long and was my first experience of service flying. I had originally joined up at Lords Cricket ground in 1943 but was taken off aircrew training on eyesight grounds until I had spend about a year on ground staff duties, including Meteorological Observations in France, Belgium and Holland early in 1944. From there I went to A.C.R.C. at Paignton and got my Sgts Stripes before being posted to Millom in Cumberland for basic navigation training and cross country exercises, all flown in Avro Ansons.

I can recall flying up the Cumberland coast with F/Lt "mad" Kelly at the controls when the ack-ack guns near St Bees opened up on a test firing exercise. With a grim look on his face he remarked how unpleasant the "real thing" was. On another occasion I managed to get us lost somewhere over the midlands and our pilot had to call for help from "Darky", the scheme designed to help distressed and lost aircraft fix their position. As it turned out we found our way home safely, and I can only imagine the lives this system must have saved during the war years.

After our course at RAF Millom it was off to an Operational Training Unit for us all, (most of us went to Turnberry) and then on to join our squadrons in early 1945. I was posted to 518 squadron on the Isle of Tiree in the Inner Hebrides, which is of course still a Met station and a small civil airport. However, the crew I trained with were posted to Gibraltar the lucky so and so's! 518 stayed on Tiree until the autumn of 1945 when we moved to Aldergrove. A year later it was merged into 202 squadron which survives to this day I believe as an air/sea rescue helicopter unit.

Neville Beale 1997

MR JIM P. BAILEY – 1944 – 1945

Although I have lived in Canada for many years my home was originally in Sedgley, West Midlands. I joined the RAF in 1939 and from then to 1941 I was stationed at St Eval with 217 Squadron. I completed two years operational duty with coastal command before being posted to Canada as part of the RAF's overseas training scheme, I liked Canada a great deal. I returned to England in 1944 and was posted to RAF Millom in Cumberland where I found myself actively involved in mountain rescue. After all these years my memory fails me but I do remember the Jeep I used to drive to the crash sites and the sick quarters ambulance, which was really rigged more for rescue work than an ambulance, I think it was a Humber vehicle. I used to live part time in the station sick quarters as part of my call out duties and I recall that a Sgt Hans Pick was in charge of rescue operations, he was Swiss, and an expert mountaineer. Whilst I was not a climber by any means I accompanied the team on most of their call outs.

I remember two crashes in particular, one was a heavy bomber which crashed in an area where mining was taking place, it may have been a place called Coniston, and all the crew were killed. I had found a way to get closer to the site by Jeep and met the stretcher parties coming down with the bodies.

The second was around Christmas 1944 and was a plane which had been missing for a week or more. The plane had crashed into Black Crags on Black Combe and all the crew had been killed outright. I was given the job of driving a Canadian Officer up to the crash to take photographs of the wreck. We set off from a small village at the foot of the mountain and I was able to take the Jeep right to the summit. When we arrived at the edge of the crags we both remarked that ten or fifteen more feet of altitude would have taken the plane safely over the mountain.

Many of the crashes were like this one and were a result of pilots descending to get below bad weather. I was posted overseas from Millom and returned to England just after VJ day. From then on I have lived in Canada with my family – being first of all a policeman till 1970 when I joined the Royal Canadian Mounted Police. I retired from the "mounties" in 1983 and went on to be a Justice of the Peace until I reached the age of 70.

I returned to Canada to enjoy the freedom and the way of life I wanted to pursue, I have hunted game and fished many of Canada's lakes and rivers and our country remains yet, a hunter's paradise.

Jim Bailey 1994

MS MOLLY BAKER WAAF 1942 – 1943

I am afraid that the information I can remember for you is not very important from a flying point of view. I do recall that the under training Observers did a lot of night flying in Ansons and I was nearly knocked off my bicycle one night by an Anson when going on night duty at the watch tower!! I say watch tower because there was no Flying Control just a single storey wooden building that connected with the operations room and Met Office. When signalling by Aldis lamp to the aircraft was necessary, on-one bothered to use the door but leapt in and out of the windows, it was quicker!

The radios in use were rather ancient TR9's, VHF was still top secret at this point, so secret in fact that in the radio school at Cranwell, we were not permitted to take notes on VHF equipment but had to memorise it, seems crazy to think of it now! The TR9's had a reception distance of about 50 miles ground to ground and just about the same when used ground to air. The TR stood for Transmitter / Receiver combined but as you can image RT contact was zero once our aircraft were outside the 50 mile range. The U/T Observers came to the watch tower to be issued with "crystals" (a bit like a square pin electric plug) each one of different kilocycles, so that the aircraft could keep WT contact. These crystals were issued, usually about 5 or 6, in a Cadbury's Cocoa tin (!!!) and were to be handed in again immediately the crews returned. On reflection, it may have been the Wireless Ops who collected the crystals, rather than the observers. Anyway, we used to plot the cross country route on a large Perspex covered wall map with chino graph pencils. One of the routes covered Millom / Calf of Man / Point of Ayre / Chicken Rock (fascinating name!) still can't find it BUT I know it's out there somewhere!

I was the first WAAF RT Operator posted to Millom, the others being male and I recall the look of utter horror on the signals officers face when I reported in. He was a pre-war regular who was obviously against the idea of women in the services. He spun the dials on a TR9 all over the place, and ordered me to tune it in. I had just completed my radio course at Cranwell and stood there frozen to the spot, I hadn't a clue, and everything I had learned was blotted out through sheer terror. However, I must have done it correctly, as I was told that I was now a member of "B" Watch. The male operators were absolutely marvellous and looked after me like Dutch Uncles. Not too long afterwards another WAAF operator was posted in which helped things a lot.

In those days there were no headphones or telephone type microphones. The "mike" (a large unwieldy thing like a pre-war BBC microphone) hung from the ceiling on an elastic cable about as thick as a finger. You had to be careful after using it since it was liable to bounce up to the ceiling and come back with a clunk on one's head.

Heating consisted of a very small pot bellied stove in one corner, and since the winter of 1942 was a cold one, night duty was a miserable affair at times. The usual routine was to go to the airmen's mess for dinner at about 02:00hrs but I soon gave that up. I wasn't afraid of the dark, being a country girl, but the long walk to the mess (before we were issued with bicycles) all alone between great big hangar doors which clanked in a most sinister manner was too much. Anyway, the food was pretty foul. The answer was to buy Bovril which was unrationed, get bread and margarine from the mess at the previous meal, toast the bread on our small pot bellied stove and cover it with Bovril. To this day I am inordinately fond of Bovril on toast!

Favourite pubs for the RAF and us WAAFs were the Plough in Millom and the Miners Arms at Silecroft, bicycles being our usual method of transport, we used to call the Plough Inn the "Pluff". There was a wonderful pantomime at Christmas 1942 staged by station staff called "Ali Babs and the Four Tea Leafs", the theme of which, if I remember rightly, was how to steal coke from the fuel dump without being caught, the fuel dump being behind wire. One of the airmen played at part of the C/O, wearing a GRP/CPT's hat but in a uniform that had tapes on it all the way down from the waist to the shoulder. There was also a fancy dress dance that Christmas, a great success.

The WAAF's were billeted in huts of 30 but at least the ablutions were attached to the end of the hut, and not a few hundred yards away as on some stations. That winter of 1942 was so cold that we slept wearing dressing gowns, socks and anything else we could find to keep warm, with our greatcoats spread over our blankets.

I don't think we had a NAFFI at Millom but I am certain we had a Salvation Army canteen, and that's about all I can recall. I can't even remember how long I spent at Millom exactly but it couldn't have been much more than six months because fairly early in 1943 I was posted to Bomber Command in Yorkshire. I remember Millom as being a happy station, and was there a hill near the airfield called the Black Mount?

Molly Baker 1993

MR JOHN BRANDON – 1943

I was in fact posted to RAF Millom for only a short period

during which I trained as an Observer, or Navigator. I was fortunate to be at the unit during the five months of that summer and with the passage of time have only one clear but amusing (I hope) memory from my time there. I was a keen swimmer as a young man and the beach at the end of one runway shelved gently and bathing was good. I had a lovely swim one day and the very next day a young WAAF who had seen me marching off with my towel asked me if I would teach her to swim. So on the next fine afternoon, off we went to the beach and I began by demonstrating the basic breaststroke and in due course when she was lying in the water with my hand supporting her as she "attempted" to swim. It was soon obvious that she was a good swimmer and that the swimming lesson was an excuse! Soon we were swimming happily around quite some way off the beach when we heard the sound of an approaching aircraft overhead. Next thing, smoke bombs began to fall into the sea close by! We were offshore very close to the bombing target but I had thought the range was not in use that afternoon. The target they were aiming for was moored very near us and when my companion began to scream and panic I told her to make for the floating target. We got there and clung to the side until the Anson had finished its bombing runs, I was right – it was the safest place to be! Not one bomb came near us! Honest!!

John Brandon 1992

MR REG BEINT, RAF MILLOM – 1943

I had just reached my 21st birthday when I was posted into RAF Millom in Cumberland. I was posted to No. OAFU for flying training as a navigator – having begun my training in South Africa. Sadly I have no photographs from my time at Millom, but I do recall that one of the unit's fitters took some photos of the station aircraft and left them at the chemists shop in Millom to be developed whilst he went on leave. He had asked his pal to pick them up for him but the chemist upon seeing the pictures, thought that they might be of use to the enemy and contacted the units C/O. When the poor chap arrived back from leave he received a very severe reprimand and his photos were of course confiscated.

On the side of the airfield was a set of small circular rails upon which a bogey travelled. Mounted on this bogey was a wooden aeroplane target which was used by the air gunners to practice deflection firing from a turret, which was positioned at a central point. I recall also that at Silecroft there was a large concrete arrow pointing to the offshore bombing range and further inland, two range plotting towers. Further up the coast at St Bees Head was the site of the stations airfield identity beacon. This beacon flashed a letter of identity which was changed every night. We would only be told the letter if detailed for night flying on that night. The only other thing I can recall is the two three storey buildings used for bomb aiming practice. The pupil would position himself over a bomb sight up on the top storey and below him would be a slowly moving picture of an industrial landscape. Instead of bombs one would drop marker pellets onto the landscape and it was a surprisingly good primer for the real thing.

Reg Beint 1992

MR E. BARCLAY – 1943

I was stationed at Haverigg airfield in 1943 as a trainee navigator, I remember that our training was done in Avro Ansons and that we had to wind the undercarriage up and down manually!

My first trip was on a map reading exercise from Millom to Whitehaven, then to Stranraer and back to Millom. All went well but on our return trip the pilot, who was a Canadian called Sgt Tobias, took us down to zero feet and flew home along the coast at that height which was interesting to say the least! Pilots, by the way were forbidden to engage in low flying unless ordered to do so as an exercise.

I also remember night flying exercises and being careful to avoid Black Combe on our return. Also in addition there were a lot of Barrage Balloons over Barrow-in-Furness to protect the town and one had to steer well away from those too. I do believe at some point that an aircraft from Walney did crash into them.

I lost a pal whilst at Haverigg, his name was Harry Sapsed and he was killed when his Anson crashed into the sea, he is buried in the local church yard.

I completed my training at various RAF stations in England and finally flew a Wellington bomber to India via Iraq and Iran finishing my RAF career by completing a tour of operations against the Japanese over Burma, but that however, is another story!

Mr E Barclay 1993

JOHN BROWN, 1943 – 1944

My first recollection is of arriving in Millom on a cold dark and wet evening with about twenty other air bombers and being directed to a Nissan hut which was to be our billet for the next six weeks. The hut had the usual iron stove for heating which was not only unlit, but its two coke buckets were empty as well. Having noticed the coke compound on the way in, half a dozen of us set off with the two buckets and soon found the wire fence of the coke compound.

Having only just completed a 'Commando Course' at Whitley Bay we soon scaled the fence and having filled our buckets we were almost back over the wire when suddenly the door of a small hut inside the compound burst open and out rushed a raving airman flashing a torch, unfortunately in our direction and shouting 'alright'! I've heard you buggers, I'll 'ave you'! I might only be an A.C.I but I'm bloody I/C coke'! We managed to make good our escape before being spotted; he's probably still looking for us!

The Ansons at Millom certainly earned their keep, they were flown all around the clock with little respite and into winds which really made them puff and pant as illustrated by the following anecdote – now and again after being briefed for a map reading exercise we were told to pick up a pigeon in a cage from the Corporal I/C pigeons and take it up in the Anson and then on landing return it to the pigeon keeper. This seemed rather pointless to me as well as being a nuisance as we had to keep an eye on the bird in case it passed out through lack of oxygen. If we saw that it was flat on its back we had to tell the pilot who would then lose a bit of altitude to bring the bird round again. So I asked the Corporal why we were not instructed to release the pigeon at some stage during the exercise, he said, *"until recently the pupils were releasing the birds during the flight, usually on the 'back to base' leg of the trip about 50 or 60 miles from Millom, however, the releasing was stopped because the pigeons were getting back to base before the Ansons and it was thought that the crews might be de-moralised"*!!

My final clear recollection of RAF Millom is of a day time simulated bombing exercise. This exercise was carried out by two bomb aimers in each Anson. I was detailed to fly with Stan Walters who was one of my best pals, we both got "washed off" the pilots course in Canada where upon we both re mustered to the trade of 'Bomb Aimer' and we stayed together for the rest of our training until being posted to operational bomber squadrons. Stan went to 44 squadron at Dunholme Lodge and I went to 467 at Waddington.

Stan and I were always trying to 'get one over' on each other, a sort of anything you can do, I can do better, relationship, though Stan was far more dedicated to the art than I was. And so we mustered for briefing and each pair of pupils were allocated a pilot except for Stan and myself. It appeared that our pilot had reported sick, not because he was due to fly with us two, I hasten to add!! Anyway, the station C/O happened to be attending the briefing and promptly volunteered to be our pilot, this took the smile off our faces to say the very least! So off we went, Stan completed his exercise, I have forgotten what it was, and I moved over into his position over the bomb hatch and over the intercom. I told the C/O the target I had been instructed to 'bomb', with the camera of course, (white bomb tit, NOT the red one) the C/O said *"forget that' your target is Blackpool Tower, when we get there I will line the aircraft up and you will direct me on the bomb run right over the top of the tower and when you bring me your photographs tomorrow morning all I will expect to see will be a square of iron work being the base of the tower superimposed by a dot which will be the pin point top of the spire."* Swallowing hard I replied, *"very good sir"!!* Stan's job on the way to the target was to go to the rear of the Anson and level the camera, which he did. On arrival over Blackpool the C/O gave me an excellent run up to the tower and took great care in responding to my directions and I pressed the bomb tit as the tower passed straight down the sighting wires of the MK9 bomb sight. I was absolutely delighted and next morning could not get around to the photographic section quick enough to see the results. The corporal handed my photographs to me, I noticed he had a bit of a smirk on his face and when I looked at them I could not believe what I saw. Each photo was a picture of the tail wheel of the Anson! I was horror stricken and realised immediately that Stan; knowing that I had to show the photos to the C/O had accidentally on purpose forgotten to tighten up the camera adjusting screws. Consequently the vibration of the Anson had tilted the camera backwards, needless to say, I 'forgot' to visit the C/O and fortunately heard no more about it. I also managed to re-fly the exercise and get a good result, albeit without Stan.

On the subject of Stan Walters, following his posting to 44 squadron his brave actions won him the Conspicuous Gallantry Medal, second only to the VC. Unfortunately not long after that he was shot down and finished up in a German P.O.W. camp. I myself was shot down on the 19th July 1944 over Revigny in occupied N.E, France but managed to join up with the local resistance group and got back in the UK in September 1944.

A big horse's head and two small saucepans

Following the invasion of France along the Normandy Coast by the Allied forces on the 6th June 1944(D-Day), the British 2nd. Army, under General Montgomery, had been held in check by the Germans for the past six weeks at their bridgehead near Caen. Although most of the railway junctions in northern France had been attacked by the Allied Air Forces there was still one small rail junction, on the outskirts of the town of Revigny in the meuse Department of north eastern France, that the Germans were using to supply their defending troops in Caen with reinforcements, so it was now vitally important for this junction to be put out of use.

Two attempts had been made to bomb this target by No.1 Group of Bomber Command - one on the 12/13th July 1944 and the other on the 14/15th July 1944 - both attacks failed because the rail junction could not be definitely identified. With two attempts having been made within two days even the Germans twigged that Revigny was down for a clobbering. And it came to pass during the morning of the 18th July 1944 that the Lancaster bomber squadrons of No. 5 Group were duly informed that the railway junction at Revigny was their target for tonight.

In the afternoon a coded radio message *"nous allons rendre visite a Maginot ce soir"* was broadcast to warn the Revineens of our coming (not to mention the Germans!) - Andre Maginot was the French Minister for War who gave his name to the defence line and was born and lived in Revigny.

At 22.45 hours that night the first aircraft of a force of one hundred and ten Lancaster Bombers took off from their airfields in Lincolnshire bound for Revigny. Three 'Lancs' had to return early for technical reasons but the remainder pressed on, only to be met by the whole of the German night-fighter force based in north eastern France and as a result twenty-four Lancasters failed to return - a loss rate of 22.5%. This was probably one of the highest loss rates for attacks carried out by 100 plus aircraft that was suffered by Bomber Command during WWII. Of the 169 aircrew casualties, 129 were killed 11 were captured and 29 evaded capture. The attack was successful and included a direct hit on an ammunition train which was blown to bits. Three days after this raid the British 2nd. Army broke out from the Caen bridgehead and the liberation of France got underway.

I was the bomb aimer in our Lancaster bomber crew, we flew with No. 467 (RAAF) squadron in No. 5 Group based at Waddington two miles south of the city of Lincoln, almost in the shadow of Lincoln cathedral, four of the crew were Australians and three were RAF. Also based at Waddington was our sister squadron No. 463 (RAAF).

Ten crews were selected from each of our two squadrons to join up with the other ninety crews from 5 Group on this third attempt to bomb Revigny railway junction.

Some of the crews on this attack had only just returned a few hours earlier from a 1,000 bomber daylight raid on the German troops in and around Caen so they were a bit short of sleep. Our crew should have been on that trip but 36 hours earlier we had taken part in a 5 Group attack on a railway junction at Nevers due south of Paris, unfortunately during this attack, a bomb had been dropped through the roof of Nevers cathedral and all the returning crews were grounded until the guilty one was identified - it wasn't our crew, we had hit the target.

Boarding our Lancaster - which has been likened to a herd of sheep going up a ramp into an abattoir - we took off from Waddington at 23.01 hours with a full load of bombs (mostly delayed action) and full petrol tanks. Having successfully negotiated the two main hazards - getting airborne before running out of runway and having enough height to clear Lincoln cathedral - we set a southerly course for Folkestone, nearing the French coast the German searchlights were already probing the night sky and it was not long before the coastal 'flak' started coming up to welcome us, so I despatched a couple of packets of 'window' (aluminium strips) in acknowledgement. We reached our last turning point without encountering any serious trouble but had been aware of quite a lot of night-fighter activity going on around us by the streams of tracer bullets that pierced the darkness from time to time.

Turning north east we headed for the 'waiting area' about 10 miles south west of Revigny and arrived at 01.25 a.m. The waiting area was where the main force Lancasters had to circle whilst the target was being marked by the pathfinder squadrons. 5 Group had its own pathfinder squadrons - one of which was 617 (Dambuster) squadron -who practised a low level system of target marking, this was carried out by pathfinder Lancasters dropping a series of extremely bright flares over the target area to provide illumination for a squadron of Mosquito aircraft to fly in very low to identify and accurately mark the target with coloured Target Indicator flares. In overall control of the target marking was a Master Controller who, among other names, was called the M.C.(on this attack he was Wing Cmdr. Jeudwine flying in a P38 Lightning). When the M.C. was satisfied that the target had been accurately marked he would call in the main force Lancasters to commence bombing and also indicate which colour T.I. flare the bomb aimer should aim at.

We had an excellent navigator in our crew (Eric Brownhall), who seldom looked out of the Lancaster to check his lair' position, he relied on his dead reckoning navigation and occasionally on my map reading to get us to the right place at the right time and this night was no exception. All was quiet as we started our orbiting in the waiting area, when suddenly the sky above us was ablaze with German chandelier flares which not only ruined our night vision but also made the silhouette of our Lancaster stand out like a sore thumb making us, and all the other main force Lancasters orbiting in the waiting area, sitting targets for the German night-fighters that were now flying in the darkness below. To make matters worse, the waiting area was quite close to a large German night-fighter base at St.Dizier and also a high powered radar installation. Due to the ground haze and the smallness of the rail junction our pathfinders were having great difficulty in finding the target and getting the target indicators correctly positioned required the patience of a brain surgeon. We were kept circling for about fifteen minutes - it seemed like a couple of hours - and during this time 4 Lancasters and one German night-fighter spiralled down in flames, our eyes had to be everywhere not only looking for fighters but with 180/90 Lancasters turning, weaving and diving about within such a small area it was an absolute nightmare. Adding to the confusion the usual strict radio silence went by the board as frustrated pilots exchanged 'heated' words with the M.C. - I had never heard so many rude interpretations of the 'pull your so and so finger out' cliché. At about 1.45 a.m. the M.C. called the depleted main force in to commence bombing and there was one almighty scramble to get out of that 'hells kitchen' with 'Lancs' coming from all directions heading for the map reference point from where we were to commence our bombing run to the target.

Switching my duty from front gunner to that of bomb aimer, I took up my prone position in the nose of our 'Lanc' and made the necessary wind speed and direction adjustments to my mark 14 bomb sight and checked that all bombs were fused and ready to go, the pilot told me we were now on the correct heading and I soon saw in the distance the red coloured target indicator that the M.C. had told us to aim at. It was most important to aim for the M.C's coloured T.I. as our camera was loaded with coloured film and started to operate when the 'bomb tit' was pressed releasing at the same time a one million candle power flare to enable a strip of photographs to be taken of what you aimed at and where your bombs would approximately fall, if the resulting photograph showed you had aimed at the wrong colour T.I. and your bombs were off target you were in for a right rollocking from the squadron C.O.

The Lancaster is an easy target for night-fighters whilst on the 'bomb run' as the pilot has to keep a straight and level course until the bombs are released and the camera work has been completed. As I was looking through the graticule on my bomb sight and giving directional instructions to the pilot that would get the Lancaster to track exactly over the T.I., I noticed a stream of tracer bullets going over the top of our starboard wing, not hearing any reports of damage from the crew over the 'intercom' I thought it was our lucky night and carried on concentrating on getting the aircraft lined up. It is a cardinal sin for the bomb aimer not to have the aircraft in the right position to release the bombs by the time the T.I. is reached because the pilot then has to turn the 'Lanc' in the bomber stream and make a fresh circuit which not only incurs the risk of collision but also the danger of running the gauntlet of the 'flak' and night-fighters whilst doing a second bombing run, if you do over-shoot you can never ask the pilot to go back a bit!

Having asked the pilot to open the bomb doors and with the T.I. perfectly sighted I released the bombs, just as I had finished reporting to the pilot 'bombs gone steady for camera' our Lancaster suddenly shuddered from the nose to the tail section, it sounded and felt as though the Lancaster was being attacked by a dozen pneumatic road drills and almost immediately our starboard wing burst into flames. I realised at once that we were being 'shot up' by a night-fighter fitted with vertical firing canons flying underneath the wing and firing incendiary canon shells into the wing petrol tanks inside which there was still about 700 gallons of 100 octane petrol - the Germans called this type of attack "schrage musik". My bombing compartment in the nose of the 'Lanc' was flood-lit in bright orange light from the blazing wing and although I could not see the fighter it was either a JU 88 or an Me110. The pilot and flight engineer were pressing buttons and switching switches left right and centre to try to quell the flames - I was told later that it was a fantastic sight from the ground!

In the meantime, as the front escape hatch cover was underneath the mattress I was laying on I started to clear the exit in readiness for a hasty departure and also clipped my parachute on in the process. By now the wing was a blazing inferno so I put my hand close to the ring pull plunger that would release the escape hatch cover so as not to waste any time when the order to 'jump' came. Almost at once the pilot gave the order to 'bale out'. Just as I was about to slip my finger through the ring pull most of the blazing starboard wing broke off, the Lancaster immediately whipped over on to its back and went into a very tight spin. I was thrown against the side of the bomb hatch and was pinned there by the force of gravity completely unable to move, the tightness of the spin was caused because the two Rolls Royce Merlin engines on the remaining port wing were still running flat out.

It was always difficult to escape from a Lancaster once it got into a spin, on this occasion it was almost impossible because being a French target we had to bomb from low level to reduce the risk of harming the local French residents. Our bombing height over Revigny was 7,500 feet and having already lost a considerable amount of height I knew my time had come, and began to think of the sadness and grief I would cause my mother and father when they received the dreaded telegram advising them of my demise and also the 'thank you' letter that most air crew types left in their rooms to be forwarded on to their wives/ parents by the squadron C.O. should the occasion arise.

Suddenly I was hearing whistling noises. I opened my eyes and literally saw stars but these were for real. I quickly realised that our Lancaster had blown up and I was falling through the air with pieces of the 'Lanc' whistling passed me. Remembering having clipped on my parachute I glanced down to my chest and saw that it was still there, so losing no time, I pulled the rip cord and the 'chute' shot out passed my face and my free fall descent was abruptly reduced.

It is difficult to describe my feelings at that moment as it all happened so quickly, but it was an amazing change of experience from having been trapped in a blazing Lancaster spinning down to certain death one moment then to find yourself dangling on the end of a parachute in the cool night air the next moment.

I was a bit peeved hearing the fading engine noises of the still airborne Lancasters making their way back to Lincolnshire where the crews would soon be tucking into a nice bacon and egg breakfast, then I looked down to see where or on what I was going to land - I had a fear that if ever I had to 'bale out' I would probably land on a church spire or slip down a factory chimney like a rat up a pipe, but all I could see was ground haze. I then started thinking about the fates of my six crew mates and wondered if they had also got blown out of the 'Lanc' .

My thoughts were soon scrambled as I hit the ground with a heck of a wallop and a sharp pain shot through my left foot as the top bone fractured - I finished up lying on my back gazing up at the night sky.

The thought that there would probably be a crowd of German soldiers out looking for shot down aviators soon brought me to a sitting position from where I could see I was in a field bordered by hedgerows with a copse of trees behind me but thankfully, no Germans. Remembering the advice given to me during 'escape and evasion' lectures at No. 17 OTU Silverstone, I quickly released my parachute and painfully got to my feet, gathered up my 'chute' and hid it deep inside the nearest hedgerow, then I scrambled over the hedge and landed on a cart track, looking to my right I could see that the track was completely blocked by the tail unit of our Lancaster so I turned left and started a very painful walk. Shortly I arrived at a minor road and approaching from my left I heard footsteps, from the cover of a bush I spotted a shortish stocky man pushing a bicycle, he did not look like a German but I was wondering why he was out at this time of morning (just after 2 am) pushing a bike - I found out later that he worked for an electricity company and was out checking to see if any damage had been done to the overhead cables resulting from our attack on Revigny.

I approached him warily just in case he turned nasty, and having been told that the best way to make contact with one of the 'escape line' organisations was through the resistance network via the local priest, I asked him where the local church was - hoping he could speak English - but he replied in French which I could not understand then pointed to the sky and then at me, he seemed quite friendly so I nodded. Just then I heard some foot steps behind me, looking around I saw it was our flight engineer Bill Johnson(a Liverpudlian with the dry sense of humour to match), on asking him if he was alright he replied 'Yes but don't make me laugh I get a pain in my chest every time 1 breathe'. Getting his cigarettes out and offering one to the Frenchman Bill said 'who's your mate'?

The Frenchman, whose name was Georges Mandet, was very pleased with his cigarette and turning his bike around he beckoned us to follow him. After a while we came to a cottage and he showed us inside and into the living room and departed. Looking around the room I saw six wooden boxes dispersed along the bottom of the walls, taking a closer look I saw that there was a very young child asleep in each one. Having been told that the Germans had been known to execute whole families for helping shot down aircrew to escape we decided to leave. Just then Georges reappeared with his wife who was carrying a tray of food, she was quite disappointed when we shook our heads but eventually we managed to convey to them that we wanted directions to the nearest church. Georges showed us where it was on a local map and insisted on Bill taking the map with him. We thanked them both and left.

The church was in the village of Laheycourt which was half a mile up the road from the cottage to a 'T' junction and then turn right for a further half mile. As we were nearing the 'T' junction we heard the noise of a motor cycle coming from our left and getting louder, so we got down into a ditch at the side of the road from where we had a view of the junction. The motorcycle duly arrived and stopped, the rider was a German soldier who, after having a good look around, turned and sped off in the direction from whence he had come.

We arrived in Laheycourt about 3 a.m. and walked as quietly as we could so as not to alert any Germans that might be on duty. Passing the first house our footsteps started a dog barking and as we walked on through the village dog after dog joined in shattering the silence of the night. Not knowing the French term for 'belt up' there was nothing we could do to stop the barking so we pressed on until we found the church at the far end of the village.

The church was situated some thirty yards off the road and a pathway led to quite an impressive entrance, unlatching the large door we walked into absolute pitch darkness. I knocked against the end of a bench type row of seats and the loud grating noise it made scraping the floor echoed around the church and aroused several hundred birds roosting on the roof rafters. It felt and sounded as if all hell had been let loose as they all took off and started screaming and swooping around us, it was quite frightening in the dark especially as our nerves were still a bit jangled from being blown out of our 'Lanc'.

We decided to sit down on the floor and rest by the slightly open front door and wait for the dawn and the priest to arrive, eventually the dawn turned up but the priest didn't, Bill said not to worry he will come along shortly for morning mass. As the village began to come to life we kept a sharp eye on the road whilst discussing our chances of getting back to the U.K. via the organised escape lines, not knowing that, as from the 6th. June 1944(D Day) they had all ceased to operate -I can't re-call the RAF telling us about that!

We watched and waited all the morning but not a soul came near us so during the afternoon, with the help of our escape maps, we plotted a route to the south of France and, via Spain down to Gibraltar. Fortunately, although my left foot was quite swollen it did not hurt too much when I walked with it, but the thought of walking all the way to Gibraltar was a bit daunting. As we were folding up the local map that Georges had given to us we saw that his name and address had been written on it, so not wanting to get him into dire trouble had we been caught with it, Bill tucked it behind the font that stood against a side wall of the church. The decision to go south rather than west towards

Normandy - which was over two hundred miles away - was because that area would have been packed with German troops and seeking help from the French people would have put them at risk

By now it was about 5 p.m. we were sitting in a store room at the altar end of the church, it had a window we could escape through if necessary and a view of the church entrance door. Suddenly we heard the entrance door latch click, taking a discreet look we saw an elderly lady (perhaps into her 80's) enter the church and make her way to the lady chapel to pray, by the time she had finished we had decided to ask her if she could contact the priest for us. Not wanting to frighten her, we made sure that she was aware of our presence, as we approached her she turned towards us with a lovely smile on her face and far from being frightened it seemed as if she was expecting us to be there. We told her we were RAF aviators and with the aid of our French/English phrase card from our escape kit she appeared to understand that we wanted to speak with the priest. Nodding her head and making gestures with her hands for us to stay in the church she departed.

We kept a close watch on the road in case she had gone off to tell the Germans of our presence although we had not seen one all day. After twenty minutes or so a young girl of some seventeen years and a boy of a similar age came up the pathway and into the church, she was a very pretty girl with long blond hair and she spoke perfect English, greeting us with a delightful smile she said good evening and we shook hands, then she told us that her name was Antoinette and gave me a bottle of champagne, the boy told us his name (which I have forgotten) and gave Bill a bar of chocolate. We explained the reason for our being in the church and asked if it was possible to speak to the priest. Accepting our story without question Antoinette said that the priest would arrive at 7.30 p.m. to hold a choir practice after which we could meet him and she would act as interpreter. We thanked them both for their help and presents then, with another flashing smile from Antoinette which nearly made me drop the bottle of champagne, they left us. Bill was not so smitten by Antoinette as he was some years older than me, was already married and two months previously, I had chased all around RAF Winthorpe (1661 Heavy Conv. Unit) to tell him that he had just become the father of a bonny bouncing boy, so I thought that I was in with a chance!

We retired to the store room and tucked into the 'champers' and chocolate and by the time the choir arrived and started singing we were quite 'merry' and making sure that the door was shut, we joined in with them. Eventually the singing stopped and at last we got our audience with the priest (Roger Guillemin) accompanied by Antoinette and her boy friend. Through Antoinette we asked the priest if he could put us in touch with a local resistance group, he was, understandably, very non-committal but said that we could stay in his house for the time being. Antoinette then told us that there were no German troops based in the village but motorised patrols arrived from time to time.

The five of us set off back through the village, it was still light and for Bill and me it was a case of re-tracing our steps of the previous night and, although no dogs were barking their heads off, we felt rather conspicuous strolling along in enemy occupied France wearing RAF battledress uniforms. On reaching the priest's house we were ushered in and introduced to his house-keeper who had prepared a meal for all of us. We had just started eating when there was a knock at the front door, after peeping through the window the priest opened the door but soon shut it again, on his return Antoinette explained to us that the caller was a man from the village who had seen us walking to the house and had recognised our RAF uniforms (No. 1. Fighter squadron RAF had been based in a near-by field in 1940) thinking that the village had been liberated he was enquiring about the celebration arrangements! After the meal Antoinette wished us 'bon chance' and departed with her 'boy friend'. After we had helped with clearing the meal table the priest made a sign to us that indicated it was time for sleep and as he pulled back a curtain along the living room wall a recess was revealed in which was a double bed, he bid us 'bonne nuit' then left and within minutes we were fast asleep.

After a good nights' sleep, we were up and dressed by 9 a.m. next morning (20th July 1944) and the house-keeper gave us some bread and coffee during which we noticed that there were a couple of young children running around, Bill tipped me a wink which did not mean much to me as my religious knowledge at that time was restricted to knowing how to get out of attending Sunday morning church parades, anyway, we both took off our thick white woolly air crew sweaters and gave them to the house-keeper to unpick and re-knit into clothes for the kiddies as clothing was in short supply.

Around mid-day the 'town crier arrived outside the house banging a drum that was strapped to his waist, he then started shouting the news that there were some aviators on the loose in the area and offering a cash reward for any information that would lead to their capture, threatening dire consequences to anyone giving them help. Bill suggested that I should go out to ask him to move up the road a bit, fortunately no one paid any attention to him and he soon tucked his drum-sticks into his belt and shoved off.

We did not see the priest until the evening meal when he told us that we would receive a visit to-morrow. Sure enough, just after our mid-day meal, an old car with a large cylinder attached to the back pulled up outside the house and a rather unkempt typical French man quickly got out followed by the driver a burly tough looking character whose name was Colombo. As they entered the house the priest made himself scarce leaving us alone with the two 'ruffians'. After giving us a thorough visual check over the smaller man, who turned out to be Louis Chenu the leader of the Revigny resistance group and could speak very little English, asked us some questions about the air raid on the railway junction, making sure at the same time that we could see the large revolver that was poking out of the top of his trousers. He was soon satisfied that we were genuine RAF types and not German 'plants', we all shook hands then Colombo went out to get the car started which was quite a noisy and complicated procedure - lots of bangs and clouds of smoke as it was propelled by burning charcoal, then Louis signalled for us to follow him to the car and after pushing us into the back seats he jumped into the front seat as the car chugged off leaving us no time to thank the priest for his help and hospitality. We learned later that Colombo was a 'general dealer' by trade and among other things sorted and disposed of scrap metal for the Germans who in turn, granted him a permit to drive vehicles to conduct his business. He also used this facility to offset his 'collaboration with the enemy' activities by providing transport for Louis Chenu's resistance group as and when required.

We trundled along some narrow roads for about ten minutes then turned on to the main road into Revigny where two nights previously we had bombed the rail junction. On entering the town we caught our first daylight glimpse of German soldiers walking about, they all looked about seven feet tall and three feet wide, Very soon the car pulled up outside the end elevation of a house (No. 1. Avenue de Paris) and after a quick glance around Louis got out telling us to follow, he quickly opened a small door at the side of two large wooden entrance gates leaving Colombo to drive off trailing a cloud of black smoke. We found ourselves inside a large courtyard facing the front of the house where a couple of days earlier, the Germans had parked a large tracked troop carrier vehicle all day under guard because, due to the continuous day light attacks by our 'tank busting' fighters on German military vehicles, they could only travel mainly at night.

Entering the house we followed Louis up a flight of stairs at the top of which was a kitchen on the left and a living room on the right, going into the living room we were met by a group of lads among whom we quickly spotted our Australian rear gunner, Fred White. Fred had been 'standing in' for our regular gunner Bob Rust who had gone sick, and had only just returned a few hours earlier from a 1,000 bomber day light attack on Caen having flown with his own crew in the squadron's famous old 'Lanc' S for sugar - 137 trips (now on display in the RAF museum at Hendon). We were delighted to see him but saddened to hear the news that our pilot Dave Beharrie, wireless operator Keith Schott and mid-upper gunner 'Buck' Rogers (all Australians) had been killed, and that our navigator, Eric Brownhall, had broken a few bones making a heavy parachute landing was unable to do a 'runner' got captured and was made prisoner of war by the Germans. Also in the group were two other RAF types, Dick Greenwood who was a bomb aimer (103 squadron) and sole survivor from his crew of seven shot down on the first Revigny attack, and Denys Teare another bomb aimer (also 103 squadron) shot down returning from a raid on Mannheim in September, 143 - his book 'Evader' tells the story.

Denys, having been in France for the last ten months or so, with no English being spoken, was quite good at speaking French but had difficulty in stringing two words of English together. Being a 'gen man' I immediately thought that he might be a German 'Plant' but dare not mention my suspicion in the hearing of the French lads for the fear that they might put a bullet through his head. Denys, in his broken English, introduced Bill and me to the French lads starting with Louis and his younger brother Jean.

Louis was slightly built and had a rather serious disposition was twenty six and Jean was seventeen years of age and a 'happy go lucky' sort of lad, they owned the house, their parents having died in 1940 and Louis, being a German P.O.W at that time, was allowed to go home to look after his brother and carry on the family business of furniture making. The other four tough looking lads - all in their 'twenties' were deserters from a branch of the French police - an armed unit - called the Vichy Guarde Mobile and they had brought their rifles and ammunition with them. There had also been two escaped Russian P.O.W's in residence but on hearing that Bill and I were coming to join the group decided to leave and take their chance hiding in the forest a few miles away. Denys told us that there were several hundreds of German troops billeted in Revigny, some in barracks and others in neighbouring houses together with a Gestapo unit, so a continuous watch had to be kept on the road outside the courtyard gates from the upstairs living room window. The civil population of Revigny was about 2,500 but because the German troops were concentrated in a smaller area they appeared to outnumber the French people.

Denys then took us on a tour of the house so that we would know which way to run should the need arise. The main escape route out of the house was by way of a ladder into the loft and through a hatch door onto the sloping roof slates, you then had to leap across a six feet gap - with a twenty five feet drop on to concrete - and land on the sloping roof of the house next door!, I said to Denys you would never clear that gap from a standing start on a slope, he said you would if you had a German behind you with a machine gun!. I soon latched on to the train of thought that it would be better to kill yourself rather than give the Germans the pleasure. On the ground floor at the far end of the house was an adjoining out-house, inside was a nanny goat and her recently born kid, noticing that the nanny goat's body was wrapped in sacking Bill said to Denys, that's the first time I have seen a nanny goat wearing a 'bra'. Denys then explained to us that food was in very short supply especially now we had arrived, so the nannie's milk was used to make cheese to supplement the daily ration of potatoes and to make sure the kid goat did not guzzle all the milk, he kept the nanny - affectionately known as Ninette - wrapped up. He did add that after milking Ninette each morning he always let the baby have the last few sucks before replacing the covers.

The first week in Revigny passed quite quickly because we had to get used to a totally different way of life to that of the RAF One of the French lads called Ta Ta 'acted' as cook, he was thick set dark and swarthy, never washed and wore P.T. shorts, socks and heavy shoes, each morning he got us to peel about fifteen potatoes which he boiled in a couple of old saucepans on a rather ancient iron cooker range for our mid-day meal, keeping the peelings to stew up into soup for supper, with each meal we had a small measured piece of bread and a glass of red 'plonk' - pinched from the depot next door- which took the enamel off of your teeth. An occasional extra was a small piece of goat's cheese full of maggots. Beyond the courtyard was a large garden with a working well containing clean ice cold water and at the far end was a cluster of apple trees that reached to a fairly high hedge which also housed the back entrance gate, on the other side of the hedge was the railway junction we had bombed a few nights ago. As about five hundred of the eight hundred bombs that had been dropped were delayed action bombs they kept on exploding well into August, The lavatory was situated in the garden by the courtyard, it was of a rusty corrugated iron sheeting construction about three feet square by six feet high covering a hole in the ground and when you opened the door you wished you hadn't! To answer my calls of nature I preferred to take a garden spade and retire to the far end of the garden under the shade of the trees. This practice was a bit hazardous at times when having just got settled in a somewhat undignified position, you would hear the crunch of heavy boots on the gravel track the other side of the hedge and then see a couple of German helmets and rifle barrels go bobbing along the top of the hedge as a railway patrol strolled past, just having regained your composure the ground by the rail track, some fifty yards away, would heave up as one of our 1,000 lb. delayed action bombs detonated sending tons of earth, bricks and rubble high into the air to come cascading down all around your ears etc. at which point you decide to beat a hasty retreat back to the house before our cannon firing fighter aircraft arrived to make their regular daily low level sweeps to rake the rail junction with their missiles.

On the Monday morning of our first week in Revigny the town crier arrived across the road to shout a proclamation for all the men in the town to report to the railway station with shovels, Louis and Jean duly obeyed the order and were instructed to fill in bomb craters around the junction. They were there for three days and never managed to throw one shovel full of earth in the right direction, at which point the Germans realised that fresh craters were appearing faster than the original ones were being filled so they sent all the shovellers back home again.

At set times during the day the 'illegal' radio would be switched on to receive the BBC London news broadcasts and the coded messages in French that were given out for the resistance area commanders. Our resistance group was controlled by a 'Captain V, his real name was Jean Jeukens and he operated from Bar-le-Duc which was about eight miles east of Revigny where he owned a chemist shop. In between his dispensing work he advised and passed on instructions to the resistance groups in his area. From the news and information we got from the radio we were able to plot the Allied armies progress each day on a large wall map in the living room and although their daily advance was rather slow at this time (last week of July) the messages from London to the numerous resistance commanders were coming through thick and fast - I used to go to sleep most nights with the sound of 'ello Pierre' ringing in my ears.

Outside the house on the main road there seemed to be a lot more German troops marching about, their singing was very good and well orchestrated - much better than our troops renditions of 'it's the wrong way to tickle Mary'. We got to know some of their songs and used to sing along with them especially 'Lilli Marlene'. Louis had taken notes of our service numbers, names and ranks for transmission by radio to London so the thought that our relatives would soon be informed that we were alive and well - albeit half starved - was quite comforting, I did ask Louis if there was any chance of getting a flight back to England in a returning Lysander aircraft after unloading it's 'parcels' he shook his head and said 'no but perhaps by submarine', as the nearest stretch of water was the river Rhine I quickly abandoned any thoughts of a speedy return to the U.K.

On Saturday, 27th. July, Denys told us some good news and some bad news, the good news was that three more RAF types had been located in a forest about ten miles away and Louis had agreed to take them in, the bad news was that our already meagre daily potato ration would have to be reduced to feed them! It was just as well that the two Russians had departed to the forest a few days earlier else we would have finished up eating each other. A plea was made by the RAF lads that a 'no vacancies' notice be put up outside the front gate. The three new lads duly arrived but this time they were delivered by a smartly dressed middle aged man wearing glasses - as it was safer not to know people by name we called him 'Specs', his real name was Luccioni. He owned a soft drinks business and similarly to Colombo he traded with the Germans who gave him a permit to drive and own vehicles which enabled him to enjoy quite a high standard of living, but now that the Allied armies were getting a firm foothold in Normandy he started offering the use of his vehicles to Louis hoping that the risk he was taking of being shot by the Germans if he got caught, would off-set his collaboration activities with the enemy.

The three new recruits were named Redmond (Red) Banville a Canadian pilot, Harry (Nicky) Nicholson flight engineer and Ken Hoyle mid-upper gunner, they were all members of the same crew and flew with No. 166 squadron, all three had received burns to their arms and hands when their Lancaster got shot down in flames during the first attack on Revigny (12/13th July). 'Specs' got to know of their hide-out in a nearby forest and volunteered to collect them with the help of Colombo. Fortunately, a young French medical student had been tending their burns during the two weeks they were hiding in the forest and he bravely agreed to continue to treat them in Revigny at grave risk to his life. I met up with him again in 1992 during a visit to the Revigny area, he was then a retired doctor and it was a great pleasure to see and speak with him again after nearly fifty years. Although the treatment the three lads required was very painful for them, and they needed a bit of helpful restraining whilst the burnt tissue was removed, within a few days new skin started to form around their wounds and the healing process quickly followed.

Our ration strength had now increased to 14 - 6 Frenchmen and 8 RAF types and very shortly the reduced potato ration got a bit too much for our 'cook' Ta Ta, he got caught 'nicking' an extra measure of bread and was immediately relieved of his cooking duties. Spotting the chance of getting an extra piece of bread, I volunteered to take over. RAF wise, I was fully qualified for the job as I had never cooked anything before in my life. The first day I managed quite well but the following morning I heard some excited chatter coming from the kitchen so in my capacity as 'cook' I went to investigate. As I entered the kitchen there was Denys and all the French lads gathered around the meal table in the middle of which was an enormous head of a horse with large brown eyes that followed you about. The poor old nag had had a massive heart attack as it trotted along a nearby road pulling a cart driven by a German soldier, by the time it had been officially pronounced dead a crowd of local people had gathered equipped with cleavers and choppers etc. including two of our French comrades who must have arrived late as all that was left was the head.

After the excitement had cooled down a bit I said to Denys, hold on a minute how am I going to cook that big horse's head I've only got two small saucepans! There followed a lot of typical French discussion and arm waving as to how it could be reduced to small pieces suitable for cooking in a small saucepan. I suggested that we took it across the courtyard to Louis's workshop and put it on the circular saw set at No. 8 and get a nice lot of rashers! Louis was a furniture maker by trade and the mere thought of using his prized circular saw for that purpose made him screw up his unshaven face until he looked like a hedgehog. Eventually, some hand saws, choppers and various other tools were produced and after a couple of hours of blood sweat and tears the kitchen table and most of the floor was liberally covered with pieces of meat and bits of bone. From some of this I made a nice horse head stew a la carte avec spud, the rest was put into preserving jars which were then placed in a dust bin half full of water and boiled up on a bonfire in the garden for future use.

During the first week of August the Allied Armies were making good progress in north west France especially the U.S. 3rd. Army led by General George (blood and guts) Paton, there also appeared to be more urgency in the movement of German troops through Revigny. We were quite excited one day when Louis received a message from 'Captain X' in Bar-le-Duc informing him that a German troop train would be passing through Revigny junction just after midnight via a stretch of rail line that had been temporarily repaired and that he had got the job of derailing it. In due course some large heavy wrenches and spanners were delivered to the house and it was decided that the six French lads would carry out the task as they knew where to go and how to do the job. The timing of starting and finishing their task was crucial, so they carefully worked out that by leaving the house soon after dark they would arrive at the pre- determined location with enough time in hand to dislodge a section of rail and be well on their way back to base before the train, hopefully, went sprawling.

Just before departing the saboteurs blackened their faces and hands with charcoal and then, heavily laden with tools, they made their way up to the back garden gate and disappeared into the night. The next five hours or so were going to be extremely dangerous for the French lads and also quite a bit hairy for us eight RAF types left behind because if anything went wrong during the mission and they had got caught or killed by the Germans the house could be easily traced and raided by the Gestapo. So we kept very quiet and extra alert just in case the worst should happen to gain as much time as possible to get away should a convoy of black Mercedes cars suddenly arrive.

It seemed a very long wait but as dawn began to break

the lads came lumbering down the garden and into the house, they were absolutely shattered but delighted to report 'mission completed,' They were too excited to sleep so we all kept a close watch on the approaches to the house and eagerly awaited news of what had happened to the troop train. Mid-way through the morning Louis 'heard news' that a troop train had been de-railed with many German casualties. The French lads were cock-a-hoop at their success and we all hoped that the non arrival of the train at its destination may have saved the lives of many Allied army lads. The Germans, of course, would be making a strong effort to find the resistance unit that was responsible for wrecking the train, so for the next few days we took our watch duties much more seriously.

With so many German troops billeted in the town, 'Captain X' and Denys had for some time been trying to convince Louis that having fourteen young lads living in a house that was officially listed as having only two occupants was asking for trouble, but Louis would not listen, however, one afternoon he did agree to go with Denys to the nearby forest and look for a suitable hiding place for some of us. While they were gone Red Banville, who was the only officer amongst us and could speak French - albeit with a strong Canadian accent - asked us RAF types to stand by the front gate ready to let him in as he was going out into the road to ask a German soldier for a light for his cigarette and off he went. We watched quite anxiously through cracks in the wooden gate as we saw a German offer up his cigarette to Red, after two or three puffs Red nodded his thanks to the soldier who then went on his way, Red did not come back immediately and seemed to be waiting for the German soldier to get out of sight, when he did return he told us that he had 'hung about a bit' to make sure the German had not suspected anything because as he was getting his cigarette to light he noticed that the Canadian brand name printed on it "Lucky Strike" was in full view of the German's gaze! We certainly let him know that we were far from happy about the un-necessary risk he had taken as it put us all in jeopardy and I am sure the lesson was learned.

It was now about the middle of August and the U.S. 3rd.Army had altered course from thrusting south and was now heading east in our direction although still some two hundred miles away meanwhile, the argument between Louis and Denys about moving some of us to the forest was still un-resolved when Louis received another message from 'Captain X' saying that a delivery of arms and ammunition was going to be made during the night, they would arrive by air packed inside containers and dropped by parachute into a certain field near the village of Laheycourt and it was his job to collect and conceal the containers. Denys told us that eight lads would be required to locate and collect the containers, he was going with the six French lads so one more collector was needed. Red Banville and his two crew mates were ruled out because their burns had not completely healed, so it was down to Fred, Dick, Bill or me. As none of us could speak French I suggested that two of us should join the party and I would like to be one of them. After having a few words with Louis - in French of course - Denys was quite adamant that only one could go This puzzled me a bit as I could see no valid reason for only wanting one of us and it re-aroused my suspicions as to Denys's true identity - was he setting a trap?. I think my feelings were picked up by the other RAF lads but of course nobody dared to say anything in case the French lads latched on to what we were talking about. Anyway nobody volunteered to go and Denys got quite angry saying that we were all cowards where upon Fred, the Australian, who had got friendly with Denys - in the nicest possible way of course

- said that he would go. I was a bit miffed at this because I wanted to go and had now missed out, but I didn't fret for long as after Denys had had another chat with Louis he came across to me and said "you can come as well Ginger".

This was good news for me because not only was I going to take an active part in the work of the resistance but also by taking two of us it dispelled the slight suspicion I still had about the possibility of Denys being a German 'plant', I now saw him as a very courageous lad who, having decided that he had no chance of getting back to the U.K. via the organised escape lines had bravely thrown in his lot with the French Resistance to help liberate France - he tells his remarkable story in his book "Evader".

It was just getting dark as the nine of us set off for the 'dropping field' near Laheycourt, I felt sorry for the five lads left behind because in addition to the ever present threat of the house being raided by the Gestapo was now the unknown danger of the possibility of us getting caught and leaving them 'sitting ducks' for the Germans. It was a fine night with quite a chill in the air, we walked in single file and complete silence, armed with revolvers, Louis and Denys were up front followed by Jean, Fred and me, then bringing up the rear were the four deserters from the M.G.R. Although it seemed ages, it wasn't long before we were clear of the built up area of Revigny and having crossed two or three fields we were approaching a road along which we had to walk for a short distance to gain entry into the next field when, in the distance to our right we heard the engine noise of a heavy vehicle coming along the road. There was no cover that we could take advantage of so we laid face down in the short grass, the vehicle lumbered passed us about twenty yards away fortunately we were not spotted and as the noise died away we got up and continued on our way - the vehicle was probably a troop carrier on its way to the front line.

We had no more trouble until we got to the edge of a field where there was a five feet drop to the road below, which lead on to a small iron bridge that we had to cross, all the lads jumped down quite safely but unfortunately when I landed on the road an agonising pain shot through my left foot which I had damaged on my parachute landing, our rendezvous was still about two miles away so I had to ignore the pain and press on regardless. After skirting the small village of Brabant-le-Roi we eventually reached the 'dropping zone' which, strangely enough, was the field where the main part of our Lancaster had crashed killing three of the seven members of our crew. The wreckage had been removed (probably by Colombo) but there was still plenty of evidence of the crash remaining which brought back sad memories for Fred and me of that traumatic experience, so we moved off to the area which had been designated for the drop so that we would be ready to flash torch signals to attract the pilot of the expected supply dropping aircraft. We would know how many containers had been dropped as each one would have the same number painted on it i.e. 8, 10 or 12.

The first two hours passed quite quickly as we were all listening intently hoping to be the first one to hear the noise of a low flying aeroplane approaching, but as time went by and nothing was heard our previous high spirits, together with the night air temperature, began to drop. We had to run around to keep the shivers at bay. At 4 a.m. the sky was still silent so we sadly decided to make our way back to Revigny which was about six miles away, we needed to be well on our way before dawn to reduce the chance of being caught especially as the curfew still had two hours to go. Except for the pain in my foot all went well until about two miles from home we reached the place where we had to take to the road for a short distance, walking in single file along the side of the road we had just reached the start of a cornfield which we had to cross via a narrow pathway, when, through the half light, we glimpsed an armed German foot patrol coming towards us on our side of the road about forty yards away, in a flash, like one man, all nine of us disappeared into the cornfield - luckily the corn was at its highest growth and gave us good cover. We ran as fast as we could with our heads well down but were still expecting a hail of bullets and a few hand grenades to come whizzing up our backsides. For some reason fright I suppose - I didn't feel any pain in my left foot until we broke cover on the other side of the field, not one shot had been fired and, glancing back over our shoulders we saw that the Germans were not even chasing us! It may be that they had not seen us or didn't fancy a fight; anyway we did not hang around to find out and continued on our way back to base without further incident but were very disappointed that our mission had been in vain.

We had a nice surprise during the morning when Colombo stopped his car outside the house, as Louis carefully opened the front gate Colombo quickly thrust a skinny wild piglet under his arm saying that it had been killed by a German shooting party the previous day, he got back into his car and drove off. It wasn't easy cutting it up into small pieces for boiling as it was all bristle and gristle but when I mixed it with our bland midday meal of potato soup it made it quite tasty and all the lads thought Christmas had come a bit early this year. The next day however I had my first cooking disaster when trying to make use of some flour 'Specs' had slipped us a few days earlier, I thought I'd give the lads a treat and make an apple tart, so I put a few handfuls of flour into a bowl and adding some water I mixed it into a nice lump of dough. Finding a baking tin and a glass jar I flattened the dough and lined the tin with it. One of the French lads cut a couple of apples into segments and spread them around the tart casing in ever decreasing circles like the petals of a flower, it looked so appetising I thought I had found my vocation at last. I popped it into the old iron oven and waited eagerly for it to cook, after about an hour I took the tart out of the oven and it really looked delicious. Explaining to the French lads that it was an old English custom for the cook to have the first piece, I plunged the point of a large kitchen knife into the centre of the tart piercing the apple with consummate ease but could get no further; my dough casing had turned into concrete! It was quite amazing to see the change of expression on those thirteen hungry mouth watering faces and for me it was a bit scary as the French lads always kept their loaded rifles close to hand, but after shrugging my shoulders like a typical Frenchman they dispersed without a shot being fired.

It was now the middle of August and despite the pressure that was being put on Louis by 'Captain V, not to mention the local Gendarmerie and Denys, to disperse his 'band of brothers' to a safer location he was still adamant that we should all stay together in his house with him in charge. It all came to a head on the 15th August when, after having some quite heated words with Louis, Denys announced that he and Fred were going to move out at nightfall. By the time they were ready to leave tempers had cooled down and there were hugs and handshakes all round and, with wishes of bon chance Denys and Fred made their way up to the garden gate and disappeared into the night. The next morning Louis must have made some hasty arrangements -nothing to do with my apple tart I would add - because about 10 a.m. 'Specs arrived and had a brief conference with Louis and Red Banville after which, Dick, Bill and me were told to follow 'Specs' up the garden as he was going to take us to a 'safe house' in his lorry. So after more hugs and fond farewells off we went up the garden and through the gate to the lorry that was parked nearby, unfortunately there were three German soldiers leaning against it but luckily not looking in our direction, 'Specs' signalled us to go back and by the time we had reached the courtyard 'Specs' had brought his lorry around to the front gate. Dick sat in the back of the lorry amongst a load of rubbish, whilst Bill and I had pride of place sitting in the front. With a few bangs and leaving a cloud of smoke in our wake 'Specs' drove off heading south east out of Revigny. It seemed rather unreal as we drove along the main road passing German soldiers we had been keeping watch on over the last four weeks or so and now pretending not to have the slightest interest in them!

It was slow going at first as we had to pull in and stop several times to allow columns of German troops on the march to pass by. They appeared to be in good spirits and un-concerned about the possible fate that was in store for them some 150 miles to the west where their comrades were suffering heavy casualties trying to stem the rapid advance of the U.S. 3rd Army. We bypassed some of the German hot-spots known to 'Specs' by leaving the road to drive cross country along cart tracks, regaining the road at one point we could see it led onto a bridge over a canal and was guarded on the far side by a German soldier, as we started to cross 'Specs' put his finger to his lips signalling us to keep quiet - he need not have bothered as neither Bill nor I had any false identification papers to present and were not in a very chatty mood at that particular moment to say the least. As we trundled over the bridge 'Specs' took his drivers permit from his shirt pocket and began to slow down a bit as we approached the armed guard, whilst Bill and me assumed an air of complete indifference to the world around us but I am sure that if our blood pressures had been taken the readings would have gone right off the clock! Just before we reached the stopping point 'Specs' put his hand through the open side window and began waving his permit - no doubt to reassure the guard that he knew the drill and was going to stop, now whether or not they were both masons I do not know, but the guard took one step back and with a snappy flourish of his rifle free hand he signalled for 'Specs' to keep going and gave us a wave and a smile as we passed, I was so relieved I almost gave him a victory salute in return. 'Specs' looked across at us and winked so Bill gave him the 'thumbs up' but no questions were asked. Meanwhile Dick was still sitting in the back of the lorry amongst the rubbish quite blissfully unaware as to how close he had been to being captured, tortured and possibly shot.

We were now getting near to the small town of Ligny-en-Barrois (about 20 miles south east of Revigny) when 'Specs' stopped the lorry, gave us a smile and got out signalling for us to also dismount, as we were helping Dick to get off a tall young lad emerged from the forest that bordered the road, 'Specs' had a quick word with him then shook hands with us and drove off. Introducing himself as Peter Ivanoff and speaking very good English, he promptly led us away from the road and into the forest. As we walked through the trees and undergrowth he told us that we were going to stay in his parents week-end chalet which was about a mile away, he said his father owned a pharmacy shop in Ligny - which was a coincidence as 'Captain X' owned a similar shop in Bar-le-Duc, he went on to tell us that he had a sister who was married to a Dutch artist and the family all lived together above and behind the shop. On breaking cover from the forest the ground immediately ahead dropped quite steeply away with a canal flowing along the bottom and right in front of us was the roof top of the chalet which had been built into the top of this one sided valley. Leading the way Peter clambered down a roughly stepped track to the ground floor level and entrance to the chalet. Going through the front door there was a living room on the left and a kitchen on the right, upstairs were two bedrooms

We had an excellent view of the canal which was just as well because, about fifty yards along the canal was a set of lock gates together with a lock-keepers cottage which housed the German soldiers who patrolled the canal. Peter warned us to keep a close watch on the long steep path that led from the side of the canal up to the chalet because on two recent occasions German soldiers had broken in and had stolen crockery and cutlery. At the top of the stairs Peter showed us how to operate the escape exit which allowed quick access to the forest should the need arise. We were on a much better diet now as there were numerous cartons of porridge oats in the kitchen and a dish in the living room was kept topped up with vitamin tablets. Peter with his married sister Anne Marie, and her Dutch husband Tony Christians came to the chalet every morning bringing a light lunch for all of us, they were usually accompanied by an American chap - about thirty years of age - who said that he was a seaman and had got stranded in Greece when America came into the war and couldn't get back home, whether that was true or not we never found out but he was a very friendly sort of a guy.

In the small front garden was a pile of 4"x V' wooden boards so, as there were no toilet facilities in the chalet we asked Peter's father, on his first visit to us, if he would like us to construct the housing for a chemical lavatory with them which we could install at the back of the chalet by hewing into the hillside. He said "obi oui" (excuse the pun) and the necessary tools were provided. The work kept us fully occupied during the next four or five days and also, was a useful ploy to kid the Germans down below that we were local construction workers. It was so hot (temperatures well into the 80's) we had to make several trips down to the canal to have a cooling off swim, needless to say, keeping a sharp eye on the Germans as we did so. A few days later the housing was finished and the toilet was completed when, Monsieur Ivanoff arrived to place a galvanised iron container with chemicals and a fitted seat into position and proudly declared the 'thunder box' open. We were pleased to have been able, in a small way, to show our appreciation to the Ivanoff family for their bravery and hospitality in giving us food and shelter at the risk of severe retribution from the Germans.

In the meantime, the Allied air activity around the Ligny area had been increasing daily but our excitement was often dampened when we saw black smoke trails suddenly stream out from some of our fighter-bombers as they spiralled to the ground after getting caught by the German defences. We had no radio but Peter kept us informed of the rapid advance being made towards us by the American third Army. During the early evening of the 30th August, we began to hear the sound of heavy gunfire echoing in the distance we knew then that the 'Yanks' were coming. I am sure all three of us felt a lessening of tension that had built up in our minds over the last six weeks but was not outwardly shown, having a price of 10,000 francs on our heads for information that would lead to our capture must have been very tempting for some of the poorer French people who, by helping us, had put their own lives in danger. Some RAF evaders were not so lucky and over sixty of them were captured and sent to Buchenwald concentration camp. The sound of the gunfire must have also brought great joy to the local French people who, for the last four years, had suffered severe hardship at the hands of an often cruel German occupying force.

As dawn broke on the 31st August 1944, the American big guns opened up again only this time much nearer to us, probably from the road where Peter had met us some two weeks ago, as they did so the German artillery also opened fire from the eastern outskirts of Ligny and we were now caught in the crossfire with American and German cannon shells whistling over our heads far too close for comfort. Fortunately it wasn't long before the Germans had had enough and their gunfire ceased as they hastily retreated eastwards. The ensuing silence was truly golden.

At about 9 a.m. Peter and Marie Anne with her husband Tony and the American seaman arrived bursting with excitement to tell us - as if we didn't know - that the town had been liberated. After a lot of hugging and hand shaking the chalet was locked up and we made our way to the chemist shop in the town centre. Our arrival in the main street went un-noticed because as some of the last Germans were leaving Ligny a stick grenade had been thrown from a departing troop carrier into a gathering of women and children on a street corner causing many casualties. We were taken into the living quarters at the rear of the shop and after some celebratory drinks Bill, Dick and I had our first bath in hot water for two months! In the meantime Madame Ivanoff and her daughter were preparing the mid-day meal and the towns' folk, now confident that all the German soldiers had gone, started putting up flags and bunting and were giving a very warm welcome to the liberating American 3rd. Army troops perched up on their fast moving tanks and armoured vehicles as they sped through the town in hot pursuit of the Germans.

After a splendid champagne lunch Madame Ivanoff asked the three of us if we would go with her to attend a thanks-giving service at the nearby church which we readily agreed to do. After the service we joined a large crowd of people celebrating their liberation, it was not only exciting to be there and witness such a unique occasion, because after all, the liberation of a country that has been occupied and oppressed by a cruel foreign enemy regime for over four years doesn't happen very often during one's lifetime, thank goodness, but to have also made some small contribution in bringing it about made it a very memorable experience indeed. It was also a sad occasion for Bill and me when, being surrounded by so much happiness we remembered our three Australian crew mates who were killed when our blazing Lancaster bomber blew up and were now lying buried in a small French village churchyard thousands of miles away from their homes and grieving families. We remembered also our navigator, Eric Brownhall, who had been injured and captured and was now confined behind barbed wire. There is a strong bond of comradeship between the members of a bomber crew mainly because we are so dependent upon each other when flying on operations and it remains with us during our off-duty activities. Our sadness was not relieved either when we saw a group of women being forcefully paraded in front of the Marie (Townhall) to have their hair cut and shaved off as a mark of shame for having consorted with German troops during the occupation. To Bill and me this seemed very harsh treatment because after all, there were very few eligible Frenchmen around as they were either in German P.O.W. camps or forced labour camps together with a small number who were hiding in the forests etc. and operating with the resistance. These 'consorting' Iadies (known as 'Gerry-bags') however, did not do themselves any favours because having received presents, clothing and extra food etc. from the German troops as a reward for their favours, they then flaunted these 'benefits' in front of their fellow townsfolk who, although very impoverished, only spoke to the enemy when they had to. Unfortunately, most of these 'consorting ladies' together with the members of their respective families suffered severe humiliation by the rest of the community for many years after the war had finished and in some cases with tragic consequences.

About 5 p.m. with the celebrations in full swing, news was received by the chief of the local resistance group - who had now taken temporary control of the administration of the town that the German troops whom had retreated through Ligny a few hours earlier had fanned out, leaving the pursuing American troops to charge on ahead, and were now on their way back to recapture the town! So all the flags and bunting was quickly removed from the houses and shops etc. and all the fit males were told to report to the Marie. Having lost track of Dick Greenwood some time ago, Bill and I made our way to the Marie and joined the queue, after signing our names in a book we were given a Resistance arm band each then Bill was directed to help man a barricade on the west entrance to the town and I was sent to one on the eastern side, rifles and ammunition would be available on arrival. With a group of middle aged Frenchmen I duly arrived at the barricade that was still being constructed, some of the Frenchmen were checking out the rifles and exploring how to load them, I was a little bit wary because the next step would be to see if the triggers worked. Fortunately there was an American army tank parked at the road side - two or three had remained in the town to take care of any Germans that had been left behind the tank crew were standing chatting nearby and seemed to have positioned themselves so that their armour plated vehicle gave them some protection should the odd stray bullet be accidentally fired off by this newly armed group of gallant Frenchmen determined to uphold their renowned motto 'they shall not pass', so I went over to them and introduced myself to the officer in charge. He was quite surprised to come across an RAF 'bombardier' helping to man a barricade so far into France, when I told him that I had been 'on the run' in the area for the past six weeks he was quite impressed and said he was pleased to have me around as my experience might come in useful. Meanwhile, the Frenchmen were getting excited about the prospect of having a crack at the Germans with their newly acquired rifles but, having recently been within touching distance of some of the massive German 'Tiger' tanks during our journey to Ligny, my enthusiasm was at a somewhat lower key.

The evening passed with no sign of a German counter attack, a scouting party was sent out but returned without sighting any enemy tanks or troops. About midnight a roster was drawn up of those required to keep watch for two hourly periods until dawn, the rest of us were told to 'kip down' nearby. I wandered across to the Americans and was handed a nice thick slice of white bread well buttered which went down a treat, then the officer got his sleeping bag from the tank and threw one to me, we pitched down under a tree and I was off to sleep in no time. Waking up at first light (1st Sept.) my face was ice cold and covered with dew -I hoped it was dew anyway - I thought that I had been captured as 1 couldn't immediately recognise my surroundings, then I spotted the American tank and all was well. It got even better when, as I sat up a kindly French lady handed me a steaming cup of 'ersatz' coffee - no beans but you couldn't half taste the acorns! Nothing had happened during the night but as the U.S. 3rd Army were advancing so rapidly nobody really knew where the 'front line' was - I think the official term was 'a fluid situation' - anyway, it was decided to keep the barricades manned for a further 24 hours but some of us were allowed an 'on call' break until 6 p.m. So I made my way back to the pharmacy where Madame Ivanoff gave me a continental breakfast, Bill arrived a little later so we spent the morning and afternoon celebrating with the townsfolk and helped them drink a never ending supply of champagne which they had hidden away from the Germans over the last four years.

At 6 p.m. Bill and I returned to our respective barricades, albeit a little bit the worse for wear. During the evening the American officer mentioned that he would be 'pushing on' in the morning and said I was welcome to come along with his crew, I thanked him for his 'tempting' offer but said that I was duty bound to return to my squadron as soon as possible as (I hoped) 1 was still on the pay roll, as we were talking two Frenchmen joined us, one was quite elderly the other was much younger and could speak English, addressing the officer, he said that the old man's wife, who was very ill and hadn't got much longer to live, had expressed a wish to see a soldier of the liberating army and asked him, on behalf of the old chap, if he would pay her a visit as the cottage was nearby. After giving the request a few seconds consideration, the officer said to me "what do you think is it alright?", feeling a bit flattered at having my opinion sought I gave the old man a quick 'once over' and assuming all the authority I could muster I said oh yes he's quite genuine and if you decide to go I'll come with you if you wish. So picking up an automatic rifle he said OK lets go. The old man's face seemed to light up as he led us down the road to his cottage. It was beginning to get dark as the old chap took us to the back door and as we went in the officer released the safety catch on his rifle and was now holding it in the 'on guard' position, we followed the old chap through the kitchen with the officers combat boots and my 'escape shoes' making quite a noise on the linoleum floor covering, as we were about to pass by the kitchen table there was a sudden rustling sound coming from beneath it, in a flash the officer brought his rifle down and aimed it towards the table, as he did so an un-shaven face poked out with tasselled hair flecked with pieces of straw and bearing a terrified expression,- probably thinking that the Gestapo had arrived by now the old man's hand was resting on the rifle barrel and he was shaking his head appealing to the officer not to open fire. After some hand gestures by the old man and some shrewd guess work by us, it appeared that we had startled the old man's son whose sleeping quarters were under the kitchen table on a bale of straw - he was very lucky not to have had his head blown off. The old chap took us into his sick wife's bedroom where the frail old lady lay looking pale and drawn, the officer put the back of his hand to her cheek and she bravely gave him a weak smile, I am sure she was indicating that she was now happily satisfied that the town had been liberated.

We made our way back to the barricade where I shook hands with the officer and his tank crew and after thanking and wishing them the very best of luck I reported back to do my spell of guard duty. Just around mid-night the guard commander stood a few of us down and confirmed that the barricade would be dismantled at day-break. So, with no Germans left to fight I made my way through the dark deserted roads accompanied only by the sound of clock chimes coming from the houses and cottages all striking mid-night at different times as I passed by, I must have walked through twenty or more time zones during the fifteen minutes it took me to reach the pharmacy and a good nights' sleep.

During the next morning, Monsieur Luccioni (Specs) arrived with his car to take us back to Revigny which had also been liberated on the 31st, August. Dick Greenwood had gone off somewhere with the Dutchman Tony Christians so as 'Specs' was rather anxious to get going Bill and I thanked the Ivanoff family for their hospitality and great bravery in giving us shelter etc. Madame Ivanoff said she would like to adopt me I don't know why, I told her I had a mother already waiting for me in England, so after some hugs, kisses and handshakes Bill and I got into 'Specs' car and departed for Revigny.

Our arrival in Revigny must have been expected because as we drew up outside of the house Louis, Jean and the four French lads were waiting, they hauled us out of the car and greeted us as if we had come back from the dead, we were soon hoisted into a large open topped Mercedes car - no doubt taken from the Germans and still standing up, as there was no room to sit down with about a dozen other Frenchmen on board, we were driven around the streets of Revigny to the cheers and waves of the still celebrating Revineens and finally finished up outside of the Marie where we were hustled into the council meeting room which was packed with noisy people. Eventually, a modicum of order was restored and Louis introduced us from a raised platform but could not finish his impromptu speech because the cheers and hand clapping broke out again and this time it was accompanied by the noise of popping champagne bottle corks. Needless to say neither Bill nor I remember much about the next two or three hours.

Around mid afternoon, 'Specs' turned up again in his car to take the two of us to Laheycourt, so after some tearful farewells from Louis, his brother Jean and the French lads, together with our heartfelt expressions of sincere gratitude to them for risking torture and certain death for helping us to evade capture, Bill and I swept out of Revigny not knowing whether it was Christmas or Easter. It did not take long to cover the eight miles to Laheycourt and arriving in the village we stopped outside one of the larger houses, as we did so the big front door swung open and out ran the very pretty Antoinette to greet us which made all that we had been through during the last seven weeks all worthwhile! Her parents invited us in for drinks etc, more champagne and several small glasses of eau-de-vie which nearly blew my head off. We didn't have to tell them what we had been up to as it seemed that they had been kept informed of our movements, so after thanking Antoinette profusely for risking her own safety in contacting the priest for us - she had covertly slipped me a couple of snap-shots of herself during the drinks we said our farewells and got back in the car again with 'Specs' who told us that we were now going to his house in the near-by village of Neuville-sur-Ornain for our evening meal and to stay over-night.

We were disappointed not to have met up with the priest, Roger Guillemin, during our short visit to Laheycourt but as it happened he had left the village and had given up his church vocation to marry his house-keeper. He and his wife Therese came to England in 1979 and stayed with Bill in the Wirral and me in Hove, sadly the church in Laheycourt collapsed in 1984 and had to be demolished. Bill and I met them several times on our post war visits to Revigny and on one such visit, when they were staying in Laheycourt with their war-time friends who still ran the village grocery shop and who 'illegally' supplied us in Revigny with sticks of bread in 1944, we asked them whom the elderly lady was that we had met in the church on the 19th July 1944 at about 5 p.m. and had made signs for us to stay in the church. After some discussion Roger said that he and his grocer friend knew everybody in the village around that date but neither of them could recall such a person who would have been in there, especially at 5 p.m. and he seemed to be doubtful of her existence, but we knew she had been there - or had she?

It was not long before we arrived at M. Luccioni's house where his wife, assisted by a lady of the village, had prepared a very nice meal for us which we all tucked into in a rather 'posh' dining room where, no doubt, over the last four years German army officers had been entertained - all in the line of business of course. As it happened, Red Banville and his two crewmates had also been given a meal there whilst on their way to Revigny six weeks previously and the lady from the village had given Red a packet of Goldflake cigarettes, she told him that they had been given to her by an RAF man from a nearby airfield (No. 1 Fighter squadron) just before he flew off in haste in May 1940 and that she had vowed to give them to the first Allied serviceman she met when the village was liberated. She was a bit premature with her offering but after four years of waiting who cares!

Next morning, 3rd September, 'Specs' took Bill and me in his car to Bar-le-Duc and dropped us off at the local hospital as he had heard that Denys Teare and Fred White had been admitted as patients suffering from a skin complaint, so after thanking him for his hospitality we said our farewells and entered the hospital which was staffed by nuns. We were soon directed to our two comrades who were lying propped up in comfortable beds with sparkling white stiff sheets. Denys was suffering from malnutrition and scabies which he had passed on to Fred. They both had blue ointment plastered all over their faces so we told them that they need not have bothered to put makeup on just because we were coming! We soon had them laughing even though they were in severe discomfort from the sores on their faces and bodies. On leaving them, Bill promised Denys that he would call on his parents as soon as he got back to Liverpool to let them know he was 'OK' and would be home in a couple of weeks or so having given our names and service numbers to Louis for transmission by radio to London we assumed our parents etc. would have been informed that we were still in the land of the living but that was not so - little did Bill know that the last notification Denys's parents had received regarding his welfare was from Buckingham Palace in May 1944 signed by George R.I. expressing deepest sympathy for the loss of his life.

On leaving the hospital we spotted a building that was being used by American army troops, Bill suggested that we went in to enquire if there was any chance of getting a flight back to the U.K. as St.Dizier airfield was nearby, so in we went and I saw, through the half open door of the first room we came to, a sergeant sitting at a large desk busily writing. I said to Bill this will do and we walked in. The sergeant was still writing as we reached the desk so as there was a sturdy cabinet at the side of it I casually leant against it to wait for him to finish writing, when he suddenly looked up at me and said 'stay where you are and don't move', gently getting out of his chair he walked to the door telling Bill to follow him, when they got to the hallway he called back to me to very carefully move away from the 'safe' that I was leaning against, I then twigged that there was something rather unpleasant inside it. So I carried out his instruction implicitly, after a few anxious seconds and nothing untoward had happened, they both came back into the room and the sergeant explained that the building had been used by the so & so Germans until they evacuated the town a couple of days ago and the safe I had been leaning against had been left with the key still in the lock and was, probably, 'booby trapped' and he was in the process of writing a notice to stick on the door of the room to warn people like me to KEEP OUT. After telling him who we were and what we wanted he said that there was no chance of getting a flight to anywhere around here adding 'this is the front line buddy" but he did direct us to their very recently acquired army supply line depot where we might be able to 'hitch' a lift on a returning truck going in the Paris direction. He forgot to mention however that, due to their very rapid advance, this was a hastily organised supply line better known as the notorious 'Red Ball Express', the truck drivers were mostly black troops and had been quickly 'trained' at the 'Kamikaze Truck Driving School'

Arriving at the depot we soon got a lift from a very friendly, all smiling black American P.F.C. driving a covered "deuce and a half truck - his term for a 3 tonner. He said there is no seat up front you will have to park in the back, so we clambered up over the tail board and found that the truck was loaded with empty petrol jerry cans in between which, after a struggle, we managed to wedge ourselves. As we did so, the driver started the engine and the truck roared off through the main street of Bar-le-Duc like a rat up a drain pipe, and for the rest of the journey we very seldom had all six wheels on the road at the same time. There were shell holes and other obstacles blocking our way at times so detours across fields had to be made, we were kept quite busy in the back fending off loose jerry cans that were flying about like 'bingo' balls only they were much heavier, how we didn't get our skulls fractured 1 don't know. Our speed never slackened as we belted through villages and hamlets where, clouds of feathers would suddenly appear in our wake as we ploughed through flocks of free range chickens whose status was instantly changed into 'oven readies' and omelettes. In fairness to the driver, getting supplies to the front line troops in the quickest possible time was paramount, and trying to keep up with the very rapid advance of the U.S. 3rd. Army made this task extremely difficult for the 'Red Ball Express' operatives to say the least, so we were very grateful to the driver for giving us a lift. Eventually we arrived at the driver's depot where he had to re-load and return to Bar-le-Duc.

As we waited outside the depot to cadge a lift on a truck returning to Paris, we noticed a group of Frenchmen across the road having a heated discussion and kept looking over at us, fortunately, there was an American military policeman close to them directing traffic who must have over-heard the gist of what they were getting worked up about, because, he came over to us and asked who we were, then he told us that the group of Frenchmen had got the idea that we were German army deserters and were going to capture us and cut our hands off! Thankfully, he stayed with us and stopped the next Paris bound truck and we were soon aboard sitting up front with the driver this time with only sixty miles to go.

We had a much smoother ride on this part of the journey, fast, but straight and level for most of the way. As we entered the outskirts of Paris, evidence of the bitter street fighting that had taken place during liberation of the City a few days earlier was plain to see. The avenues and boulevards were littered with burnt out wrecks of the hastily departing German tanks and troop carriers that didn't get away. The Paris Resistance fighters had played a big part in the re-capture of their capital but had also suffered many casualties in doing so. Our driver dropped us off in the Place-de-Concorde by the Hotel de Ville, we shook hands and thanked him for our having had the pleasure of travelling with the 'Red Ball Express' and he drove off. We had a brief look around the opera district but, although Paris had been liberated for some eight days, there was still the occasional burst of machine-gun fire to be heard, so as it was about 9 p.m., and feeling whacked out, we started to look for somewhere to sleep, Having managed to hold on to the French currency that was part of our escape kits, some of which we had offered to Louis in Revigny but he refused to take it, we found a small hotel in a back street and lashed out on a room for the night.

As this was our first visit to Paris we set out next

morning (4th Sept.) to spend the day sight-seeing and left reporting our presence until the evening. The Parisians were still in high spirits though most of them were dressed in 'make do and mend' clothing which was in keeping with the rather sombre atmosphere that pervaded the city, the buildings and shops were mostly candle lit due to the severe shortage of electricity. There were burnt out vehicles in many of the thoroughfares, some were still smouldering and acrid smelling. Other than the military vehicles that were dashing about everywhere, the main mode of transport for the Parisians was by bicycle or bicycle drawn taxis. Whilst we were talking and gazing up at the Eiffel Tower a Frenchman, over-hearing our English conversation, joined us and explained that the entrance to the Tower was locked because it was thought that the Germans had booby trapped the lift cage before their departure, he went on to say that a Spitfire fighter aeroplane had swooped down and had been flown through the supporting arches of the Tower the day after the city had been liberated - the pilot, probably of the Free French Air Force must have been a right 'nutter' or a driver from the 'Red Ball Express"

As the evening approached we started looking for someone to report to, we soon found a very informative American military policeman and he directed us to the Hotel Meurice which, until a few days ago, had been used by the Germans as their military head-quarters for Paris. On arrival in the foyer we could see it was a really plush hotel despite the damage that had been done to the very ornate decor, caused by the hand grenades and bullets that had been discharged in persuading the German General Coltitz and his staff to surrender. Due credit must be given to the General for disregarding Adolf Hitler's order to totally destroy the City of Paris before his garrison departed.

The American Army was now the hotels' new residents

and we were very cordially received and promptly supplied with a meal U.S. army 'K' rations but very good - and a large sumptuous bedroom en suite. We had no idea what half the fitments in the bathroom were for, especially the two large basins near the floor about three feet apart, assuming they were for washing your feet in I said to Bill, you would have to be about ten feet tall to get your feet in those, but he reckoned that they were for two people to wash their feet at the same time!

In the morning we were interrogated by a U.S. army officer to check out that we were genuine shot down RAF air crew as there were all sorts of people trying to get to the U.K. at that time including some 'wanted' German army personnel. We were then put on a flight list and eventually, on Friday morning, 9th September 1944 we climbed aboard a U.S. DC3 (Dakota) aircraft at Orly airport bound for RAF Northolt. Not only was this our first flight since getting blown out of our blazing Lancaster but also the first time we had ever flown without the 'safety net' of a parachute which, just seven weeks earlier, had saved our lives. Luckily no German fighters came to see us off. After 'buzzing' the Eiffel Tower we set course for the Normandy coast, as we flew over the invasion beaches my thoughts were of the thousands of young Allied army lads who would not be returning to their families. Touching down at Northolt it felt great to be back in ones own country again, we were soon issued with new battle-dress uniforms (no badges etc.) and each given a letter of identification stating that we were repatriated airmen. After being taken to a small RAF hostel for the night and provided with a meal, Bill and I went out in the evening to find the nearest 'pub' and have our first pint of beer since leaving Waddington which was only two months ago but seemed much longer. We had not walked very far before we were stopped by two RAF police corporals who, thinking that we looked a bit odd, asked to see our 1250's (I.D. cards) when we both said that we had not got one their faces lit up like Christmas trees, but on producing our letters of re-partition the change of expression on their faces was a joy to behold. We knew then that we really were back in the RAF again.

The next morning we were interrogated by an RAF Intelligence officer during which we made sure that the names of the brave French people who had helped us evade capture were recorded and requested that consideration be given for their bravery to be officially recognised. We were then asked what we wanted to do now apart from going on leave, so we asked to go back to Waddington and rejoin 467 squadron to finish our tour of operations. This request was promptly refused by the I.0. who told us that we could not fly on operations over Europe anymore because we had been involved with the French Resistance and also that, we had already been credited with completing our tours of operations. The I.0. then asked if we would like to fly in the Far East with 'Tiger Force' which was in process of being assembled, thinking that flying out there would be a 'piece of cake' we said yes please and with that the interrogation was concluded.

With three weeks leave and double ration coupons we set off for our homes, Bill to Liverpool to see his wife and baby son, whom he had never met before, and I set course for Gillingham in Kent. Even though I had assumed that my parents would had been informed of my well being because Louis had sent our details to London by radio message, I was still quite excited as I rang the front door bell as I knew it would be a nice surprise for them to see me standing there, but my excitement was quickly dampened when nobody came to the door. I soon realised that as it was Saturday afternoon they would be out shopping in the town, so I went around to the back of the house and got in through a window that I knew was seldom locked. It wasn't long before I heard the front door being opened and my parents walking along the long hallway to the living room, not wanting to frighten the life out of them 1 called out hello mum, hello dad it's only me. When they reached the living room and saw me they were absolutely dumbfounded and thought that I was an apparition, it took some time before I convinced them that it really was me, and even longer for the colour to come back into their faces - talk about seeing a ghost! The reason for their shock was of course that they had not received any further news about me since getting the letter from the squadron, nearly two months ago, saying that I had not returned from air operations and must be presumed missing. Bill Johnson's wife was so surprised to see him again it brought on a state of total deafness which remained with her until she died in 1994 - six months after Bill had passed on. It leaves little to the imagination to appreciate the total disbelief of Denys Teare's parents when Bill, as promised, called on them with the news that, apart from a bit of a rash, Denys was well, sends his love and will be home shortly, when, the last notification they had received, some four months previously, was from Buckingham Palace - following a letter from Air Ministry presuming his death - expressing heartfelt sympathy in their sorrow!

The three weeks leave soon expired and I met up with Bill again in Morecambe which was the assembly point for 'Tiger Force' personnel bound for the Far East theatre of war. We had only been there a matter of days when the two of us were sent up to Nairn in the north of Scotland and told to report to RAF Brachla. Being a 'gen man' I said to Bill this is it mate, we are on our way to the boat - I had sailed from Gourock nearly two years previously to do my flying training in Canada. Brachla was an all air crew camp most of whom were wearing decorations and path finder badges making Bill and me feel like a couple of 'rookies'. There was an unusual atmosphere on this camp and the residents seemed to be left to their own devices to pass the time away, but being, as we thought, a transit camp we were not unduly concerned. When after a couple of weeks Bill and I were handed leave passes with no expiry date we thought we were going on embarkation leave. Six weeks later I was instructed to report to Transport Command H.Q. at Harrow-on-the-Hill, from where I was sent on detachment to Holmsley South in the New Forest. Holmsley was a large busy air field flying Yorks (converted Lancasters) and Liberators transporting passengers and freight to the Middle East and India. Due to my civilian occupation, I had been posted there to help out in the Pay Accounts section. Not being happy about that arrangement I got an interview with the station commander Group Captain Whitworth (ex C.O. at Scampton at the time of the Dam Busting raid), and although he didn't grant my request to fly as a 'spare bod' with the air crews, he did create a job for me in Flying Control in charge of administration and the day to day running of the airfield - I got quite well known by the personnel for my 'tannoy announcements' and by the forest ponies for my accuracy with a verey pistol to keep them off the run-way in use!. I found out some months later that Brachla was a rehabilitation centre for air crew whose operational flying duties were over, but neither Bill nor I were ever told that we had been taken off the 'Tiger Force' draft. Perhaps by us volunteering to fly against the Japanese prompted the thought that we were a couple of 'nutters', as it happened the war in the Far East finished-before 'Tiger Force' got off the ground so we would have missed the boat in any case. In March 1946, 1 was sent on an accountancy course at Kirkham in Lancashire then posted to RAF Keevil from where I was 'demobbed' in August, 1946.

I have many light hearted memories of my time spent with the French Resistance but I do not forget either the brutal atrocities committed by some of the retreating German troops against innocent French people of the Revigny area in revenge for being harassed by groups of our S.A.S. troops who were operating in the nearby Forest of the Three Fountains. On one such occasion, during the morning of the 29th. August 1944, German troops retreating through the small village of Roger Espagne, situated on the edge of the forest, rounded up all the men and young boys - fortunately some were out working in the fields - under the pretence that they were required to do some digging. They were then lined up in front of three machine-guns and shot. One village lady, whose husband had been taken away and shot, was hiding an RAF air gunner (Albert de Bruin) in her cottage and during the roundup had concealed him under the floor boards in her bed-room, but she had to quickly get him out again as the Germans had now started to set fire to all the cottages. Luckily, they managed to escape from the blazing cottage via the back door and garden to take cover in the under-growth until the Germans pulled out of the devastated village. Similar atrocities were being carried out simultaneously in the three adjoining villages bringing the total number of killings to over eighty. In recent years, together with Bill Johnson, Nicky Nicholson, Albert de Bruin and other members of the RAF Escaping Society, I have returned to Revigny to visit and thank Louis and Jean Chenu and the many brave French people who risked their lives in helping us to evade capture. On these visits our three Australian comrades who were killed when our 'Lanc' blew up and crashed are always specially remembered, their graves in the church yard at Brabant-le-Roi are visited and respects are paid. Georges Mandet and his wife have now passed on after raising a family of thirteen children, on a visit to Laheycourt church in 1981, Bill and I retrieved the map that Georges had given to us in July 1944 and gave it back to him We had had to hide it behind the font because his name and address was on it. Also during that visit, we called on the farmer who still owned the field in which our Lancaster crashed and had a look around the site. After inviting us into his house for a few drinks - it happened to be his 81st. birthday - he produced a pair of RAF suede flying boots that he had found near our crashed aircraft, they belonged to our navigator Eric Brownhall (taken prisoner) and had been jerked off his feet when his parachute opened. The farmer (Paul Thomas) gave us the boots requesting that they be returned to the rightful owner. Due to his working abroad, we had lost touch with Eric after the war but eventually found him in Reading in 1982 and gave him his flying boots back - thirty eight years after losing them!. In handing them over to Eric we told him he was lucky it was only his boots that fell off!

For his bravery, Louis Chenu received decorations from the British, American and French Governments and after his death in 1997 a square in the town of Revigny was named after him in recognition of his courageous war time activities with the French Resistance.

On reflection, it may have been unwise to have housed so many of us for such a long period of time in the small town of Revigny right under the noses of so many German troops, on the other hand, it may have been the reason why we did not get caught. But one thing that is for sure is that I owe all the French people who helped me evade capture an immense debt of gratitude for their courage and hospitality.

What happened to the very pretty Antoinette? I understand that she got married soon after the war ended and went to live in South Africa - YOU CAN'T WIN 'EM ALL!

John 'Ginger' Brown ex 'Millomite!'

MR ROSS BLANCHARD, 1944 -1945

18th July 1942 – My RAAF Training Begins!

On the above date I reported, with 250 other new recruits to No.4 Initial Training School at Mount Breckan. Straight away my drumming abilities stood me in good stead when I was quickly made a member of the units dance band. This was great because it got me out of all sorts of other military bits of nonsense, and it also helped me in another very important way, for after six weeks of this three months course I had to front up to the category selection board, who would decide what my future training would be, e.g. pilot, navigator, bomb aimer, wireless operator / air gunner or a rear gunner. Like most of the members of this course I really only wanted to become a pilot, so you can imagine my sheer delight, when the leader of the band took me aside about a week before this interview and said, 'Blanchard, don't worry about the interview next week, all members of the band get what they want'! I thought 'you bloody beauty! I'm going to be given the chance to become a pilot'! I did my elementary flying training on Tiger Moths at No.11 Elementary Training School, Benalla, Victoria and passed with an average assessment, though sadly with no opportunity for drumming. I then went on to No. 7 service Flying Training School d' Deniliquin, New South Wales where I did my training on Wirraways, once again passed with an average assessment, won my pilots wings, was promoted to the grand rank of Sergeant, and still no drumming. My postings then took me back to No.4 Embarkation Depot at Scotch College, Torrens Park, South Australia, then No.2 Embarkation Depot, Bradfield Park, Sydney, New South Wales. I was only there for six days, and the last night of my stay was very interesting, for the WAAF's put on a dinner dance for all these bold blokes who were about to head off to the much more dangerous areas of WWII.

I had a dance with a very attractive WAF Corporal this evening, and during the course of this dance I asked her what her function was in the Air Force, and she told me she was a radar operator. Now, in 1943, radar in Australia was a very mystic subject, and her comment made me very interested, so I asked her to tell me a bit more about it. She then went on to tell me about tracking on aircraft in South Western, New South Wales one night in April before finally losing contact with it. It took a tremendous amount of self control to stop me from bursting out laughing for I then told her that in all probability she had most likely been tracking me! On April the 4th 1943 I had to do a solo night flying exercise from Deniliquin to Echuca on the River Murray, a distance of about 45 statute miles, then return to base. It was a beautiful night, millions of stars, no moon, no turbulence and a very satisfactory arrival at my destination, with a very cocky pilot at the controls. In fact I was so cocky I did some aerobatics, and then headed for home and a well earned sleep. After about 20 minutes I could see no sign of Deniliquin so come to the conclusion I must have a head wind, and flew on for another five minutes. Still no base! I then went into the standard search pattern, flying 5 minutes east, 5 minutes south, 10 minutes west, 10 minutes north, and so on, expanding the pattern until I saw the lights of Deniliquin, Aha!! I had made it! Unfortunately as I got closer I realised that it wasn't base at all, and I had no idea where I was, but that I was at least in Australian territory! At this stage my fuel was starting to get a bit low, so I had to make a decision, bail out, or make a forced landing. I decided on the latter, and in a Wirraway aircraft a forced landing at night had to be done with the undercarriage retracted, for if you didn't, and you survived, you were scrubbed for being extremely stupid. I went into landing pattern, climbed to 4,000 feet, dropped flare No.1, descended to 1,000 feet and dropped flare No.2. The first flare had by this time unfortunately started a fire on the ground which was generating lots of smoke and as I turned onto my final approach and put on the landing light it was as though I was flying into a London Pea Soup Fog! As I was about to switch off the light I saw a huge gum tree flash past my port wingtip, so I knew I was pretty close to the ground, turned off the light, and went into the one landing drill for an emergency landing on instruments. When the altimeter read zero, I shut down the engine, eased back on the stick and did a very smooth belly landing. About 50 yards after this gently touchdown I ran into a wire fence, which brought me to a very sudden stop. Because the gear was retracted, the undercarriage warning horn was blaring quite loudly, so I got out of the cockpit, opened the small cover on the starboard side of the fuselage, shut off the master switch to enjoy a few minutes at least, of peace and quiet. The aircraft was pretty badly damaged, but the only injury I got was when I scratched my finger on the horn position hinge spring. I had quite an audience for this time of day, and they were most solicitous, and I found out that I had landed at White Cliffs, Bendigo, Victoria, about 96 miles from where I should have been. There was a very large army tank training unit here, and one of the Sergeants took me in hand, looked after me very well for about three days, while the air force people came and dismantled the bird, packed it on the back of a huge truck, along with its pilot, then drove back to Deniliquin.On my return to base I was interviewed by the C/O, GRP/CPT. J. Waters and had my log book endorsed, 'Forced landing, inexperience, faulty night navigation'! It never came out that I had neglected to lower the gear for resetting course for base, and this lapse could put the magnetic compass out of accuracy by up to 60 degrees or more.

The gorgeous WAAF Corporal thought this was a remarkable story and that I was a very, very lucky lad to have survived, we both chuckled over this for some time. It was now that the war started to feel much closer to me. For I boarded the troopship 'Mount Vermont' in Sydney Harbour the next day and we set sail about mid afternoon. Just after we set sail I remember all the people alongside the harbour bridge waving us farewell and shouting 'good luck'!

Our voyage was to San Francisco via Auckland New Zealand, where we were given about 12 hours shore leave. Our first view of the U.S.A was about five days later with the beautiful Golden Gate Bridge shining in the sunlight. On arrival the Americans treated us as though we had been conscripted, and the difference between their aircrew and ours was that all American pilots automatically became officers, and as we were not officers we were considered rubbish. We were not allowed to go ashore straight away but next morning we had to scale down a rope net with all our gear and taken by barge to Oakland. From here myself and some 600 other aircrew began a train journey across the United States. The carriages were very comfortable, and our attendant, a black American, was a very nice chap, who treated us very well indeed.

One of my pastimes during the trip was to measure our trains speed by timing the mile posts as they went by, it was usually just over 100mph! We stopped in Chicago at around 2 o'clock in the morning and whilst stretching our legs came across a black bloke with a tray of all sorts of goodies around his neck, a few purchases and a stroll later we were off again. My view of New York as we went through was of a station five floors below sea level, I recall it as a miserable scene. My stopping point was Camp Miles Standish, about halfway between New York and Boston. This was an American Training Camp and it was here that I was first introduced to the US Juke Box, a huge machine holding about fifty 12 inch records by, Duke Ellington, Count Basie, Benny Goodman, Artie Show, Tommy Dorsey, Jimmy Lunceford and a host of others, I LOVED IT!!

I had the surname of some family relations in New Haven, Connecticut and I went to spend three days leave with them and we had a great time. I was approaching the front gate of Camp Miles Standish at the end of my leave as a large group of Aussies were coming out the other way. As soon as they saw me, one of them said, 'we're all shipping out in three days, it might be a good idea to do an 1800 turn and go back to where you've been!' I did not need telling twice and headed off again for another enjoyable three days.

At the end of this time, on my return to camp I heard that we were entraining in one hours time and so I hastily packed my gear and made it to parade on time. The Australian Officer there was very angry with us, for out of 600 odd in our contingent, about 99% had gone A.W.A.L. He duly informed us that on arrival at our destination we would all be charged. Now, we all figured that our destination would be the UK, and if so then the Brits would be far too busy to worry about charging us delinquents. We were correct on both counts and we never heard another thing about it. Our train took us to New York where we boarded the Ocean Liner Queen Elizabeth making our way to our allotted cabins. When my group reached the aforementioned cabin, we found nine bunks and a paliasse on the floor, guess who got the floor? Still, I wasn't bothered and in fact was very comfortable during our voyage. When I rose from my slumbers next morning we were well and truly at sea and it took me almost an hour to find the other ranks mess. We got two meals a day, as I believe there were about 15,000 Government sponsored passengers on this crossing, with the America GI's being allocated a six by three feet space in all corridors to be shared by all GI's.

The first two nights at sea were spent listening to live jazz in one of the huge reception areas, played by all sorts of muso's with top quality all round. After the second night the authorities banned this function because it got too many people in the one spot at the one time, and if we had been torpedoed the loss of life would have been enormous. The Queen Elizabeth got along at about 32 knots, and used to change course about every 15 seconds, to avoid the prevalent U-Boats that were haunting the Atlantic Ocean. About half way across we had an exciting break in routine when the ships anti aircraft batteries opened fire. Fortunately this was just a practice exercise and five days later the lovely green hills of Scotland appeared on the horizon, and although it was late June, this green looked beautiful

Our transport docked at Greenock, Scotland and our 600 got on a troop train. Within 24 hours we detrained at Brighton Sussex. Very shortly after our arrival there my mate Angus Tyson, (a very good pianist in the Fats Waller style) and I were walking along the seafront, when we saw a sign which said 'out of bounds to all service personnel'. Now being Aussies, we just looked at one another, and without a word, went to investigate. We walked down a flight of stairs and came into a fairly large room with a full length bar, complete with barman, a nicely carpeted floor with about 40 to 50 tables with several very comfortable chairs to each one, a dance floor and a podium with a semi-grand piano with a full kit of drums complete with sticks and brushes. One of us said to the barman "would you mind if we played a bit of music"? His response was "no, be my guest", we had a ball, and afterwards the barman asked us if we would be interested in playing there six nights a week, for ten shillings each a night and free drinks. How could we refuse? I think we started that same night. The news got round fast and before we knew it we were a five piece band and the 'joint was jumping' every night!

My mate Angus was posted away on his advanced flying course after two weeks but we managed to recruit a good replacement and after about four weeks of great fun we were approached by the manager of "The Dome" ballroom who wanted to know if we would be interested in relieving his big band for fifteen minutes each hour. We agreed, and if you take into account the free drinks, we were being paid almost as much as the air force was paying us, for doing something we all enjoyed and TAX FREE!!!!

Down to the serious stuff!

However, on the 14th September it was 'down to brass tacks'!! I was posted to No. 6 Pilots Advanced Flying Unit at Little Rissington, and on the 28th September 1943 I had my first lesson in advanced flying, I must say, I could not have had a better birthday present! This course lasted four months, and was very advanced indeed. Not long after I started the training I figured that if I wanted to give myself a sporting chance of surviving this tremendous piece of human nonsense, then I must devote all my energies to flying. My drum sticks and brushes were put away, and never again used professionally.

My first six and a half weeks were spent flying with type experience, and cross country exercises, a lot of which was done with two Kiwi pilots, FLT/Sgt Madsen and F/O Blackwell. I did a low level cross country with the latter and when I went down to the Aussie low level of 150 feet he went right off his block and very brusquely said "TAKING OVER" and down we went to ground level! I'm sure he did some grass cutting during this display, it was most intriguing! The next twelve days were spent on the B.A.T. flight where for about an hour before flying one had to put on glasses with very dark blue lenses, and all cockpit windows were covered with dark yellow screens. This meant that all the pupil pilot could see were the luminous instruments, and he did everything from start up to shutdown, with of course direction guidance from his instructor. It was first class training which totalled 20 hours flying. After another 18 days day flying, I went onto the night flying training, and after 4 hours 10 minutes dual, I did 35 minutes with F/S Madsen and he was so impressed with my standard that he apologised for not being able to give me an above average assessment, The night flying system in England made our Australian one look as though it was still in the Bleriot days, for in Aussie all we had were six flares in a straight line with one at the end to make up an L shape, and a ground operator to give you a green light if it was OK to go or a red light to hold. The UK system was called DREM, it was magnificent, with a ring of white lights on a two mile radius of the aerodromes centre, with lead lights to the runway in use, with their lights only visible if you were flying into wind. There were also lead in lights from the perimeter, lights to the runway in use, along with green and red lights at the end of the strip to indicate your correct level of approach. For me it made night flying so much easier.

Every airfield in the UK during WWII had a red flashing beacon which spelt out two more code letters about every half minute, and these were changed every 24 hour, they were known as PUNDIT. In the UK there were four other beacons called OCCULTS which flashed a single Morse code letter about every minute, I think these changed monthly. There were quite a few other PUNDITS' around the UK which were slotted in dangerous country to entrap the enemy. We were given the means to avoid being fooled by these spurious beacons but sadly I can't recall what it was. It is really quite remarkable when I think of it now, for in those days, air traffic control was an unheard of term, and the amount of traffic flying round the UK was enormous though we were only aware of the merest inkling of it at the time.

My night flying near miss must have taught me a few valuable lessons because my night flying instructor told me at close of play how impressed he was, and that if he had any say in the matter I would get an "above average assessment" but for my strife once again when one morning myself and a couple of other diggers slept in. When we reported late to the flight centre we were hauled over the coals by Flt/Lt W. McRobbie. He really went to town, and apparently I was smiling during his rant, he went right off and I had the biggest strip torn off me to date!! When I sent my Christmas cards for 1943 I sent one to Lord and Lady Bledisloe, who had been Governor General of New Zealand. I had met them both whilst at an afternoon tea and dance at Government House, Wellington, New Zealand in 1939. I received a very nice card back from them, and because it was open for all to see, word soon got around that apparently, I was well connected. McRobbie treated me with kid gloves for the rest of my stay at Little Rissington but I was keen to be involved in the obviously forthcoming invasion of Europe and applied to become a glider pilot, my application was ignored.

Even the seagulls say "caaark!"

When my posting came, it was to No.1 Staff pilots Training Unit at Cark in Cartmel, Lancashire, and I was brassed off at the idea, not least of all because I would be flying the MKI Avro Anson which would be the most basic aircraft I had flown to date, apart from the old Tiger Moth, which was exceptional. Things were pretty quiet at Cark during my time there with the exception of a tragic mid air collision between two Ansons near the Mull of Galloway which killed a pal of mine off the same course as me. He had taken me under his wing as I was so far from home, I was greatly saddened. There were several Polish Pilots on our course, and one of these was Sergeant Shlitzinger, and there are no prizes for guessing what everybody (including the WAFFs) called him. He had a very interesting experience on one of his early solo cross country flights, for the weather was decidedly nasty, but he successfully completed the trip and made a very rough, bumpy and damaging landing following what he believed to be a good approach. He was very upset by this, and even more upset when he discovered that he had not landed at RAF Cark, but actually in the railway yards at Lancaster!! He copped a huge amount of teasing but I'm sure he only understood half of it as he always had a broad smile on his face. A great coincidence springs to mind here, all my course numbers in Australia were 30 and I was part of No.30 course at Cark too!

I join the staff at RAF Millom in Cumberland

I left Cark on the 7th March 1944 with another average assessment to my credit and was posted to RAF Millom No.2 Observer Advanced Flying Unit. I was no longer a pupil I was a member of "The Staff"! What a huge difference this made, plus the fact that I was now engaged in some positive activities. I was not at this station for long but I have fond memories of it. I had been having serious problems with my mail because all overseas mail was sent to a unit in London and transferred from there. I was not receiving any letters at all until suddenly I was deluged with mail because all my mail had been sent in error to No.6 A.F.U. instead of No.6 (P) A.F.U. Sadly, one of these letters was from a pal in the Australian Navy, to tell me that a lass I was rather keen on, had been taken very ill with Scarlet Fever. I had just read this and was walking back to my quarters when I was pulled up for not saluting the station C/O, these things happen. On the plus side, I became good pals with the WAAF from the units, parachute section, her name was Mary Howarth and she was a beauty! We used to cycle down to the beach with a host of others where we enjoyed the sunshine, and some of us took a dip in the Irish Sea!

Whilst at Millom, I remember taking off one night in pretty terrible weather for a night training exercise. We were getting nowhere with our navigators training so I put the dear old "Annie" into a climb, and somewhere between 12,000 and 15,000 feet we broke clear of the cloud layer and awful weather. Suddenly, there we were looking at all the stars and planets, crystal clear with no moon, and our trainee navigator's blood well and truly pumping! He had a ball!! When we got back on the ground at Millom our staff wireless operator said that he had been listening to a commercial radio station in New York with excellent reception. When I told him what height we had been at he almost wet his pants! Our flying roster at Millom was two weeks day / two weeks night flying and at any time if there was cloud cover on Black Combe, day flying was cancelled, but of course at night time this was not apparent, and we flew in all sorts of very nasty weather. I can recall one night in particular when towards the end of the first turbulent, training flight I was absolutely bushed, and it beats me to this day, how I got the bird down in one piece. At the second briefing on this night the Operations Officer asked if there were any pilots who would prefer to give it a miss. I was the only starter, and was excused with good grace. I think I was in the cot by 12.30am, and did not surface until about 10.00 hrs that day, which gave me about 10 minutes to get down to the next briefing. It was the only occasion that I had to do this so it got tucked away as a learning experience! Whilst at Millom I applied for a commission, and went down to the Midlands for my interview. I was successful and I became a Pilot Officer on the 24th July 1944 and one week later my posting came through.

Boomerang!

I was posted back to Cark in Cartmel as a Staff Pilot Instructor! To be honest I didn't really enjoy being at Cark but I had a good pal there who was another Aussie. I can't remember his name but he was from somewhere north of Brisbane, Queensland. Anyway, there I was, sat keeping an eye on rookie staff pilots and making the most of it. I remember as a feature of WWII night flying, that at each, pre flight briefing, every pilot was given an altitude to fly at in the event of an air raid warning, and he had to circle the nearest 'PUNDIT' at that level. Now, these were only 200 feet apart, and as a result, every pilot and crew prayed very hard that every altimeter was set at the same barometric setting! At one stage I came to the conclusion that my name must have been left off the Duty Officer tasks list. This misconception was dispelled with after a long period of being detailed no duties, I found myself on duty on Christmas day 1944, it was then that the penny dropped! During this second stint at Cark I had to undertake a night training flight with a trainee squadron leader who had joined the RAF in 1937, and had not done any night flying since his early training days. We took off into the usual British night, rain, St Elmo's fire and turbulence which did nothing to bolster the S/LDR's confidence! Anyway, very soon into the flight the dear old S/LDR went into a steep left hand turn with a frightening loss of altitude as a result. He froze at the controls despite my comments and I was forced to take over control of the aircraft. It took all of my concentration to get back to straight and level flying, but whilst I was checking our position, I got the horrible feeling that we were once again back in a left hand steep turn, I was horrified to find us on checking, that we were in fact in a tight RIGHT hand turn! Oh dear! Back to base and glad of it! As you will have gathered, some flights remain in ones memory.

At some point in February 1945 I flew a cross country exercise right up into the hills of Scotland, with a full moon, no cloud and the ground brilliant white under a covering of snow, it was magnificent! A short time later I met up with a Lancashire lass, let us call her Miss X, we would scoot off together to all sorts of places for weekends away when I was on leave. Finally, she came to me with the news that she was expecting, so I did the so called "decent thing" and married her. Surprisingly for me, two weeks after the event she decided that, no she was not expecting and I was left to accept the embarrassing fact that I had been 'conned'!

I took my last flight with the air force on the 26th July 1945 and received my next posting very soon afterwards.

Boomerang!

My next posting was back to RAF Millom! No longer a flying unit but now No.14 Aircrew Holding Unit. The station was full of Aussies like me who were waiting to be shipped home. I was back at Millom for about two and a half months during which time I did a month's course for aircrew officers down in Hereford and a two week air sea rescue course at Blackpool after which I became Millom's A.S.R Officer.

At the end of my stay at Millom, and after three weeks in Brighton, I boarded the H.M.T. AQUITANIA for a very pleasant cruise home to Adelaide, via Freetown, Sierra Leone, and Cape Town. I was given a shore pass, and with my good mate F/O John Bails DFC in tow, set off to see the sights. We met up with a mother and daughter who very kindly put us up for the night in their home, all above board, I can assure you! And set off back next morning to re-board our boat. We managed to thumb a lift off a couple of lasses but when we got to the dock the Aquitania was just putting out to sea!! We were extremely lucky for there was an escort about to go out to the ship and on our request we were given a free ride, and climbed up a scramble net to the many cheers and catcalls of our fellow passengers. I disembarked at Sydney and arrived home by troop train on the 28th November 1945. My family were very relieved to have me back in one piece! There were many renewal gatherings with old school mates, and it was here that I learnt that out of our crowd of seven lads, only one had not come back. His name was Bruce Davies, and he was killed on a heavy bomber training flight before he even began operational duties. In March 1946 I had a talk with my Dad about a photographic exhibition I saw in London and which preyed upon my mind.

The exhibition illustrated the liberation of some of the German concentration camps. I had seen this exhibition in April 1945 and had spent about an hour trying to take it all in. It was truly horrific and it took all the willpower I had not to cry. I have only ever seen about 10% of the pictures I saw there ever displayed to the public again. I was quite appalled when my father told me that the Germans should be forgiven and our paths became quite divergent after that. I had applied for a post with Australian National Airways but the course I was to go on was cancelled, I had put in some hard work in anticipation too. Anyway, following a successful interview with Mr J.P. Rayland, the operations manager for Trans Australia Airlines, in July 1946, I was engaged as a trainee first officer with effect from the 9th September 1946 on No.3 course at Point Cook, Victoria, the course was six weeks long. I completed the course OK, did my navigators studies by correspondence course, and after a further eleven months flying, I was a fully fledged F/O. In October 1947 I was posted to Adelaide as a first officer with T.A.A. and did my first flight on Saturday the 1st November 1947. This was the inaugural flight to Darwin, via Mount Eba, Oodnadatta, Alice Springs Tennant Creek, Daly Waters and Katherine. A two pilot crew, one hostess, no VHF radio, no cockpit loudspeakers, and very little gear – we were very rarely given the OK to take the controls. Once the routine started I was averaging 75 to 80 hours a month.

I remember a couple of incidents from these days, and on both occasions the skipper was Eric Kneig. Once, after leaving Alice Springs, and finishing our airborne lunch, cruising on towards Tennants Creek I was suddenly aroused by an urgent request for a position report. I looked across and there was Eric, also sound asleep! I replied and all was well.

The second thing was during a charter flight to pick up 21 immigrants from Alice Springs. After a couple of hours I had to answer the call of nature and went to the little boy's room. Shortly after closing the door we encountered a very severe bout of turbulence during which there was a tremendous crashing in the gallery area and it rained heavily in the loo! When I returned to the cockpit it was obvious that the "turbulence" was of human instigation, as Eric was laughing his head off! In 1950 the R.A.A.F. had three de Havilland Mosquitoes based in Alice Springs doing a very comprehensive photographic survey, and being in the Air Force Reserve, I was given 2 hours and 40 minutes in one of these beautiful birds. I had a ball!! In 1951, after three attempts I passed my command training and was posted back to Adelaide, flying more or less the same roster but with many more modern aids, VHF etc.

I actually began my command training with Captain Harry Locke, D.SO, DFC who had taken part in the dambuster raids, he was a great bloke and taught me a lot. Sometime in 1952 my roster changed and I had about a 36 hour stopover period in Alice Springs. It was the time when the John Flynn memorial church was being built and I had met John Flynn when I was a small boy. At a loose end I volunteered my services as a builder's labourer to his number two, the Rev Fred McKay who insisted on paying me for my efforts. I accepted but made amends by leaving most of it behind the bar of the Alice Springs Hotel. Every time I visit and see that church I get a good feeling knowing that I helped to build it. Shortly after this I came close to getting the sack after raising concerns about pilots exceeding the 8 hour flight limitation. This matter really worried me, but resulted in a hell of a mess which could have been sorted out without all the unpleasantness it incurred had a little common sense been employed. It resulted in a good deal of disruption and me being 'sent to Coventry' but I strongly believed it was a safety issue and stuck to my guns. In the end I was told by a senior staff member that no action would be taken against me, and asked if I wanted the reports I had submitted, returned to me, I declined the offer. I told him that my reports were addressed to the Melbourne Senior Route Captain and they were now his property!

I remember one DC3 night flight from Darwin to Alice Springs in the wet season, with John Dawe as first officer. The severe turbulence began almost immediately, and it was so bad that I could only hand fly for about five minutes, with the aircraft suddenly going up at about 4,000 feet per minute, indicated airspeed about 170 knots, gear down, flaps down, no power on, then bang!, down at the same rate, about 90 knots, gear up, flaps up, full power and very savage continuous turbulence, which was so bad that it gave you eyeball bounce. This is when the body is vibrating, but the eyeballs are vibrating at a different rate, very difficult to see clearly when this occurs, it was incredible. John could also only manage about five minutes, but between us we made it. All the passengers and our hostess were sick, and it was an awful night but after a while things improved dramatically. I think of all the first officers I flew with over the years, John Dawe would have to rank among the best, and I think that, had it been someone else that night I would not be here telling this story.

Keeping in mind the summary of man's 95 years of heavier than air flight, 1903 – 1998 it is satisfying to note that I have been involved for very nearly 56 of those years!

Ross Blanchard 2004

MR I. BAIN – CARK 1943

I was stationed at the Staff Pilot Training Unit, Cark, from November 16th to December 30th, 1943. It was not a happy posting. Having signed up to go anywhere and do anything for King and Country, I – along with virtually all the aircrew in the Course – was bitterly disappointed (and more than a little embarrassed) by being relegated to the flying of trainee navigators around the Irish Sea in effing Ansons.

I am sure that the Lake District lives up to its reputation as one of the premier beauty spots of Britain in summer, in winter, even the few Canadians on the Course who were accustomed to very-much-below-zero winter weather 'back home' found the Cark winter to be miserably damp and bone-chillingly cold. The Nissen huts we used as living-quarters were 'heated' by a tiny stove in the middle of the room in which we burned any unattached wooden objects and a few pieces of coal from the normally well-guarded pile. As I recall, we often slept fully clothed – and in flying suits – and more often than not, we had only cold water for our ablutions.

One entry in my log book suggests that I landed from about 20 feet – described as being "rough". That would have been an understatement if true but I do remember one occasion – at night – when I misjudged my height and thought that I would be wearing the undercarriage around my neck when we stopped bouncing.

As frightening as that heavy landing was for me and those flying with me, it was not as serious a risk as the night when I was what seemed like inches from a collision with another aircraft. The practice was for aircraft to take off on a pre-determined schedule, climb to a designated height and then fly over the airfield setting the designated course. It was not anticipated that delays would lead to two aircraft planning to set course over the airfield at the same time!

On this occasion, as I was getting ready to set course on our trip, I noticed the lights of another aircraft off to my port side. It can be difficult at night to positively determine just where the other aircraft is and what the pilot intends doing. Within seconds, it became apparent that the other aircraft was drifting in my direction and at approximately the same altitude. As I pointed the nose of my aircraft sharply down, the other pilot pulled his up and I braced for the sound and feel of metal on metal as we passed. When we assembled in the briefing–room after the flight, a pilot – obviously the other pilot – stood up and in shockingly obscene terms described what had happened and challenged the offending pilot to identify himself. Fat chance!

On happier note – local families in the area were very generous with their hospitality and I remember one pleasant occasion when several of the men on my course were invited to an evening with a local pub owner and his family in their living quarters above the pub. Their daughter had invited several other local girls and with food, beverage and music it was really as close to a family occasion as the airmen – especially the Colonials – would enjoy during their stay in Britain.

Ian Bain - 2012

MR R.A. CROXALL – CARK 1943

I arrived at RAF Cark on the 2nd July 1943 having been posted in as a Staff Wireless Operator from the radio school at RAF Madley. Having examined my log book I see that I was involved in a forced landing at RAF Millom on the 15th July after problems with our MK1 Avro Anson. Our pilot that day was Pilot/Sgt Colling and fortunately we escaped the incident without injury.

During my time at the station I flew exclusively in Ansons and my pilots were Sgt Roberts, F/O Clarkson, P/O Bowen, P/O McKillingon, Sgt Wright and Sgt Tennyson. The aircraft I flew in whilst there were J2, C3, J3, M3, N1, M1 K2, C2, L4 and K1. Our job was to take part in various navigational exercises and during my stay at the unit I clocked up 37 hours and 45 minutes; 28 hours 50 minutes daytime flying and 8 hours 55 minutes night flying. Our Senior Instructor was F/O S B Durrant and my lasting memory of Cark is that of a very happy station.

At the end of December 1943 I was posted to RAF Bishops Count in Northern Ireland as an instructor to the trainee wireless operators there. Having completed a spell there I teamed up with an old school friend who was now a pilot. The pair of us passed through an Operational Training Unit en route to 'Ops', with first of all 199 Squadron and latterly with 171 Squadron, carrying out special duties in support of Bomber Command. Unfortunately, on our fourth 'op' we crashed on take-off, with my old school pal receiving the blame and being posted out as a consequence.

I finally completed my operational tour on the 13th March 1945 and the rest, as they say, is history. For the record, the pilot who replaced my pal was S/L Sturrock, a New Zealander.

I hope my memories of Cark are of use, I do recall fondly a very cosy pub in the village where I spent some happy hours!

Mr R A Croxall - 2011

MR DERRICK WILLIAM CROISDALE

I can honestly say that my stay at RAF Millom was the high spot of my ATC Service, although it almost put an end to all my future aspirations! I was a FLT/Sgt in our school A.T.C. (Bacup and Rawtenstall Grammar School, No. 589 SQDRN), and was already in the RAFV.R having been accepted for aircrew (pilot) training. I was seventeen years old and awaiting "call-up" after my eighteenth birthday.

My time at RAF Millom was spend at ATC summer camp in 1942 and was memorable because my first flight in an aircraft was nearly my last! The aircraft was an Avro Anson and we were engaged in a bombing exercise over the Duddon Estuary. I well remember the breathtaking views of the Lake District and Irish Sea. My most vivid memory however, is of the bomb which failed to release over the bombing range. Violent manoeuvres by the pilot failed to budge it. Eventually there was no option left but to return to the airfield and hope that the pilot would make one of his better, smoother landings, he did the bomb remained firmly in situ until safely removed by an armourer.

I was duly called up in 1943 and thanks to my A.T.C qualifications my preflight training was shortened by several months. In December 1943 I found myself aboard the S.S.Mauritania bound for the new world. My flying training was at No. 4 British Flying Training School (BFTS) Falcon Field, Mesa Arizona. Between Primary and Advanced training we had a period of leave enabling us to visit the Grand Canyon, Los Angeles, Santa Monica and Hollywood. The American hospitality was overwhelming and as soon as one stepped foot on one of the boulevards in Hollywood a car would screech to a halt and the occupants would invite you to their home. That happened to me and my two colleagues and we spent three days at the home of a yacht designer and his wife who lived opposite Betty Grable in Beverly Hills. I remember midnight barbecues on the beach at Santa Monica, very heady stuff for a young lad from East Lancashire who until joining the RAF, had never travelled further than Millom!

However, I duly got my "wings" in 1944 having flown Stearmans and Harvards, and upon my return to the UK in the SS Ile-de-France, along with about 10,000 American and Canadian troops, I was selected to become a flying instructor. I spent the next two years instructing at Elementary Flying Training Schools (Tiger Moths) and Advanced Flying Units (Airspeed Oxfords). I was "de-mobbed" in 1947 having accumulated 1,100 hours flying and having attained the highest instructors qualification awarded by the RAF, the A1 category. Curiously, none of my pupils were in the RAF, they were all either Army or Fleet Air Arm pupils of all ranks. My best pupil, then a F.A.A. Lieutenant, later rose to become a Vice Admiral having captained the aircraft carrier Ark Royal during the course of his career.

My post war career was in the Civil Service, involved mainly with the use of computers for administrative purposes. I started my computing at the National Physical Laboratory using the Automatic Computing Engine (ACE) pilot computer designed by Alan Turing, the Oxford Mathematician who, during the war, broke the German 'Enigma' code. I ended my career as a deputy director at the Civil Service College.

Apart from flying as a passenger I haven't done any really flying since my RAF Service. However, on my 70th birthday my wife and sons treated me to a 'hands on' flight in a Harvard! About the same time I used some Barclaycard 'profile' points on a short flight of nostalgia in a Tiger Moth at Booker airfield, which was the last airfield on which I served. In fact I flew from Booker to Blackpool in a Tiger Moth for my 'de-mob' at Kirkham! Incredibly, the Tiger Moth I flew turned out to be the one which I had flown in 1944/45 at RAF Woodley! nearly half a century had elapsed!

As a postscript, No.4 BFTS, Mesa Arizona produced two pilots of note, one famous the other infamous. Brian Trubshaw got his wings just before I did and went on to achieve fame as Concorde's test pilot, he was the famous one! The infamous one was John Stonehouse who got his wings after me and later achieved notoriety as Postmaster General in the Labour Government when he faked his own death by drowning. After his release from prison he resumed his attendance at our BFTS reunions, but sadly died relatively young.

Derrick. W. Croisdale 1997

MR JOE CRAWFORD, 1942 – 1944

I was, whilst at RAF Millom 1688290 LAC Crawford J and my duties were those of Flying Control Assistant.

Following basic training in Blackpool I travelled with a number of others up to our new posting in Cumberland. The weather was foul and as most of my companions were Southerners, several comments were made as we approached Millom. I remember one chap saying to his mates "hide your watches lads, they won't have seen one up here, their all hill shepherds", much of this was for my benefit as I was a West Coast Cumberland lad. I spent about two-thirds of my local service at Silecroft and the remainder at the airfield of RAF Millom.

Silecroft was the control unit for the stations bombing and air to air gunnery range. It consisted of a control tower situated about half a mile north of the aerodrome, the target was a large, square, wooden structure moored about ¾ of a mile offshore due west of us. The first thing to determine before bombing could commence was wind speed and direction.

The equipment used was a large framed mirror which was approximately one yard square, sectioned off in degrees and indicating the points of the compass. It stood as a completely level concrete base and on top of the mirror was a pretty basic sighting device, we also used a stopwatch.

Before the aircraft started its bombing run it released a smoke bomb upwind of the tower. As the smoke traversed across the mirror, using a wax pencil, the sight and the stopwatch, we could work out the winds speed and direction. This information was then passed to the aircraft via Flying Control at Millom. Alongside the tower were two large oblong wooden flags pointing in the direction of the target, white on one surface and dark on the other. These flags were hinged if the white surface was uppermost it indicated to the aircraft that he was bombing on the range by himself if both white surfaces were uppermost however, it meant that two aircraft were using the range. These indicators were illuminated during night bombing.

To determine the accuracy of the night bombing we sat behind an oblong Perspex screen which was situated inside the window of the tower, which was in darkness. The screen was graduated, and in a direct line with the target. As the bombs exploded, giving off a bright flash, we marked the position on the screen, by this method we could work out the accuracy of bombing.

There was also a bombing range on the Duddon estuary used both day and night, during night bombing the crews would at odd times mistake the illuminated flags for the target and there would be a sudden flash and explosion outside the quadrant, it certainly made you jump!

I should add that there was a bombing range over at Askam but this was used for daytime bombing only. On our site at Silecroft there was a flashing beacon for homing purposes, we changed the letters of the day by moving a series of cams. The letters were issued to all crews flying out of Millom, and during the frequent poor weather they homed in on our beacon, when the weather was extremely bad, a series of paraffin flares were set out along the edges of the main runway to disperse any low lying mist, and three searchlights were crisscrossed over the airfield when necessary. This searchlight aid was known as SANDRA, (search and direct returning aircraft).

We had our own small dance band at Silecroft playing

for local dances; the Miners Arms was a popular place for us at Silecroft. In Haverigg the Star Inn and the Working Men's Club were the drinking places. I think I can speak for all the service personnel at RAF Millom when I say that the local people were always kind to us during our service at the unit. We had some great times and some very sad times at Millom. I recall one nice warm summers day I was helping to man the crash tender and watching the fitters starting up the Anson engines. I saw one fitter start the engines on his aircraft and then, for some reason, accidentally walk into the arc of the revolving propeller. He was killed instantly. It was a shocking and terrible thing to see.

Also I recall well the day a young WAAF was killed in the station sick quarters. It was a horrific accident involving a Very pistol (flare gun) and one which upset us all a great deal.

I remember too, whilst being on duty as part of the crash tender team, when a large tanker of high octane fuel ignited and we had to tackle the fire. We attempted to cover it with foam but the heat drove us back, the best we could do was contain it and stop it spreading. It was fortunate indeed that it caught fire well away from any aircraft or buildings; it could have been a complete disaster.

I also recall being on duty one night when one of our Ansons went into the sea just off Silecroft. The pilot and crew had landed safely and were taxiing their way to dispersal when Flying Control fired up a red flare, I have never been able to remember why, other than, it was a complete mistake – whatever the circumstances, the pilot believing that it was unsafe to remain on the ground, performed an emergency take off straight away. Having done this he carried out a circuit to the north of the station, carefully skirting Black Combe and whilst about to begin a first approach for a second landing dived into the sea just offshore of the old coastguard house at Silecroft. Maybe a loss of airspeed and a stall was to blame but all the crew lost their lives as a result.

I now live very near the Kells in Whitehaven and I lost several friends when one of our aircraft crashed there after coming apart whilst passing over.

I knew a lot of the crews and pilots as I used to work behind the Sergeants Mess bar; there were some mad boozing sessions in there at times I can tell you!! The sad thing about the Kells crash was that I had just arrived in Carlisle by train when it happened but I could not go anywhere near the accident as I was travelling without a pass.

I attended more than one crash scene but the worst one I was ever involved with concerned one of Millom's Ansons which crashed into Muncaster Fell. The impact must have been extremely violent and the crew were all killed as the aircraft disintegrated into a vertical crag. The poor lads will have known nothing about it but for me it was one of the most upsetting things I had to deal with during those years. I recall that when we returned to Millom having carried out our sad duties on the fellside that day we were served a late meal and expected to be hungry, such was the reality of service life in those days.

Joe Crawford – 1998

MR EDWIN 'DIXIE' DEAN – 1942–1945

I joined the Civil Air Guard in 1938 and did my first solo flight in an Avro Cadet. In 1939 the Civil Air Guard was disbanded and soon afterwards I joined the RAF. After a period of initial training I was posted to America where I completed my pilots training with the U.S. Army Air Corps.

On returning to England I was posted to RAF Millom which was designated No. 2 Observer Advanced Flying Unit. I arrived at Millom in late 1942 and flew Boulton Paul Defiants with "G" gunnery flight until this was disbanded in 1943. From that point I was appointed Flight Commander of "B" Flight flying Avro Ansons at the rank of Flt/Lt and remained as such until the unit closed down, after leaving Millom I was posted to RAF Llandwrog in Wales and ended my service at RAF Watchfield in Wiltshire. It was all rather a long time ago I am afraid but I have several clear recollections from my service at Millom, some glad, some sad.

I remember well my time flying the Defiants, they had a tremendously fast approach and landing speed due to the added weight of their gun turret. The Defiant, rather like the fighter type of aircraft it resembled, had a sliding cockpit canopy. Pilots were strictly forbidden to fly with this open due to slipstream but of course rules are made to be broken and we sometimes did.

On one memorable occasion I fell foul of breaking this rule with potentially deadly consequences. Having collected my very young, new, inexperienced, and doubtless nervous gunnery pupil, I took off out to sea towards the ranges with my canopy wide open. I never could, and cannot to this day remember how it happened, but at some point my arm became caught in the slipstream. I do remember well enough though, the agony as my shoulder was instantly dislocated! My pupil was thankfully unaware of what had occurred and must have wondered what was going on as we turned back for the airfield for what I hoped would be a safe and successful emergency landing. Flying the aircraft with a dislocated shoulder was difficult enough but as I made my landing approach I was sweating profusely and on the verge of losing consciousness. Thankfully I made it safely down and had no sooner rolled to a stop when I passed out with the pain. I cannot imagine what the bewildered pupil must have been thinking, but I always closed my cockpit canopy from that day onwards!

I have many happier memories of my time at Millom but recall a fatal crash involving one of our friends, Henry O'Gara, who was killed along with all his crew when the Anson he was piloting suffered some sort of structural failure in the sky over Whitehaven.

I have recently been flying once again, this time in a Cessna with a qualified instructor from Caernarfon Airport, which of course was the old RAF Llandwrogg; most enjoyable. In the course of our flights the instructor asked me had I ever flown an Anson or a Lysander. I told him that indeed I had flown both, at which he told me that the airport collection are hoping to have one of both types by next year! I'll let you know if they let me have a go!

Mr Edwin Dean 1993

ALFRED WISE DUDLEY - THE UNIFORM YEARS 1940 - 1946

Strictly speaking, I suppose with regard to the wearing of uniform I should start with my Home Guard time or Local Defence Volunteers (L.D.V.) as it was first known. This was formed post Dunkirk, in May 1940, and open to everyone to volunteer above the age of 17.

A bit of a "bits and pieces" arrangement to start with, but they did become more professional as time went on with the issue of uniforms and rifles, and now looking like a sort of army. Not, I think, that it would have been much of a match for any invading forces dropping out of the sky, with a maximum of 5 rounds of ammunition available per man. We had our share of "Dads Army" characters too, they were all there. If it hadn't been about such a serious business, it would have been a laugh a minute, however, I suppose it did achieve a degree of propaganda and confused the enemies thinking, it certainly confused a lot of people here!

The really serious uniform time started rather later, and my first attempt to be of assistance in the conflict was early August 1940, a week after my 18th birthday. I made my way to the joint recruiting office in Manchester to volunteer for flying duties, but after a couple of interviews and some form filling, I was informed that I could not be accepted for aircrew training, as my educational qualifications were not of the required high standard (I had of course left school at the age of 14). However, I was told I could join the R.A.F as a general duties entrant, this offer I rejected and said I would go next door and join the Navy, not that I had any intention of doing this, there was too much cold water involved there!

However, my next attempt in April 1941 did meet with rather more success, as the reality of the situation had finally become recognised, in as much as losses in personnel were overtaking new entrants coming in, and the strict educational requirements were having to be relaxed to further a push for higher numbers to be brought into the system.

The powers that be, therefore, agreed that I could be finally accepted for aircrew training, and could be actually allowed to get into one of their aeroplanes! So it was off to Padgate for the aircrew selection board and medicals.

The medical examination was giving me some cause for concern at this time, as I had rheumatic fever as a child and was aware that I had a heart murmur as is usual post this illness. I also knew that this would have precluded me from aircrew duties, so I omitted to mention this on the form I was given to complete listing childhood illnesses and hoped for the best. Fortunately, a lot of the doctors who were doing the medicals were older retired practitioners who had been brought in to fill the gaps, and were not over efficient. The sheer numbers going through meant that things were a little rushed. My murmur was not picked up, even after the preliminary checks of blowing up a column of mercury and holding it for one minute and the quick whizz round in a chair and then standing on one leg, and various other things to be completed pre-medical.

More interviews followed, the whole process taking two full days, and then, I was finally accepted as a trainee WOP/AG (wireless operator/machine gunner), sworn in, accepted the "Kings Shilling", and then designated the service number 1049069. From that point on I was indeed just a number.

After this it was back to my civilian status and also the Home Guard on deferred service to wait until my number came up in the queue for places in the training schools. This finally arrived on September 19th 1941, and it was off to Padgate again for kitting out and then to Blackpool for the start of training proper.

RAF Squires Gate

I spent 4 months at Blackpool doing all the usual training stuff, drills etc. plus a round of inoculations, anti typhoid, typhus, malaria etc. all in anticipation of overseas postings. Pretty vicious stuff it was too. Knocked me out for nearly a week and for a couple of days I didn't know whether my arm belonged to me or not. These all to be topped up at a later date; I made a mental note of avoiding the next time, thinking there had to be a way of giving it all a miss. But more of that later. The main focus of the training was on learning and using Morse code. This was relentless and aimed at getting up to speed by a certain time. There were various venues for this, the best of which was the Winter Gardens and the worst was the disused Tram sheds (which was where I unfortunately was allocated to). They were cold, flag floors wth no heating. As the weather got colder, it necessitated the wearing of overcoats and gloves. We sat on long tables with a pair of earphones clamped on over a cap, for two 2 hour sessions every day, and occasionally three. Really it was mass learning by saturation. With a test every 2 weeks and the speed being increased up to a maximum of 12 words per minute for passing out, there was only one second chance for a failed test. If failed again, it was a case of cease training – commonly known as CXd. Understandably this pressure of continuous Morse in the headset did affect a few people and resulted in a degree of temporary insanity. With 3 or 4 weeks in a psychiatric unit (Feldmans Arcade had been adapted for this purpose) they recovered quite quickly but were never allowed to return to the business of "Morse" in any shape or form.

Training apart, the things that most remain in my mind about Blackpool were, on the plus side, the wonderful efficiency of bath parades. These were twice a week at Derby Baths (long gone now of course) with thousands going through every day. If the shower was taken quickly, there was time for a few lengths in the main pool. It was all timed extremely well, with my squad allocated 5.15pm every Tuesday and Friday. The local hospitality was much in evidence too, and I remember particularly the cheap rides on the sea front trams. This was a maximum of one penny if in uniform, regardless of the distance travelled, and one could ride from Squires Gate to Fleetwood for this.

On the downside was my billet, it must have been one of the worst in Blackpool. Twenty eight of us in there, the food was awful, never properly cooked, and for example the same pudding every day of the week, and only a change on Sunday when it was rice. The landlady employed 3 or 4 young Jewish girls (refugees) and paid them a pittance. She was regularly seen going out by taxi in the evenings dripping in gold jewellery. There was a resident Corporal, who we had to address complaints to, but it didn't make any difference. I have always believed that he was getting a good pay off every week. Most of those Blackpool Landladies did a really good job and treated twi-SR boarders like their own sons, but for just a few it was an opportunity to make a lot more money than they had ever been able to make running second rate boarding houses. Afterwards I lived on many camps where cooking was on a mass produced scale, but never any as bad as my Blackpool experience. At least I was never hungry again, and didn't have to spend every penny I could spare on buying food!

Now, after acquiring the necessary speed of taking Morse, it was time to move on. After a weeks leave, it was off down to Yatesbury in Wiltshire, this being January 1942.

RAF Yatesbury

A cold bleak January it was, and turned into a long winter, continuously frozen up everywhere, and lasting until mid March. Not much heating in the huts or in the cookhouse which was a large Spartan building, with seating for up to a thousand. By the time the food had been collected and taken to the table there wasn't a lot of warmth left in it! However, one got used to the conditions eventually, and, as well as the continuation of the process of gradually increasing Morse speeds, there were now classroom and workshop periods we learned about the technical side of radio, fault finding experience mostly, to be able to decide which valve/fuse to change if the equipment went down whilst airborne. We also had some responsibility for the general electrical systems of the aircraft.

One small episode that might be worth mentioning concerns the next round of vaccinations. I didn't much fancy these, so after observing the procedure and knowing my day I prepared myself by a visit to the NAAFI store to buy a packet of plasters. Armed with these I went down to the medical hut and joined the queue waiting for injections. I rolled up my sleeve and stuck a plaster on my arm. I then joined the queue waiting to have pay books stamped to confirm injections given and displayed my bit of plaster. Result (pay book stamped and all quite painless, with no after affects at all!). As I mentioned before, there was always a way.

My time at Yatesbury finally ended in April 1942, and after the end of term exams, I was finally a fully trained radio operator. Plus I was in receipt of a 50% rise in pay, still not great but welcome nevertheless, it was actually from 3 shillings per day to 4 shillings and 6 pence. (In the metric scale this would be from 15p a day to 22p a day, difficult to make comparisons due to much changed values). Finally, it was home leave for a week and then on my way to No.10 Air Gunnery School as a staff radio operator, ground service.

RAF Walney

When I was first informed that my posting was to Walney Island I thought that I was going overseas as I had never heard of it. I suppose it was overseas in a way, being an island, but I was relieved to discover it only a short bus ride across the estuary from Barrow-in-Furness. The channel was up to the shipyards on the Barrow side, where the submarines being made were launched. I often stood on the bridge and watched, and wondered how many of their crews would survive the war. I remained at Walney for most of the summer of 1942, not leaving until mid-August. This proved to be a very enjoyable period as, being a radio operator and working shifts, I was excused all other duties and parades. I lived in a hut designated as a signals hut, with all the other signals operators – it was all very comfortable. We worked 12 hour shifts, alternate weeks on days and nights, with very little in the way of radio traffic. We were required to listen to Group Control broadcasts every hour, with an occasional individual message to 10 AGS (not that these were very important). I think it was just to make sure we were still awake! The whole network, with control at Preston, covered all the west coast, and was in place as a back-up in case of landlines being destroyed by enemy action. We had one day off a week and, as it was a particularly good summer, I made a habit of getting up mid-afternoon when on nights and going down to the beach for a couple of hours with a book, returning in time for an evening meal before going on 'watch' (the hours were 8 to 8). Sadly, as all good things must, it came to an end, and I found myself on my way down to London.

No.7 Signals School

I arrived in London, South Kensington SW7, in mid-August 1942. The whole school were billeted in a block of flats, known as Albert Court Flats, directly opposite the Albert Hall. They had been and indeed still are, "Luxury Flats". All fittings had been stripped out of course, apart from essentials, and the lifts no longer worked. Not a lot of fun when living on the 6th Floor as I was, with 2 flights of stairs to each floor. It was very up-market after living in a hut, I think nearly everyone was surprised to find baths fitted with glass doors. Some more so than others, having probably never seen a bathroom before. There were a dozen or so of us to each flat.

The course was 14 weeks duration and designated as a Radio Maintenance Course. I only discovered in recent years that after passing out I had become "*Aircraftman 1st class Radio Operator Mechanic*". I don't remember ever noticing the increase in pay that should have gone with this sudden elevation in rank – wouldn't have been much though! Our classrooms were in the science museum, which had been stripped of all its contents for safe keeping until after the war's end. Workshops were in what had been the sculpture galleries and our dining room was in the basement of the arts building. A bit of a doubtful place this for a dining area, as I remember when on one occasion a drowned rat was discovered at the bottom of one of the large tea urns, (kind of puts you off tea!). We paraded daily on Cromwell Road before going off to classes. P.T. was in Hyde Park, quite pleasant this though. In the early days when the weather was still warm, a swim in the Serpentine was the order of the day, and when the weather was inclement, P.T. periods were in the Albert Hall. Suppose I can always claim to have appeared there.

As we were now in an advanced stage of training we did not have to be back in Barracks until 23.59hrs each evening – a privilege this for a training school, it was usually 22.30hrs. I was not the least familiar with the way around London, but soon found the tube system made it possible to quickly find the way to anywhere. With very little spare cash, it was not possible to sample many of the attractions that were still available, but I did manage a visit to St. Paul's Cathedral and to Kew Gardens, plus an occasional walk along the embankment and a few visits to speakers corner. I also remember what was probably the best forces canteen I ever encountered. It was in the basement of the Brompton Oratory, and staffed by the ladies of the church. Food and drinks were excellent with occasional cream cakes on the menu. (How did they do it?) Mid January 1943 brought an end to my stay in the capital. It was a pleasurable enough period and now I found myself on the way to Madley in Herefordshire, to at last be introduced to a real aeroplane!

RAF Madley

Madley did not appear to be very hospitable on arrival. It was a wartime built establishment, hurriedly put together. Nissan Huts and everywhere widely dispersed; each section seemed to be at least half a mile apart, with a long walk to the ablution site. After the long walk for a wash, it was a further long hike to the dining hall and classrooms, with a final stretch down to the flights. never being anywhere near the point of residence again all day, and it was essential to carry small kit around all the time i.e. shave and wash gear, and eating utensils. However, the course was quite enjoyable, and mainly aimed at using the radio equipment whilst airborne. This was at first in Dominies, a twin engine aircraft that was really quite small, but with enough space for 5 pupils and an instructor plus pilot – virtually a flying classroom (which worked very well).

The last 2 weeks were spent going solo in a single engine aircraft, Proctors, with just a pilot and then doing individual work on the radio. I found the whole process very pleasant, particularly so as flying was a completely new experience, as indeed it was for most of us. I really enjoyed flying up and down the Wye Valley. This all came to an end in early March 1943, and I was on my way to gunnery school for a course in air gunnery.

RAF Mona

So now I was off to Mona in Anglesey to No.3 AGS. Again this was a somewhat dispersed establishment, with Nissan Huts for accommodation. They were very cold at that time of year, with just a shelf running down each side of the hut. Very active those shelves were too at night, with mice running up and down.

Air Gunnery practice was done from Blackburn Bothas – not a very comfortable aircraft and extremely unpopular with most aircrew. Three pupils for each aircraft were carried, with 2 machine guns in the turret to fire 200 rounds each. We fired at a drogue towed by another aircraft, the tips of the bullets were coloured in order to establish which pupil was responsible for each hole in the drogue. They were then dropped in the dropping field, where they were then collected by WAAFs and the holes duly counted. I sometimes think they would add a few more hits to the score if they thought someone had a poor score. I never heard of anyone actually failing the course! In my end of term report I see that I was assessed as above average, I think some kind WAAF must have added a few to my total.

When firing was completed, some of the pilots would fly up to Blackpool to go round the tower a couple of times. One other incident occurred after a couple of weeks when we had started with the flying side of the course. I got my flying boots off the shelf in the hut, and a dozen or so little pink mice dropped out of them. It appeared that Mr. and Mrs. Mouse had set up home there, not much fur left on the boot! So it was off down to stores to exchange them for new pair – did me a good turn actually as the ones I got were a much better style and quality than the ones I was discarding.

My time at Mona came to an end in late March 1943. With passing out this time came promotion to the somewhat exalted rank of Sergeant, and with this came a very welcome increase in pay. It's difficult to quantify in terms of today's wages, but it more or less doubled my income. With the passing out parade came the list of postings to say where I was headed off to after a week's leave I found myself due to report to RAF Cark, No.1 SPTU. I had no idea at the time what sort of establishment it was, or indeed where it was but I was soon to find out!

RAF Cark

I soon found out RAF Cark was based in Flookburgh, close to Grange-over-Sands. That set the location, but I was still in the dark as to knowing what it was. It turned out to be another course, they seemed never ending – now to turn me into a Radio Instructor, Air Operating. It all sounded very grand and I could not imagine why I found myself earmarked for this. I can only think, in retrospect that my number had just been pulled out of a hat somewhere; I'm sure it wasn't due to any special ability on my part.

This six week spell proved to be very enjoyable as it was now late spring, with a lot of fair weather periods. Not much of the time was spent in classrooms, mostly it was spent airborne without an instructor. It was really just a case of working through the syllabus whilst flying on cross country exercises. We had a second pilot, one flying whilst the other did the navigating. They were training to be navigational instructors, to fly trainee navigators around, hence the name, "Staff Pilot Training Unit". My course work consisted mainly of supplying these trainee Pilot/Navigators with enough in the way of Fixes and Bearings to enable them to plot their course.

The aircraft in use were Ansons, in which I was to spend a lot of my time during the ensuing 18 months. I found them very comfortable if a little overcrowded with 5 crew members. Nothing exceptional occurred whilst at Cark. The only thing of note that I remember was flying in formation over Carnforth one Saturday afternoon, where they were having a "Fund raising day" for the war effort.

RAF Millom

On completion of the course I found myself on my way to Millom, designated No.2 AFU (Advanced Flying Unit) where the pupils were already qualified aircrew and were there to gain further air experience.

Millom seemed to be agreeable and friendly enough on my arrival. I found my quarters were to be a single room contained in a block, very small and sparsely furnished but nevertheless a pleasant change from living in a barrack block. It contained a bed, a small but comfortable enough chair and a small table covered with a piece of old blanket. There were no facilities for hanging clothes up, but a couple of nails in the wall took care of that. Heating consisted of just a single pipe running through the room, and I noted that there would be just enough space to park my cycle. The communal ablutions were situated at one end of the block, all very nice though, particularly so as this was the first time in my life that I had a room of my own! (I was now 20 years of age.)

On checking out the routines, I found out that the mess was only a hundred yards away and Millom itself about 3 miles distance. Hence the bike was to prove very useful over the following 18 months. A private laundry service was provided through the mess, paid for through a mess bill at the end of each month. Apart from clothing, sheets were changed weekly (as aircrew an extra privilege was to always have sheets), the mess was always able to come up with extra rations such as eggs and poultry (much of it I suspect obtained via the black market and the farms of the Lake District). Meal times were somewhat changed, with the main meal of the day now being evening dinner. This was to accommodate ever changing flight times, all of which was to maximise air time at 24 hours a day weather permitting. A light meal was served at lunchtime, with afternoon tea with sandwiches available in the anteroom for those who required them at about 4pm. We enjoyed waitress service for evening dinner. All-in-all it really was very civilised.

The downside to all this, of course, was having to be available to fly at any time of the day or night when the weather was deemed suitable. We flew in some fairly dodgy conditions and, as Ansons were not equipped with any de-icing facilities, plus the fact that they had a ceiling of about 12,000 feet, and could not often fly above the clouds, meaning that on frosty nights we were briefed to take care when approaching high ground!

On an organisational level we were divided into 4 flights; 2 flights on days and 2 on nights. We flew alternate fortnights days and nights, with one day off each week. Days off were usually spent in Barrow, with evenings in Millom when not scheduled to fly. The local pubs were the favourite venues. (Not much else to do in Millom). There was always the option of an early return to the mess when the pumps ran dry, as frequently happened in those days. Home leave came quite frequently; being aircrew we were allowed one week off in every six, normally taken as a fortnight every 3 months.

However, we did not suffer anywhere near the casualty rates of Bomber Command, where life expectancy for a new crew at this time was 5 operational flights. We did however suffer occasional accidents, with the limited capabilities of the aircraft – many of which had been well used before arriving at Millom. This, coupled with the fact that servicing was somewhat minimal, did lead to some problems. It has to be said though that most accidents with fatalities occurred due to weather conditions or errors in navigation. Mountains or high ground did have a nasty habit of getting in the way! We lost about a dozen aircraft with crews during my time there, plus many other accidents of a lesser degree – not that we were any different to other air training establishments. There were crashes of one sort or another every day. Over 100 aircraft perished on the slopes of Snowdon during those years. Four of our Ansons during my period found their graveyard there.

All of this apart, I really quite enjoyed my time there. Between Walney, Cark, and Millom I spent about half of my service life in that SW corner of the Lake District. It is only in retrospect that I perceive many of the delights there were in spending time in that neck of the woods. One that I particularly remember is of returning from the west after night details just as dawn was breaking on summer mornings, and flying into the rising sun, and seeing from the observation dome the mountains casting their first shadows, with the sun's rays reflecting from the lakes. Not that this was seen as anything special at the time, all we were thinking about then was getting back to egg, chips, and often bacon. Also, that would be served between night details; and if on the final flight, hoping that the next night's flying would be cancelled so that a visit to town could be arranged!

One other duty that should have been appreciated but wasn't, occurred only occasionally (twice in my case) involved changing the batteries on the mountain warning transmitters that were situated on high ground. These were heavy duty car type batteries carried in back packs designed for the purpose (certainly heavy!). We were in teams of 6 and took turns in carrying them, the whole process in getting to the top and back down again took about 5 or 6 hours. I remember on one occasion having to use ice picks to gain access to the container housing the equipment. When the changing process had been completed the discharged batteries had to be carried back down the mountain side. I suppose I can always claim to have climbed Scafell and Skiddaw, not so much of a climb really, as we were guided up the easy route by a local guide, it was heavy going though; there was however a bonus at the end of the day in the form of a evening meal laid on at a local hostelry, on one occasion this was the Royal Oak, Ambleside.

I was fortunate during my time at Millom not to have been involved in any accidents of any description, even minor ones. I did avoid (if that is the right word) 2 accidents that led to fatalities, simply because fate decreed that I was not in the wrong place at the wrong time. The first of these occurred in my early time there before we had become established with regular crews. One of my group asked me if I would mind changing with him because he had become friendly with a particular pilot, I agreed and on their first flight together the aircraft started to vibrate and finally broke up over St.Bees Head – they were all killed. The second occasion was on a weekend leave taken to be best man at a friend's wedding. When I returned from leave on the Sunday evening, I discovered that the crew that I would have been flying with (had I not been on leave) had crashed in Northern Ireland, with 2 crew members killed and the others in hospital. Thus it would appear that the gods were being extremely kind to me.

Two other small items that just might be worth mentioning – rather amusing both of them. The mess adopted a young jackdaw that had an injured wing and had difficulty flying. It quickly became at home in the dining room due to the scraps of food readily available, and also developed a taste for beer. It would perch on the glasses on the bar and drink from them, as you may well imagine this behaviour was much encouraged. The problems started when it was introduced to whisky and had great difficulty standing on one leg after a few drops of the short stuff and immediately fell over. This led to much hilarity all round. Afterwards it settled in a corner of an armchair, sleeping off the effects before waking up with an obvious hangover – with feathers on it's head standing to attention! Sadly it only survived for about 6 months, being so slow on the wing I can only imagine that some predator had a bit of a feast.

The other small detail that may be of some interest concerns the toilet facilities on the Ansons. As the aircraft was comparatively small there was no elsan available, just a funnel with a tube leading out into the slipstream for emptying one's bladder. Bit crude this, I often wondered about what some honest citizen passing underneath must have thought – probably, "that's funny, I didn't think it would rain today".

My time at Millom came to a sudden end, as all good periods must, when I returned from Christmas leave in 1944 to discover that all flying had ceased. There no longer being the need for more and more crews, quite suddenly there were more trained aircrew available than required. The war in Europe was moving towards closure and consequently demands were diminishing. So I, along with all the other flying personnel, found ourselves on the move again. I had enjoyed a comparatively comfortable 18 months and, if nothing else I did depart with 600 odd hours of flying time in my log book and an extensive knowledge of the NW coast of Wales and the SW coast of Scotland including the Mull of Galloway and the Mull of Kintyre. I departed for pastures new on the 1st of January 1945 wondering what the next 18 months would bring.

RAF Wing

Wing in Bedfordshire was the next port of call. It was No.26 OTU (Operational Training Unit) and I found myself part of a crew of 6 flying in Wellington Aircraft, generally known as "Wimpeys". The training we did was mostly cross country navigational exercises. In fact, similar to what I had been doing for the previous 18 months, but, with the greater range of the Wellington, trips now averaged 5 or 6 hours duration. At 22 years of age, I was the oldest member of the crew and also the most experienced, with more actual flying time than the other 5 added together. My job was more or less the same as my work at Millom, but rather easier as I did not have a trainee to guide through the various procedures. We did all the fringe bits and pieces of course, Dinghy Drill, Simulation High Altitude chamber etc. I do not remember anything very special about this period, apart perhaps from a couple of trips over Normandy, (the war had by this time moved into Germany). My memories are of seeing all the dead livestock lying in the fields waiting for someone to come along and clear up. The only other point is that I had now reached the somewhat exalted rank of "Warrant Officer", a rank I was able to exploit to the full during the rest of the time I still had to remain in the RAF.

RAF Acaster Malbis

Mid-April 1945 saw me on the move again – going on leave to await instructions as to where to report next, normal procedures meant that this would be a HCU (Heavy Conversion Unit), but that was not to be. My leave was constantly extended via a weekly telegram and a fortnightly pay voucher to be cashed at the post office. This went on for 3 or 4 weeks and during this time the war in Europe ended, leaving me wondering "what next?", for the war in the Far East was still being pursued. However, my instructions finally arrived and I was on my way to Acaster Malbis, a place I had never heard of, but was relieved to find it was only about 5 miles outside York.

I duly arrived there in early May to find that it had been a Bomber Command airfield which had been mothballed, but was now being re-opened to accommodate all the redundant aircrew who were in limbo. All channels now full as replacements were no longer required. All was chaotic initially with no one seeming to have much idea about what was going on, but we were being fed and watered and indeed paid. On this point perhaps I should mention that now, as a Warrant Officer, I no longer had to attend pay parade, I simply called in to the accounts dept. and signed for my cash. Really quite civilised. Some sort of order was eventually established, with interviewing panels set up to send individuals off in various directions and career changes. Some crews, and indeed the ones from my OTU course included, were posted off to Transport Command where there was much work still to be done. Unfortunately, I was now part of a headless crew, as my pilot (being Canadian) had been sent off down to Fleetwood where all the Canadians were being assembled to await transport home – as Canada no longer had any commitments, not being involved in the war in the Far East.

Thus ended my flying days. It was to be years before I would fly again, and next time, rather than being paid to fly, I had to pay to fly! Very different now from the sort of flying I had been accustomed to, now it is just a bus ride without the scenery. It was now interview time to discover where I would be going next. Returning to flying duties was not an option, there were just too many trained aircrew in the system The choices were somewhat limited, and I finally opted for a radar mechanics course. Two reasons: I thought the knowledge might be useful after the war with the possible advent of TV and I knew the course was down at Yatesbury where I had spent some time before and I rather fancied another spell there with the new freedom that I could enjoy as a Warrant Officer. Now it was a matter of waiting for a vacancy on a course, this took several weeks, and I rather enjoyed what remained of my time at Acaster.

RAF Yatesbury (again)

Thus the beginning of July 1945 saw me settling in down in Wiltshire. Nice homecoming in a way, and comfortable in the knowledge that all that cross country running was no longer a threat. I was actually in a unique situation, as the remainder of my group were all new recruits, subject of course to all the parade ground stuff and other pastimes that passed for initial training. With my new rank I could avoid all this and I went on to exploit my new situation to the full. Classroom work and technical work in the labs was the general order of things. I made a point of attending those but nothing else. In the classrooms I found we were on a course of mathematics, and I rather enjoyed the opportunity to extend my somewhat elementary knowledge of that subject. I also picked up a few bits of know how in the workshops, e.g. using a soldering iron for much finer work than that met with a couple of years earlier at No.7 signals school. I also learned to use a Vernier, a Micrometer, and a slide rule – skills not much in demand these days. Apart from course work, my time was my own and this I spent between my quarters (I had my own room again), the mess, and later in the day the Lansdowne Hotel down in Calne. With a break for tea in one of the cafes, which all seemed to be owned by Harris's – (the well known pie merchants). All things considered it was an enjoyable period. In retrospect I suppose my life then was equivalent to that of a college student today – only turning up in the training wing when I thought it was worthwhile, with the advantage of course that I did not have any financial obligations. This all came to an end when the war in the Far East ended, and forces requirements were again reviewed, with information starting to come through about demobilisation dates.

The radar course that I was on was a long one of two years duration, split into ten week segments. I had just finished the first one and learned that I had the option of taking a shorter course, or signing on for five more years and completing the course. Five more years was too much to contemplate and so I settled for a driving course lasting six weeks. I thought that this might prove useful and interesting, and would give me a driving licence when I eventually got out. Also the driving school was at Weeton nr. Blackpool, handy for weekends at home.

RAF Lyneham

After two or three weeks I was on my way again, this time to Lyneham in Wiltshire, which then was, and still is, a large transport airfield, and I actually thought I was about to resume flying duties, but I was sadly mistaken.

Arrived at Lyneham to find that I was unexpected (again!) and by now I was beginning to think that no one wanted to know me any more, not that I was too concerned. I quickly found myself some comfortable quarters, booked in to the accounts dept (just to make sure the money kept coming in), and checked out the local geography, i.e. the way to the nearest pub. I then sat back and waited for the next development. Nice relaxing time really, but I was soon on the move again, February 1946 found me on my way at last to my driving course.

This proved to be quite enjoyable, with a gradual progression from 16hp cars up to 5 ton heavy goods vehicles. The driving part was only 2 hours per day. I made use of my rank again and did not participate in any of the other activities. I also took advantage of the fact that I was close to home and went there every Friday night for the weekend – all very sociable. Finally passed out, now with a licence to drive anything apart from articulated vehicles, and on my way on leave again to wait to see what my next move would be. I knew at this stage that it wouldn't be long before I was saying goodbye to the RAF, as it was possible to roughly estimate when my number for demobilisation would come up. I thought about mid-summer which turned out to be about right, my number was 41.

RAF Handforth

The telegram with instructions duly arrived, and I found that I was to report to the MT section at 61 MU Handforth. This sounded ideal and I cycled down to book in and make arrangements to live out. I thought this would be a good introduction to civilian life; living at home and cycling to work, but events were to take another, and final turn. I introduced myself to the MT officer in charge, a gentleman by the name of Quant who took an immediate dislike to me, which was reciprocated, I don't think he really wanted me in his department, difficult for him I suppose as I was still carrying my Warrant Officer rank but now only employed as a driver. Still there was nothing he could do about it, my rank was sacrosanct and I was still getting rank pay and flying pay.

I collected the lorry allocated to me. It was a somewhat worse for wear Canadian 3 ton Dodge. Difficult to drive and requiring constant double declutching and gear changing just to get up the smallest of inclines. That said, it had to do. On checking the work schedules I found that there was the odd load to be picked up and taken over to 7 site (which I discovered was in Adlington) where the Industrial Estate is now, which I thought would be ideal for me. So I used my rank again to establish myself as the regular driver covering 7 site. Handforth was overloaded with equipment for storage and made use of several sites over a wide area to store surplus materials – 99% of which was never used and would end its life in some scrap yard somewhere but it had to be stored and documented. I remember on one occasion taking a load of Lancaster spares to Woodford (Avro's as it was then). At first they refused to accept it, but eventually realised they had no alternative, and took it to some far off hangar. They too were getting desperate for space, for no longer required parts were still coming off the production lines.

I made the most of my daily runs to 7 site, usually going home first after collecting my vehicle from the yard and having an early morning break before going to the site to check if there was anything to move before going back to the main site for lunch. Another run to Adlington in the afternoon, before returning to the yard, parking up and going home. I often saw the MT officer watching me through his office window and looking quite concerned. Don't know why, as although I was usually the last one to leave the yard at the start of the day, I made up for this by being the first one back in the evening. One afternoon a week was given over to vehicle washing, but as there were a few Italian prisoners of war working in the yard. It was quite possible to get a good job done for the price of a packet of cigarettes, with half to get the job started and the other half on completion. It was just a case of sit in the mess until they came to tell me that the job was finished. This rather comfortable period came to a sudden end when I was summoned to see the MT officer to be informed of my next move. He informed me that I was to be posted to Wickenby, which was a storage site for the main depot; to go there and take charge of the MT section. (I think he was pleased to have the opportunity to get rid of me!) My old Dodge had finally given up the previous afternoon, pronounced irreparable and presumably written off, but I was pleased with the replacement, a two ton Austin Tender straight from the factory, similar to a pick-up and a delight to drive.

I picked the truck up the following morning, called at home to collect my gear, and set off to Wickenby – which I ascertained was a disused airfield about seven miles east of Lincoln. When I arrived it was to discover all signs of flying had long gone. Hangers were full to bursting point with spares that were no longer in demand. On further investigation I discovered that the MT section consisted of one other truck and one driver, a young lad only recently called up. Further enquiries produced some unexpected results. We were a mixed group of about 23 or 24, with 3 cooks, 3 telephonists, and a larger number of armourers making safe and disposing of bombs, ammunition, and other military hardware that was still lying around. I was informed that an administrative officer had been in overall charge until the previous day when he had left to be demobbed, but his replacement had failed to arrive. As a warrant officer with no other senior officers on the station, I had become de-facto the commanding officer of the whole establishment. A most unusual situation, but one which was to become quite interesting.

It soon became clear that I was also responsible for seeing that everyone got paid, relieving the telephonist when one of their number was absent on leave, and so providing short term cover. Although there was very little traffic, the telephone line had to be kept open 24 hours a day. I did make full use of this facility to make a few private calls. Rations were collected every other day from a depot in Market Rasen and, as we were such a small group these were more than adequate. We all dined together and really lived very well. I went over myself for the rations or occasionally sent my one and only driver. There was also a daily run to Wragby to pick up any post, as postal services were no longer available. Pay day became my responsibility and involved a trip over to Scampton to collect the money along with a list with the amounts due to everyone. This only happened a couple of times as I was only there a few weeks. On returning with the cash I was wondering how I could get in touch with all as they were scattered around the airfield. I needn't have worried as the bush telegraph had been at work and all and sundry were waiting around the MT office when I returned.

One unusual occurrence that I have a vivid memory of was concerning the main runway, now out of use of course. There were a team of contractors working at one end making repairs to the surface, whilst at the far end of the same runway were another group engaged in digging it up, taking all the surface material away and ploughing up the land prior to it being returned to agricultural use. This all seemed very odd to say the least, so I enquired as to why the repair work was still going on. The reply, and I quote *"The contract still has two years to run"*, unbelievable! I often wondered what the outcome would be when the two groups met, but I was long gone before then.

I made full use of my new found power as MT officer, e.g. I made a habit of driving home for most weekends on Friday evening I armed myself with suitable cover notes to cover my journeys, one for the trip home and another for the return journey on Sunday night. To say that I was picking stores up to take to store at Wickenby. I should perhaps mention that the cover note was a form to cover all transportation, with 3 sections, one requesting transport and saying why needed (this I duly signed as Commanding Officer), the second part to be signed by the MT officer and stamped with the official stamp, (this I complied with), and the third part to be signed by the driver on completion of the journey (this I duly signed on my return) then I filed the form, don't know why! Fuel was never a problem as I had sole access to the one remaining pump. When I was home for the weekend, I parked the lorry in a disused sandpit behind my home in case anyone passing became curious. On my return on Sunday evening, I stopped off in Lincoln, parked in the station yard, and went into the nearest pub to await the arrival of the last London train. There were always one or two people travelling up from points south who had been on weekend leave, looking for a lift back to Wickeriby. Generally speaking the whole establishment ran very smoothly, everyone getting on with their own jobs and waiting for the next pay day!

De-mobbed at last

My time at Wickenby passed very quickly and the time when I would part company with the RAF was fast approaching. My demob number (41) came up in early June 1946. The 11th found me on my on my way down to Uxbridge to go through the demobilisation process. I collected my civilian suit (not much choice, there were a lot of look-a-likes walking around). I could have a cap or trilby, mac or overcoat, grey or fawn suit all parcelled up in a cardboard box. All back pay was collected, plus civilian documents and ration book. Uniform handed in, apart from that being worn. I received a one-way ticket for the journey home. Now I was on my way on a month's demob leave, finally severing all links with the RAF in mid-July – just before my 24th birthday. A final twist when I was on the train on the way to Manchester. An airman got into my compartment, it was my soon to be Brother-in-law, also carrying his little box.

Life in 'Civvy Street' was now very close. I had to seriously rethink my lifestyle, with an immediate 50% reduction in pay, my own clothes and food to buy, and very soon a young family to be responsible for.

On reflection, I have to think that my uniform years had been a rewarding experience, having seen and done many things that would have been outside my orbit, yet of course, I had been very lucky. So many of my acquaintances and indeed friends had perished over the skies of Europe. Now it was farewell to the uniform times, and I could finally shape my own destiny about where and when. In short I was no longer just a number.

A. Dudley (1998)

MR JOHN EDMUNDS – 1941-1942

I arrived at Millom in late 1941 as a Corporal Fitter after training at Halton. Life in general was quite bearable at RAF Millom. The huts and washing facilities were somewhat basic however, and it was very cold out on the airfield during the winter months. At the airfield itself, my main memory is of the constant westerly wind blowing in from the sea which made a nuisance of itself when we were trying to do some fiddly job or other and when working with or handling cowlings or detachable panels. Occasionally, in clear weather I recall seeing the Isle of Man over the distant horizon. We were made very welcome down at Haverigg Working Men's Club where we all joined the 'Glee Choir' singing with great gusto!

Looking at diary notes I made at the time I see that from December 1941 to July 1942 I was involved in quite a good number of air tests, in fact I note that on 12th July 1942 I took part in an air test of Anson No. 23, of some 20 minutes duration over the Duddon Estuary. I do remember that the shortest trip I ever made by Anson was to RAF Cark near Cartmel. I recall that the runway was covered with rubber chippings and that lines representing field edges, had been painted across it as camouflage. When I first arrived at Millom the unit was flying a good number of Blackburn Botha aircraft but were very wisely in the process of "phasing them out" due to their lack of reliability. The Botha was very prone to engine failure and had a well earned reputation for being unable to fly on one engine. One day I was detailed to

119

fly to Silloth as a passenger in one of the units Botha's, to collect some Anson spares. On the take-off run the port engine suddenly failed but the pilot was luckily, able to stop the aircraft just before we ran out of runway. I recall that a dispatch rider was sent instead! A second Botha incident occurred very soon afterwards when someone ran its engines too fast at the dispersal site and the thing tipped up onto is nose! A crewman was sent up the sloping fuselage to fix a rope for us to set it down again. He had just got astride the tail section when his weight caused things to right themselves. The speed of the tails descent and the effect on the crewman sitting astride the fuselage was painful to behold! We had many scrapes and japes, I saw a Defiant making the take-off run with its propeller in coarse pitch one day. This is like trying to drive a car from a standing start in top gear, no acceleration, it ran off the end of the runway and was badly damaged but the crew escaped with a few bumps and bruises.

We watched one day, as a Fleet Air Arm Swordfish (who had obviously come to show the RAF how to fly), sweep downwind along the runway at low altitude, pull up into a half loop, and rolling upright, diving down to land gently into wind. However, the landing was rather harder for himself and his undercarriage than he intended, which did rather spoil it for him. On another occasion a B17 Flying Fortress requested a landing and was given clearance. It was the first four-engined bomber I had ever seen. On rolling to a halt the skipper leaned out of the cockpit window and shouted "is this Blackpool"? When I shouted back "no it was not" he asked "well where the hell is it"? I pointed south and shouted "that way" upon which he took off again flying off over the estuary, it was an almost surreal experience. My group of fitters was under the command of a chap called Flt/Lt Boxall, and I think it is fair to say that he was disliked by everyone.

The MKI Avro Ansons of those days had air operated brakes supplied by a high pressure air bottle which had to be pumped up by the ground crew between flights; Foot pumps were issued for this purpose and required a lot of effort on our behalf. We used to walk around with an exaggerated limp to indicate that we were "Boxalls foot pump boys". The unit came under enemy attack once whilst I was there. A lone Junkers 88 machine gunned the airfield one summer's day about lunch time. After all the commotion, FT/LT Boxall phoned our flight hut to ask what was happening. I identified the German aircraft for him and confirmed for him that no one had been injured in the action. This was not strictly true however, as many fitters suffered sprains and bruises as they were leaping from the aircraft they were working on in order to take cover! My final recollection is of an Anson whose brakes did not work at all. A very headstrong young pilot arrived to taxi it back to a hangar for repair. We urged him not to do so but he would not be swayed and off he went. We watched as he crashed into the hangar door unable to stop the aircraft. I do not recall what happened to the pilot after the event but it's fair to assume that he "got a rocket"!

Mr John Edmunds 1997 (Ex Halton Brat)

JOHN (EDDIE) EDMONDS

As a young fellow I was somewhat obsessed by all things mechanical and would take anything to pieces just for the sheer joy of putting it back together. Some sort of engineering would naturally have been a preferred career option however the war intervened.

I mustard for aircrew but was most disappointed when I was told my eyesight was not up to the mark, though not entirely bereft when I found myself in RAF Blue in spite of this and being paid to take aircraft engines apart and put them back together again – a step up from my motorcycles and the sundry gadgets I would tinker with in my dad's shed in the black country.

And so to RAF millom. I was posted there in January 1942 and oh my it was so so cold. Our bullets were heated by two stoves which never seem to be lit for very long and the station's location on the Cumberland coast left us prey to the most bitter of winds straight off the Irish sea.

I loved the work itself, the unit was mostly flying Avro Ansons, and their radial engines were a delight to work on even though on many occasions this had to be done on the airfield out in the open.

The Anson engines were Armstrong Siddeley Cheetah Radials, beautifully engineered and could be run for many hours between servicing. This was done out at a town some miles away from Millom. I once travelled on a tender carrying four Cheetahs there. The town was called Ulverston and I remember being perplexed by the fact that it had a landlocked lighthouse above the town.

It was not all work and I enjoyed a good social life at Millom, my pals and I frequented two excellent pubs in town – the John Peel and the Plough or the 'pluff' as we renamed it. The locals were very friendly and often invited us back to their homes, I remember the town fondly.

I left RAF Millom in the autumn of 1944 being posted to RAF Wombleton in Yorkshire, a station flying Lancaster Bombers. We called it 'Wombleton on the mud' and it never failed to live up to its name.

After demob I became a motor mechanic and following my retirement I continued to tinker and disassemble things just for the sheer joy of reassembling them... old habits die hard!

John Edmonds 1996

MR EDDIE ELLIN – 1942

I did my 'Square Bashing' at Blackpool in Lancashire. My flying career as a Wireless Operator / Air Gunner was less than assured however as I suffered from severe airsickness from the outset. So severe was this in fact, that I was grounded several times as a result. After a great deal of perseverance I was able to beat the problem and was posted to RAF Millom in 1942.

I remember the remote location of the station and recall many of the people you spoke of, Dave Waters, Bill Gracie (of course) Willie Williamson, Des Jones, John "Tiger" Timms to name a few. Also I recall Ken Wolstenholme who went on to become a famous sports writer and who is best remembered perhaps for his remarks in the closing moments of the 1966 world cup. We flew our exercises by night and day in Mk1 Avro Ansons, though there were one or two other types around the airfield I remember that the instructional airframe we had was an Avro Manchester which landed at RAF Millom during this aircrafts development phase and test flights due to the technical failings which required an emergency landing at Millom or damage sustained during that landing, the aircraft was declared a write-off and retained for training purposes. The Manchester was the lighter forerunner of the Avro Lancaster and only saw limited use. Further recollections of Millom are few but I do see from my log book that I was part of an aerial search in October 1942 trying to locate a Lockheed Hudson aircraft which was missing, presumed lost in the Lakeland Mountains. We did not locate the Hudson, my pilot during that search was John Timms.

The Hudson aircraft had gone missing from a navigational exercise from I.O.T.U. RAF Silloth and was eventually found on the 10th of November 1942 having collided with high ground at Beda Head near Ullswater. It was Hudson AM680.

I left Millom along with John Timms to commence training on Wellington Bombers at RAF Edgehill in January 1944. From Edgehill I was posted in February to 12 O.T.U. at RAF Chipping Warden (again on Wellingtons). I stayed there until April when I joined 1678 Lancaster Conversion Unit at RAF Waterbeach near Cambridge. In May I became a member of 514 Squadron in the role of Deputy Signals Leader and in December completed my tour of operations. I then was posted to a Flying Control Officers course which I remained part of until the close of hostilities and my "demob".

Eddie Ellin 2007

MR ARTHUR J. EVANS 630683 – 1941-1942

After enlisting in the RAF 12.1.1939 I had of course various stations, training and experiences on an O.T.U. plus a short spell at Markam from where I was posted to Millom and arrived there in February 1941 (as a FITT 11E) where I found it like a graveyard after previous stations. As far as I can remember there were few, if any, aircraft, and lots of workmen working on the airfield. The 'tin' hangars were all up and billets of course.

The first impression was that of the arctic, icy winds (and strong) and had plenty of sand at times, in the mouth and eyes etc but we soon got used to it and when the wind wasn't too rough it was beautiful fresh air.

We soon had some Blackburn Bothas, Avro Ansons

(Faithful Annie) and a variety of aircraft used to 'drop in' for visits etc including Boulton Paul Defiants and one visitor I remember in those early days was the first Spitfire I saw on the ground and was able to do a D.I. on it.

Soon, I hadn't a lot to do with the flying side as I was given my stripes and had a squad and we mostly did 'period' inspections, engine changes etc. etc. The one occasion when I got airborne was when an Anson force landed on the east coast of Ireland, I took a fitter with me and we were dropped off by another Anson with spare parts, tools etc and after checks, ground testing etc, the pilot flew us back to Haverigg. The fitter I took with me was nicknamed 'Professor' and he looked and behaved the part. When for instance some of us had been to the 'Star' (I think that was the name) for a few pints, 'Prof' would be sat up in bed with one of his thick books. (One of them, if I remember right was on Astronomy.)

Our billets were handy for the Star as we were down near the farm and the lane ran straight to the pub and Haverigg main street. We helped to get the harvest in at least one time during our leisure.

One memory I have of that time was a chap in our hut was a right 'moaner' and coddled himself. Going to kip at night he kept his underclothes on and his socks then his pyjamas went on top with another pair of socks over the bottoms of his pyjama legs. One night a few of us had been to the pub and late on decided we would give him some fresh air. He was fast asleep and stifling our laughter we carried his bed outside. As I remember, he must have been in a heavy sleep because it was some minutes before there was one hell of a tirade of foul language and with a lot of laughter we relented and carried him in. He was going to report us and all that sort of talk, "I could have got pneumonia" he said, but nothing happened. I must add that my taking part in this episode was before I was made corporal. A lot of the names of friends and companions of those days I've forgotten, but some, Jimmy? Devon Malcolm, Harry Cowling and George Umpleby (who was later to be 'Best Man' for me) and the Professor, I can't remember his name.

During this period, I was in a canteen in Millom and a helper there, Mrs. Margaret Braithwaite invited me back to her house in Market Street where I met and liked her husband Ron and two children, Norman and Marion. (I think those were the children's names). Very kind of her, as were many people toward servicemen in those days.

On one of my visits to Barrow I met my future wife to be - Joan, a Walney girl. We got on fine and got serious and one day (I think it was a Sunday) we were walking by the Coliseum, Barrow, when a threatening storm erupted. Thunder and lightning and one of the flashes struck some of the Barrage Balloons which of course burst into flames and the cables fell across building and road. I saw Joan home and returned to camp. Later on when Barrow got the raids, I remember watching the flames and explosions from Haverigg and 'wondered' (fingers crossed.)

We later married in June 1942. My stag night ended up at a pub near the slag bank (Devonshire?) About six of us went the 'rounds', but by the time we were walking back to camp via the short cut past the church, there were about a dozen of us. What I remember was a great night.

One thing I must mention, especially during the early days at Haverigg was the wonderful ladies of the W.V.S. who were out to us daily with big pots of tea and giant slabs of cake (plain or fruit as required). Especially on cold days (mostly cold anyway) this was a godsend. They were wonderful and the sight of their van on the way was a tonic.

Some months earlier I had put my name down for aircrew and received the posting to St. Athens for a Flight

Engineers course late 1942 and was accepted operational at last.

Mr A. Evans 2007

WARRANT OFFICER PETER FEAR

Wireless Operator / Air Gunner. RAF Millom.
Member of the Training Staff – March 1942-April 1945
I enlisted in the RAF as a volunteer in February 1941.

The joining venue was at Blackpool. At this time the town was used for the introductory discipline course combined with training in the early stages of Morse code. For those who know Blackpool a large section of the Winter Gardens was set aside with numerous tables upon which Morse Code Keys were available to the trainees. Civilian instructors provided training in Morse code, up to a speed of twelve words per minute. The training course at Blackpool lasted three months. Each month a test of the speed attained by the trainee was taken. The testing was conducted in rooms above a branch of Burtons clothing store. If a trainee failed after two attempts he was removed from the course. The expression often used in the RAF "Gone for a Burton" was thought by some to have originated from a failed Morse code test at Burtons store Blackpool.

At Blackpool all aircrew trainees were issued with a white flash to be worn in the fold of the forage cap. A card authorising the display was issued to each trainee. In between instruction periods at the Winter Gardens, my squad consisting of thirty men joined many hundreds more marching and drilling on the promenade, also using the Beach area for keep fit training.

I completed the course at Blackpool in December 1941 and was posted to an advanced Wireless training establishment at Yatesbury in Wiltshire. In addition to increasing the Morse code speed up to a minimum of eighteen words per minute, operational training in the use of radio equipment and message procedures were taught. A part of the training also included flying when the practice of radio communication was introduced. This was also of three months duration.

On completion of this course I was posted to perform duties as a ground wireless operator, pending the availability of a further flying training course. This entailed duties at various airfields in the south and midlands.

In November 1942 I resumed my flying training at an advanced flying training school in Gloucestershire. It was in December of that year just a few days before Christmas that I arrived in Barrow-in-Furness to commence an air gunnery course at RAF Walney. This town subsequently played a major part in my life. I met and married my wife in Barrow.

The gunnery course consisted of learning the techniques of a gun turret, using and maintaining machine guns, etc. Flying in Defiant fighter planes over Morecambe Bay gave the opportunity to take part in firing at a drogue target towed by another aircraft. This course was of ten weeks duration and in the last week examinations were taken in the knowledge gained.

Having gained marks to bring me within the first ten trainees, I with the other nine men was informed we would be posted to an advanced flying school as staff instructors. Five airfields were listed and we were given the opportunity for two airmen to be posted to each of our own choice one such airfield was RAF Millom. I together with a colleague John Hoskison, who later became a life-long friend, met on the course at Walney, applied for and was posted to Millom. We arrived as newly promoted sergeants having completed our flying training.

For the next two years we performed flying duties as wireless instructors. This consisted of supervising trainee operators in all aspects of radio communication from aircraft. The training involved flying in Anson aircraft. The pilot and the staff operator being regular crewmen, with a trainee navigator, wireless operator and sometimes bomb aimer, completing the crew. The flying periods were approximately three hours duration. Two such periods during the day, and two during the night. A meal break intervened between the flights. We performed the flying duties week about, nights and then days.

A briefing was given at each flight. The course to be undertaken being indicated a wall map and consisted of the North West region of the U.K. Most trips involved a great deal of flying over the Irish Sea, making land fall at various points, such as the Isle of Man, the coast of Anglesey, Northern Ireland and many locations on the south and also western coast of Scotland.

I was regularly crewed with a pilot named Gordon Wilkinson. Many hours were flown during the two year stay at RAF Millom. The total bordered on 1000 hours. Needless to say our trust and reliance on one another made for a special association.

Many incidents occurred during this period, which at that time were considered of minor importance. To mention one, on landing one night after a three hour cross country flight, the starboard undercarriage gave way causing the plane to swerve to the right, across the airfield and ending up colliding with a parked unattended aircraft. To walk away was always considered to be a satisfactory landing. One major incident will always remain in my memory. We had just arrived back over Millom airfield and were about to call for landing instructions. Dawn was just creeping up over the hills of the Lake District. Instead of landing instructions being given we were informed that an Anson had overshot the runway when attempting to land. It was known to have come down in the sea just off the coast line. We immediately carried out a search of the area and in the poor light we thought we saw wreckage. I recall signalling towards the object with an Aldis lamp to indicate to any survivors that help was at hand. The sea rescue launch was already at sea. We then returned to land. It was some time later that with great sadness that I learned that all the crew had been killed. The staff wireless operator was Ron Clayton a colleague of mine and greatly missed.

Due to the location of the airfield the mountain Black Combe was always a hazard especially at night, more so in the winter nights. In day time it appeared to be a friend guiding us in from our many trips out over the sea.

After one year at Millom I was promoted to Flight Sergeant, then after two years to Warrant Officer.

Social life involved a visit to Millom cinema, and pubs if only a few hours were available. When I had a day or two off a visit to Barrow-in-Furness was undertaken by train. As I had met my future wife in the town I of course visited Barrow whenever possible. There were occasions, especially in the winter months, when I phoned the control room at Millom to see if flying had been cancelled due to bad weather. If so my stay at Barrow was extended.

During my final month or so at Millom I was invited to take over as a direction finding station operator. This was brought about by the shortage of trainee flying courses. A hut approximately ten feet by ten feet was situated in a field a short distance from the main airfield. The unit was manned twenty four hours a day giving bearings, (QDM) to aircraft calling by Morse-code for such navigational aids. Mainly aircraft from Millom used the station, but aircraft from many other stations which were flying in the area called for a QDM. At times when giving bearings, points of various degrees from 0 to 360, aircraft literally queued up to avail themselves of the navigational aid. One bearing after another being passed out to the relevant aircraft.

In April 1945 1 was posted to an operational training unit at Abingdon RAF station in Oxfordshire. There I was crewed up with a pilot, navigator, bomb aimer, and two air gunners. Flying was in Wellington Bombers and the course lasted six weeks. From there with the crew I had joined I was posted to RAF Woolfox Lodge, Rutland. We converted from Wellington bombers to Lancaster Bombers. The course lasting six weeks. After a short while our crew like many others was disbanded. The reason being that the war situation had reached a point where we were no longer needed.

This meant that I was off flying duties and was posted to RAF Cranwell in Linclonshire as a ground radio instructor. I remained so until January 1946 when 1 was informed that my demobilisation papers were in the office for signature.

Having married in 1943 the thought of being released was pleasing, although 1 left the RAF with a certain amount of regret, having spent four years and five months in a service I had wanted to join and respected. The personnel with whom I shared my service life have always been held in high esteem.

Peter Fear 1997

Formally Warrant Officer, Royal Air Force

MR GEOFF FROUDE 1941 – 1943

I joined the met office in 1937 and spent time at RAF Leuchars, Marham and several other Group 2 stations. I then joined the RAF – VR in June 1939 just ahead of the first "call up", but as with most forecasters on "home" stations, was not mobilised until April 1943, about the time I left RAF Millom for HQ 3 Group. The panoramic photograph I have sent you was taken in 1941 from the roof of our "met" building and shows RAF Millom its early days, as you can see, work is still being done on the hangar roofs. We took this sort of picture to show "visibility points". I remember that on my way to night duty one evening during blackout, I was knocked down on the perimeter track. An Anson was being towed behind a tractor with very dim headlights. The driver shouted something which I could not make out and the aircraft was invisible in the darkness. I collided with the Anson wing at chin level and was carried to the stations sick bay unconscious. The memory is quite strong for in the next bed to me was a Lysander pilot who had landed his aircraft on its nose and was busy coughing up chunks of the airfield! The met office was the meeting place for the "odd types" who had little else to do, the oddest of which was a Flt/Sgt or Flt/Lt pilot who had "worked his ticket" and become among other things, the local rabbit catcher. I went shooting with him on the Duddon Estuary after duck and geese several times. He eventually married into a farm near Lady Hall on the Duddon where he lodged and was renowned (early 1960's?) for declaring Unilateral Independence for 'his' property, perhaps you can put a name to him?

I recall also the Silecroft Coastguard, his name was John Grimes. John had little to do and always welcomed a chat, his armoury consisted of one Tommy Gun and not much ammunition, strangely his married daughter lives not far from my present home down here and her son still has a property up at Silecroft.

A final memory is of a Fairey Battle being taxied into the met hut on one occasion which startled the occupants and loosened not a few bricks! Having left Millom in Spring 1943, I was back there briefly in November of the same year to complete a quick navigational course on my way to becoming a Met Air Observer, this occupied me for the next eight years, the last four of which I spend running courses at RAF Aldergrove.

I stayed with the RAF as a Civilian Met Forecaster through to 1978 with overseas postings to Gibraltar, Habboniya, Singapore and Aden. I am surprised but pleased that I can still splice a number of service memories together after all this time!

Geoff Froude 1998

Author's Note:

I can indeed put a name to the "odd type" who hung round the met hut and became unit Rabbit Catcher and Wildfowler! The gentleman in question was no-one other than Mr Victor Craven-Hodgson, one of Britain's great eccentrics! In the early 1960's, Victor was so disenchanted with the government that he declared his property to be independent territory, and wrote to the queen to say he had done so! Victor was given to wearing a kilt (an obscure tartan) and drove a Land Rover which had a flashing light on its roof. Much to the consternation of the local constabulary, he would park it just about anywhere, When approached he would declare diplomatic immunity, pointing to the plates he had fastened to the front of his vehicle indicating that he believed himself to be visiting a foreign country quite removed from his own "land"! The media loved the story and though Victor has sadly passed away, he is part of local lore yet!!

MR KENNETH R. FULTON −1943 R.C.A.F

I graduated from High School in Windsor, Nova Scotia,

in June 1941, at the age of eighteen years. I joined the Merchant Navy, and spent one year, serving on two ships, both of which were later sunk by the enemy.

And so to my time at RAF Millom. I remember well that our group of navigators were very disappointed with the posting as it rained most the time. I understand that the course was supposed to be four weeks long, but due to the weather, it took seven weeks for us to complete our training – we lived in mud and rain.

We had a Brazilian Flight Commander who was not very well liked, one of our favourite staff member was a RAF Wireless Operator Air Gunner who had completed 2 tours, had applied for remustering to Pilot, and was accepted. Whilst we were there I remember that he was due to go to Canada for training at any time. During the first week at Millom we were all greatly saddened when Sgt Murphy, one of our student navigators was killed in a flying accident.

We had dinner in the West County Hotel in Millom on many occasions and visited Barrow-in-Furness a few times also. We spent an awful lot of time having a get together in Ed Emmersons room, sharing parcels from home and just putting in time indoors out of the rain. Some of the navigators who had trained with me, and who were posted to Millom with me are Ed Emmerson, Ralph Emmerson, John Harvie, John Brock, Cliff Cameron and Stan McPhail. Ed Emmerson completed a tour and received a D.F.C., sadly, Ed Emmerson's brother Ralph was killed on ops, they were both from Toronto. John Harvie from Montreal was shot down near Paris in July, was picked up by the French Maquis, and was eventually turned over to the Gestapo by a traitor. John was then taken to Buchenwald concentration camp, and eventually transferred to Stalag Luft 3. John Brock, Cliff Cameron and Stan McPhail all completed operational tours.

Ken R. Fulton 1996

MR C.K. GARNER – 1941

My recollections of the five months spent at Millom are still very kaleidoscopic, so many new experience, so much excitement and also a great deal of hard work. To set my place in the scheme of things – together with about forty other hopefuls, we were the very first to arrive for training. The folk of Haverigg and Millom must have felt completely taken over with 250 arrivals every six weeks, and a staff of 1,400.

We were No.1 course No.2 Bombing and Gunnery School RAF Millom, and as such were in almost at the birth of the new station. Our arrival, on a dark Sunday evening in late February 1941, after an all-day train journey from Cambridge, was less than auspicious. The domestic area of the camp was still uncompleted and thick mud meant that movement between buildings was only possible by using duckboards, and care had to be exercised to avoid deep trenches and equipment of all kinds.

Also, in the early days our sleeping quarters were set up in a section of the dining hall. To be fair though, things improved rapidly and before long we moved into single rooms in concrete buildings.

The Station Commander at that time was GRP/CPT Wray, who went by the nickname of "father" (because of his concern for his men) or more unkindly "hoppy" because of his game leg, the result of a wound sustained during his service in the First World War.

I only recall two other senior ranks, W/CDR Hadow, who was overall in charge of training, and "Dutchy" Holland, a Civilian Bombing Instructor, an ill tempered

135

man, as I recall. But as he was disabled in some way, and we, his pupils, were all very green, he had reason to be less than friendly I suppose. Not one of the forty of us had any previous flying experience so our excitement was unbounded when, on the fifth of March in groups of five or six we were taken up for a short familiarisation flight, my own group being fortunate enough for our first flying experience to be piloted by the Station Commander himself! The aircraft on which we trained were the much mistrusted Blackburn Bothas. Believe it or not, we came to rather like this aircraft as our confidence grew, though we were fortunate indeed, that in all the time we trained at Millom there were no accidents or serious mishaps, the odd early return from exercise maybe, but nothing more. I must say though, that some of the staff pilots were deeply suspicious and wary of the poor old Botha. As my flying log reminds me, the staff pilots themselves were a mixed bunch, they included several Poles, who feared nothing and spoke little English.

The majority of them were survivors of earlier campaigns, the Battle of Britain, Dunkirk etc and few of them I suspect, enjoyed stooging around with crews of beginners, and getting lost over North West Scotland.

By the time our course was completed in mid July 1941, although several of our number had either been washed out or had departed voluntarily, most had done sufficiently well to pass, to be subsequently dispersed to the various operational training units. All I have now to remind me of them are several course photographs taken during our time together. I know the fate of two of them, but as for the others I have no idea whether or not they survived the war. Following my departure from RAF Millom the station passed into history for me. I remember it in a kindly way and it's good to know that something of its spirit still survives to this day.

Ken Garner 1993

Ken and I were able to establish that he had actually flow in Botha L6446 whilst training at Millom. Following our excavation of her crash site at Dernarglar Loch and the recovery of her wing, I sent him her wing electrical junction box as a keepsake.

MR D. J. GRIFFITHS – 1941 - 1943

When I arrived at RAF Millom training was in full swing and the station had been re-designated No.2 Observer Advanced Flying Unit following its formation as No.2 Bombing and Gunnery School in January of the same year. I flew 9 hours and 25 minutes on the ill fated Bothas thankfully without mishap! In actual fact I made several flights down to RAF Aldergrove in my role as Wireless Operator to pick up Millom crews who had been flying the units Bothas down there for disposal. This was pending their replacement with the far more reliable Avro Ansons.

I arrived at Millom in December 1941 and after 14 months flying duty as a Staff W/OP, left the station in February 1943 for No.22 Operational Training unit, RAF Wellsbourne Mountford, training on Wellington Bombers. I became part of the all RCAF Crew of skipper Sgt George Neale and in April 1943 we were posted to RAF Topcliffe, 165 Heavy Bomber Conversion Unit, flying the big four engine Halifax Bombers. I cannot recall under what pretext we did this, but I had a very dear pal still serving at Millom by the name of Bill Gracie. He, like myself was a Staff W/OP and so we decided to land at RAF Millom so that I could pay him a visit!!

We landed at the unit by the skin of our teeth using every bit of the length of Millom's runway, and causing quite a stir into the bargain! Bill was astounded, and after our social call we duly took off once again using the full length of the runway to get the giant airborne and causing a minor sandstorm in the sand dunes at the end of the strip as we departed. The Halifax, by the way was Topcliffe's 'S' for sugar. Our Operational posting was to 419 Squadron R.C.A.F at RAF Middleton St George, early in May 1943.

On June 24th 1943 we took off to bomb a target in the Ruhr. Upon nearing Cologne we were attacked by night fighters and had both our starboard engines put out of action during the attack, which also ignited fires in our starboard wing. At the time of the attack we were flying at 22,000 feet. The loss of the engines put us in to a spiral dive and we were down to an altitude of 3,500 ft before our skipper could regain sufficient control to level us out. Our navigator had been wounded and so I obtained radio fixes (over the northern Ruhr) and we set course for the North Sea, with the possibility of ditching there. However, we gradually lost height and our skipper had no choice but to make a forced landing wherever he could. In fact George set us down safely in a marsh near Arnhem in the Netherlands. According to our squadron records, this was the only known episode where an RAF plane successfully landed in occupied territory after being crippled by enemy fire. We managed to evade the Germans for a few days but were eventually caught and found ourselves in Stalag Luft VI from which we were transferred to Thom in Poland. Our first period of imprisonment was spent at Fallingbostel near Hanover, and close to the infamous Belsen concentration camp. We were eventually liberated from there on April 18th 1945.

Jack Griffiths 1997

My research has led me to conclude that the Topcliffe Halifax, 'S' for sugar, in which Jack made his visit to RAF Millom was LL505. This is the Halifax which crashed into the Coniston fells on the night of the 22nd Oct 1944 killing her 8 RCAF crew. How strange is fate that it would be Millom's Mountain Rescue unit who would attend the scene of her destruction?

MR BOB GILLESPIE 1943 – 1944

I was a Staff Pilot at RAF Millom from July 1943 until December 1944, flying navigators under training at what was No.2. Observer Advanced Flying Unit. In addition to the quota of Navigators, Wireless Operators and Air Bombers were also undertaking various courses at the station.

My memories are of a happy, but very hardworking unit with very variable weather; our Met Officers were all knows as "Cloudy Joes"! I recall once, however, returning from a night exercise early one morning and approaching Millom from the Irish Sea. It was one of the most beautiful sights I have ever seen. A ruddy coloured sun was just starting to rise and the Lake District Mountain peaks were all covered in snow. Millom and the low levels were still in darkness with a light mist just above them. Here and there an odd light pierced the blackness and the snow which covered Black Combe slowly turned into a brilliant red with the light from the rising sun. I, and my crew for that trip, were speechless with the beauty of the scene and it remains with me in my memory to this day.

My memories of RAF Millom are not all good however! Whilst at the station I had to make a forced landing in Ireland, another vivid recollection! I was the pilot of Anson MG395 on the night of March 26th 1944. We were flying a navigational exercise and returning to base, coming in over the Isle of Man when my Wireless Operator for that trip received a message from base telling us to divert to Bishops Court in Northern Ireland because of a rapidly developing and thick sea mist at Millom. We did an about face and headed back but decided to head for the American base at Knutts Corner as the food was much better there. Shortly after crossing the Irish Coast one engine cut out. This was quite normal as to stretch our endurance we flew on outer tanks until one was dry and when we experienced an engine cut out, changed onto our full inner tank. When I tried to do this, the other engine stopped and no amount of juggling the fuel cocks would re-establish the fuel feed. This happened at an altitude of 4,000 feet. I realised the situation was hopeless and gave the order to bail out. The pupil Wireless Operator went first, pulled his ripcord too soon and was caught up on the Ansons tailplane, the navigator went next but forgot to tighten the leg straps of his harness, fell out, and was unfortunately killed. My staff wireless operator followed them and in the process, struck his pupil (who was still stuck on our tailplane) knocking him free, after which they both made a safe descent. My pupil bomb aimer panicked and nothing I could say would induce him to jump and so I had no choice but to attempt a forced landing in the pitch dark. As I came in I spotted two trees in the dim light and steered between them. Both wings struck a tree which cut our speed a great deal and we came to rest in a field, facing the way we had come in. My aircraft was a write off but my bombardier was fine. I suffered a broken femur, ankle and foot, but was glad to be alive!

I returned to flying in November 1944 and left Millom to fly Wellingtons and Lancasters when the station closed down. I left the service in late 1945 and never did I expect to return to Millom with ex comrades and find a museum of our old station! During our reunion visit whilst being given a tour of our old runways, I looked around and quite honestly tears came into my eyes at the thought of how it all used to be and all those people I once worked with gone. Happy memories though!

560' North 80' West

In 1943 I was a staff pilot with an advanced flying school at a small airfield on the Cumberland coast. We did navigational training trips over the Irish Sea in Ansons with a crew of five - staff pilot and wireless-operator, and pupil navigator, bomb-aimer and wireless-operator.

As most pupils were destined to fly in Bomber Command, the air training was generally at night. On occasions the monotony of our flying was broken by making air searches of the nearby peaks in the Lake District and sea searches for overdue aircraft.

One night I landed back at base about midnight. I was asked by the duty officer if I thought the weather was fit for more flying. It was worsening, but I said: "If take-off time is advanced we should manage to do an exercise and return before the bad weather finally closes in."

I went to the dining hall to have my night-flying supper, the usual egg and chips, washed down with mugs of hot, sweet tea. I met my staff wireless-operator and told him to collect our pupils from the briefing room and meet me at our Anson.

Aircraft overdue

As soon as my crew were aboard the aircraft I started the motors, taxied to the runway in use and took off. After climbing to 2,000 feet I swung the Anson round on a course to take me back over the centre of the airfield and asked the wireless-operator on the intercom for our instructions for the trip.

He told me it was a combined search and navigational exercise. Apparently an aircraft being ferried from Gander in Newfoundland to Prestwick in Scotland was overdue and the last contact had been made when it was at 56 degrees north 8 degrees west. We were to fly to that position and check on any lights on the surface of the sea or any signals from dinghy emergency radio transmitters.

My navigator gave me a course of 285 degrees at 4,000 feet. He warned me not to drop below this height, because our track would take us near 3,500-foot-high Mountains in Scotland. Flying a small aircraft at night with a trainee navigator meant a great deal of work for the pilot. He had not only to control the plane but also to keep a navigational plot going, in order to check on his pupil. To add to my difficulties, patches of cloud kept drifting across, necessitating complete instrument flying. Consequently, I had no time to look round the aircraft cabin or check on my crew.

Nothing seen

After about an hour and a half we reached our destination and I dropped the aircraft down to 500 feet to see if any lights were visible. Nothing could be seen, and my radio-operator reported "negative" on his radio watch as well.

Disappointed, I turned the aircraft on to a homeward course and began climbing back to our safety height of 4,000 feet. I had been on the course only a couple of minutes when we plunged straight into an extremely solid-looking bank of cloud and I was compelled to go back on to complete instrument flying.

My troubles did not end there, for I felt the aircraft swing to starboard and noticed the revolutions per minute on the starboard engine indicator plunge back to zero. I trimmed the aircraft to fly on one engine and pushed the port throttle fully forward to maintain height this time 3,800 feet.

I felt no worry because an Anson, even loaded with all the crew and equipment we had, would maintain height on one engine, though there was no extra power available for any height increase. However, when I glanced out of the cockpit window I did feel most uneasy, for I could see the onset of that most dreaded of all flying hazards - ice forming rapidly on the wing.

It was obvious that action had to be taken - and taken quickly. The only thing I could think of at that moment was to dive down to about 500 feet and fly home keeping over the sea all the way. But I knew this would add another 40 or 50 minutes to our flying time - and I doubted very much if our fuel would last out.

In the clear

While these thoughts were going through my mind one of the crew members came and sat beside me. "Can you hold this height for another five minutes, Skipper?" he shouted. "By then we should be in the clear."

Thinking base had radioed this information, I kept the aircraft at 3,800 and, as predicted, we broke out of cloud, though we still had a layer both above and below us. Nevertheless, at our height the air was clear, with no danger of picking up more ice.

I turned to the chap sitting beside me and said: "Thank whoever it was who gave us that information - they've probably saved us from a long swim home." Whether he misheard me or not I do not know, but he said: "Ken - Ken Russell," and added: "If you don't need me any more I'll get back." He disappeared down the aircraft.

From then on the flight was uneventful. We maintained a steady course back to base, homed in on the radio beam, let down through the cloud and landed.

As I had only one functioning engine, I couldn't taxi the aircraft, so as I waited for a tractor to come and tow us to the parking area I decided to fill in my log. For the first time that night I looked round the cabin and was surprised to see only two pupils.

"Where's the bomb-aimer?" I asked my wireless-operator. "He went sick at the last moment and cried off," he replied. I then assumed it must have been the navigator who gave me the vital message to maintain height earlier and I carried on filling up my log.

My wireless-operator gave me the name of his pupil, which I wrote on the log-sheet, and I then turned to the navigator and said: "I know your name – Ken Russell, isn't it?"

"No", he said. "I'm Tony - Tony Russell. Ken's my brother and he certainly is not here. He's not even in the country!"

Thinking I must have misunderstood earlier, I gave the matter no more thought and carried on writing down the details of our flight.

Very upset

A few days later I was in my room when a knock came on the door. Opening it, I was surprised to see the pupil navigator standing there looking very upset. He said: "You remember that trip we were on the other night, when we looked for that ditched aircraft?" I nodded.

"Well, my brother was flying it and I heard today that he's been posted missing, presumed killed."

Feeling helpless, I said: "Come on in," and muttered a few consoling words like "There's still hope." But I knew for certain there was no hope.

We talked for a while about the flight and by careful questioning I confirmed what I already suspected. No-one had come forward during the trip to give me any message from base.

Bob Gillespie 1992

144

MR BILL GRACIE –1942 – 1944

Where's Millom?

One day in mid December 1941I was one of nineteen young airmen standing expectantly on a parade ground at RAF Penrhos, near Pwllheli in North Wales. The previous day we had completed our training as wireless operator/air gunners. Although already qualified as wireless operators, in addition to the gunnery course we had an additional nine weeks intensive radio course which included a lot of flying and now we were about to be awarded our sergeant stripes and given details of our first posting as air crew.

There should have been twenty on parade but two days previously, on the last flying day of the course a Blenheim crashed on landing killing the pilot and the navigator and badly injuring Bill Elliot, the wireless operator. Bill and I were friends, we lived in the same small town in central Scotland and had been at school together, the crash cast a shadow over the passing out parade and made us realise that wherever there was flying there would be accidents and casualties. Bill died a few days after I left Penrhos.

When the top ten on the course, including myself, were told we were posted to RAF Millom we all looked at each other and whispered "where's Millom?" We were told an important job awaited us there but were given no details. Worse- we were given no leave!

The first thing we noticed on arrival at our new station was that the aircraft in use were Blackburn Bothas and

Avro Ansons so we knew immediately that this was not an operational unit. With all due respect to the said aircraft we hoped that this was the case! RAF Millom was then in the process of changing to No 2 (O) Advanced Flying Unit where navigators and wireless operators would come on a six weeks course to gain more flying experience before passing on to an operational training unit. Most of the navigators had trained abroad so it was essential they gain experience of flying under war time conditions, particularly at night in the black-out.

A permanent staff of pilots and WOP/AGS was being assembled and soon the ten of us, by mutual agreement, had each paired off with a pilot to form a two man crew. We were soon spread out among the four flights which had been formed and quickly settled into a routine of ten days day flying followed by ten nights of night flying, normally doing two flights per day. Training flights were usually of around two and a half to three hours duration, mostly over the Irish Sea area with landfalls on the north Wales coast, Northern Ireland, southern Scotland and the Isle of Man which allowed for a variety of routes. The two pupil navigators aboard were on their own while the pupil WOP/AG was under our supervision sending and receiving base messages and obtaining bearings and fixes from ground direction finding stations which were welcomed by the navigators. It was mainly routine stuff but there were the occasional moments of anxiety at night when the navigators had to admit that we were a bit lost.

The ten of us soon agreed that this was not a bad life. Millom was regarded as a good station although perhaps a bit in the backwoods but the local people were friendly and welcoming and on a day off it was only a short train journey over to Barrow-in-Furness or up to Coniston. Most aircrew had single rooms and rarely was a complaint heard about the food. We had to accept that there would be losses even in Flying Training Command but thankfully they were few and not all resulted in casualties. One crew had to bale out one night when flying above ten tenths cloud, completely lost and running out of fuel but confident they were over land. Fortunately they were! On a not very pleasant winter night when over the Irish Sea the engines on an Anson cut out, the pilot successfully ditched and after some hours in the dinghy by a stroke of good fortune a small ship appeared and took the very wet five airmen aboard. In poor weather one day an Anson landed on Snaefell on Isle of Man with no casualties apart from the aircraft which had the belly ripped out. A couple of days later back in the comfort of the mess the Scottish wireless op. who was aboard, hands still shaking and threatening to spill his whisky, described how "the aircraft just stopped suddenly and when I looked down my feet were in the heather." One morning when heading to the mess for breakfast a few of us were astounded and amused to see an Anson sitting on top of the coal dump, scarcely damaged. An "Error of Judgement" by the pilot that night.

After about eighteen months the ten of us, known as the Penrhos Ten, began to split up. While our work at Millom had given us a degree of satisfaction it was time for us to pass on to operational flying. We were all agreed that our posting to Millom had probably extended the flying career of some of us and very soon this became a fact. The first three to leave joined a Stirling squadron of Bomber Command and within a few weeks the names of all three appeared on the casualty lists. Five of us survived to the end of hostilities and sometime later, thanks to the efforts of John Nixon and his band of willing helpers, some of us have been able to return to Millom for an annual reunion at the fine museum which is on part of the site of the old camp (now a prison) when hands are shaken and memories revived. While there on such occasions I always had a nostalgic walk over the old airfield and tried to recall details of some of the 334 flights I took part in during my stay in that friendly corner of north west England.

Bill Gracie 2007

ALAN F. HELMSLEY - 1942 R.C.A.F

A Millom winter

I embarked from from Halifax, Canada with some five hundred other RCAF aircrew, we had begun the eight-day Atlantic crossing aboard the Royal Navy armed merchant cruiser "California". There was an escort of two destroyers and a minesweeper. Landing at Greenock on 17 December.

It was a grey morning when we arrived at Millom Station at 0800 hours, 6 January 1942. The greyness foretold the character of our existence for the next three months. A kind lady took pity on four RCAF flyers shuffling about in a vain attempt to keep out the cold dampness. We were invited in for tea and bread and marmalade. We were grateful.

Our first glimpse of No.2 AFU Milom was not encouraging. It was, however, a day of poor weather. The damp cold under sunless sky did little to relieve the soreness of the grey concrete buildings.

Also, frowning down upon this bleak picture was Black Combe, two thousand feet of mountain inconveniently located near the end of one of the runaways.

The sleeping quarters were in a long, narrow concrete building furnished with two rows of cots and two small coal-burning stoves, both cold. The washing facilities were in a separate, unheated, concrete building with about two inches of water on the floor. There seemed to be no visible means of drainage.

My only memory of the sergeants mess is of the dining room with its round, tall coal-burning stove located at the mid-point of one wall. This was a very busy place each morning as we endeavoured to make toast by pressing slices of bread against the stove sides. Most times it was successful: other times it produced burnt offerings.

It was a difficult time and the war was not going well. The meals were probably adequate but one day the Australians promoted a hunger strike. Everyone waited until all the meals were on the tables and then walked out. This left the unfortunate WAAFs with all the work of cleaning up. A few days later, the meals seemed to improve.

On our first day, we were assembled on the parade square for the commanding officers welcoming address. In very few words he indicated that we colonials knew little about discipline but that would soon change. For Canadian and Australians this was a great beginning.

Later, the same officer attempted to carry out a drill. Thanks to the Australians with some help from us, the entire exercise became a shambles. We were quickly dismissed. Next, an order was issued prohibiting us from wearing our regulation overshoes and black leather gloves. This we ignored and nothing came of it. At the end of February, we were criticised for lacking discipline and failing to salute officers. I had no personal knowledge of this behaviour but punishment came in the order for everyone to fall in on the parade square at 0745 hours for inspection drill and to be marched to classes. Finally, the Commanding officer must have been having a difficult time because he threatened to have the stripes of the next man to be brought before him. Much later I learned that after I had left Millom some Australians had a wild time, broke into the bar by smashing down the door and generally caused a major incident.

The purpose of Advanced Flying Units was to provide us with the opportunity of gaining practice in map-reading and navigation over unfamiliar country, especially in the blackout and to occupy our time white waiting postings to Operational Training Units. This was a good idea but the winter weather with frequent days and night of rain, fog and snow was very restrictive. Day after day flying had to be cancelled. Sometimes flights that were started were compelled to return. On some occasions poor weather prevented a return to base and we were directed to another airfield, where in one case, we were fogbound for two days.

Other reasons for cancelled flights included faulty radio equipment and engine failure. There was no doubt about the difficult working conditions experienced by the ground crews. Finally flying was restricted by illness from common colds and bronchitis among some of us. During my three months at Millom my flying consisted of eleven day and five night navigation exercises plus one for air-firing practice.

There were flying accidents. On the night of 9-10 January an Anson lost a tailplane when it struck a landing flare. The aircraft was missing until the wreckage was found in sea or the end of the runway. Five men were lost.

On 28 February a plane with four men was reported as missing. A diary entry for 10 March noted that all flying had been reduced to short trips because too many aircraft were being lost, not crashing or mining, but just lost - floundering about in the bleak night.

The classroom work was insignificant and seemed to suffer from a lack of proper structuring of the course.

Sometimes, we did plotting and chart work as assigned by an RAF flight-sergeant observer instructor Many times, we just sat huddled in greatcoats. Our only hope was posting to an OTU.

Every week or ten days we were given a day off. Usually, we left the evening before on the train for Barrow-in-Furness, about twenty-five miles away. Barrow is on the coast but protected from the Irish Sea by the long Isle of Walney. This was once an important ship-building centre which seemed to have failed to recover from the depression of the 1930s. We'd take rooms in the Imperial Hotel, have few a drinks in the bar then dinner in the hotel or the West Country Hotel and return to the bar, this was attended by two jovial local girls one of whom was Kitty. After the departure of the locals the bar was opened for hotel guests almost always us!

Compared to camp it was warm, it was wonderful and there was bacon and eggs in the morning. Next day would usually be spent wandering about the stores and going to the cinema.

A good day in Barrow was on 3 March. We had lunch at the Criterion, saw a film at the cinema, dinner at the Armadale, saw a variety show at the Majestic Theatre, and had time for a bar visit at the Imperial before boarding the Millom train at 2120 hours!

During weekdays, there were frequent visits to Millom. There was a cinema and we usually had dinner at the West Country Hotel. The most frequented pub was the John Peel near where we got the bus. There were no dances in Millom and only two in Barrow, both at the town hall. One night, the WAAF held a party with games and food.

At the airfield there was a gymnasium. We went once to play badminton but there was snow in the middle of the court. We amused ourselves on the bars until an RAF type invited me to do some boxing. I had never boxed. but he was not very big and I accepted. To my sorrow, I learned that he held the junior lightweight championship for the British Isles.

The mention of exercise reminds me of snow-shovelling. This we were required to do in order to clear the runaways. There was lot of snow. It may seem unusual for non-commissioned officers to shovel snow, but we were the largest workforce available and it required a lot of men. Anyway, it was better than sitting idle in a cold classroom.

It was a great day on 21 February when an invitation was extended for three aircrew to spend a weekend with some families in Seascale. We three quickly accepted. Issued with tea and sugar ratios. We left on the train for a thirty-mile trip north of Milliom. A Mr. Pattinson met us at the station and drove us to his home for a cocktail party with many friendly guests and no scarcity of gin and vermouth. After the party, each of us was taken to a different home for dinner and overnight. My charming hostess was Mrs. Keene. It was a lovely dinner after which her daughter and I played shove ha'penny and had some beer to complete the evening. I had a glorious room with a fireplace. No 2 AFU Million seemed far away.

In the morning. I was awakened by a maid with a cup of tea. Then there was a large breakfast with two eggs! While Miss Keene had to meet with a Sunday school class I enjoyed a quiet time in the library while I basked in glorious sunshine slanting through the French doors. Later. I helped Miss Keene pick Brussel sprouts from the garden. At noon, a Colonel and Mrs Johnson arrived for coffee and/or beer. We talked mostly about hunting. After lunch, we were joined by Mr and Mrs Wrigley for a very pleasant walk. After tea at Colonel Johnson's and beer at Mr Squance's, Mrs Keene drove us to the Seascale Station.

We were each presented with an egg which we nursed all the way back to Millom.

Our usual flight-sergeant instructor who was posted to Canada as navigation Instructor. Was replaced by an RAF officer who was a friendly type with an appreciation of our situation. On 14 March. he organized a bus trip for twelve of us to visit Preston for a guided tour of an aircraft plotting station. It was a pleasant ride with a lunch stop en-route. The interpretation of the operation and procedures of the station held our interest as did the great number of WAAFS, all very attractive.

On the return trip the driver was encouraged to stop at pubs along the way. At one, we purchased at least two dozen bottles and restocked the supplies as we progressed. By the time we approached Millom, all the songs had been sung and all the beer consumed. We must have realised that we were in trouble when we asked the driver to stop so that we could get rid of the bottles. We could have done nothing about the sticky mess on the floor. The driver assured us that he would take care of the bottles for the refunds. A quiet entry into the camp was attempted but there was no need. Almost the entire camp was drunk! Next morning after the mess in the bus was reported, our officer lined us up outside and gave us a bad time. He promised that our behaviour had put an end to any future trips. He, of course, was right. As he continued berating what must have appeared as a sorry looking lot of sergeants, he could hardly prevent the beginning of a smile. We were quickly dismissed.

Postings to Operational Training Units were rare. As postings became available we drew from a hat. My lucky day came on 3 April when I held a piece of paper labelled "No. 14 OTU, Cottesmore". Ken Macdonald also drew the same posting and from that time we became close friends.

For us, that was the end of Millom. Was it all that bad?

Probably not. It may have been the gloomy weather, the days of cancelled flying, little being accomplished, and no immediate end in sight. There were good days with trips into Millom and Barrow. There were the sporting challenges of sneaking about to steal coal from the coal pile and paying an airman not to put out our fire after we had gone to classes or flying when he was receiving less pay for damping out the fires. This effort of ours, of course, was soon discovered and stopped. It was probably a very difficult time for the training staff who had to organise the flying time for numbers of trainees during such adverse conditions.

On 7 April, Macdonald and I boarded the train for Oakham, near Cottesmore.

Ken Macdonald and I remained close friends until he went missing on a Dusseldorf trip on 8 April 1943. According to Allison and Hayward his remains are buried in Reichwald Forest Cemetary.

Alan F. Helmsley

MR C. KODER – 1942 - 1944

My log book for RAF Millom covers some 32 full pages. I served there as a Staff Pilot from June 1942 until May 1944 and have several memories of the station.

Whilst at the unit, I flew Masters, Ansons, Lysanders and Defiants. On the 22nd of August 1942, and following what my log describes as "local flying practice" in a Defiant, I found that I could not drop my undercarriage as I made my circuit to land. Try as I might to budge it, the undercarriage selector lever remained locked in the "up" position. The aircraft had no radio aboard and so I could not inform Flying Control of my awkward situation! I very quickly scribbled a note in the margin of my map to give warning that after flying off most of my fuel, I would be making a belly landing. Firstly, I buzzed the Flying Control at almost ground level, (to wake them up!) then during a second similar run I threw out the map. Within no time the fire tenders and ambulances were positioned at the end of the runway in anticipation of my arrival. Happily the Defiant touched down nicely on the tarmac and I walked away uninjured and relieved, but leaving the poor old Defiant with a thoroughly scragged belly!!

My second recollection is one of RAF Milloms' Ansons ditching in the sea some way west of the airfield. The date was the 13th of April 1944, it was night time and the crew managed to leave the aircraft and use the emergency dinghy. Straight away, they sent up distress signals and myself and another Anson were scrambled to locate the crew. I very quickly found the dinghy and we were able to circle the area, dropping flares to illuminate the scene until Fleetwood's RAF Air Sea Rescue launch picked up the crew some time later.

On an exceptionally low tide that same month, part of the wreckage of the ditched aircraft became visible and I was able to reach it and removed the compass as a souvenir. The crew of the wrecked Anson were all rescued without injury. I left Millom for O.T.U. and eventually was posted to No. 625 squadron at RAF Kelstron for Operational Flying. Between September 1944 and March 1945 I completed 36 operations with No, 1 Group Flying Lancasters on several major German targets and in support of our advancing land forces. I left the RAF at the rank of Flt/Lt.

Clem Koder 1992

The ditching on the night of the 13th April 1944 involved Anson R3346, Pilot FLT/Sgt Thorpe. ORB records ditching location as 5 miles west of the airfield. It appears that a substantial amount of her was washed closer in shore by the same high August tide which caused such a low water. Clem very kindly donated the compass of R3346 to the RAF Millom Collection where it can be viewed in pride of place, at Millom's Discovery Centre and in remarkable condition.

MR J. FOSTER– 1941

I actually trained at No.2 A.O.S. as part of course No.7 from June to November 1941. I can remember little of the place, other than of course, the imposing mass of Black Combe and a brilliant instructor by the name of Sgt Chadwick. The highlights of my posting were weekend escapes into the surrounding, and quite beautiful Lake District. After qualifying and 'crewing up' (on Blenheims) at 13 O.T.U. Bicester, I flew almost entirely with the same crew until my demob. I had racked up 1,500 flying hours before joining 194 and 31 squadrons (Hudsons and later Dakotas) supplying Wingates Chindits in India, (among other tasks) then back to the UK tugging gliders.

During the D-Day landings I made two glider towing flights, following the advancing army with supplies and flying back heart rendering casualties. Then more gliders and supply drops at Arnhem and for the Rhine crossing, following which I became personal crew to General Sir Brian Robertson who of course was General overall Command, in charge of the Rhine Army. I make no apologies for "line shooting" I don't often get the opportunity these days!

I was demobbed in 1946 having reached the rank of Flt/Lt.

Jack Foster 1992

HARVEY JACKSON

We left PRC Bournemouth quite early on the morning of October 16th 1944 to catch the train to Millom. As I recall there was more than one train involved but my memory fails me I do recall that we arrived at millom station between 9 and 10pm. It was very dark very windy and raining heavily as we made our way to the airfield.

We were duly assigned our hut, and as we arrived there, over the station's tannoy they were calling for the Mountain Rescue Team to assemble. We all stopped talking and looked at one another... and I venture to say that each one of us was thinking the same, that flying from Millom will be very similar to flying over the prairies in western Canada. The very next morning we were told that a Halifax bomber from a heavy conversion unit in Yorkshire that crashed into the nearby mountains.

After breakfast a few of the fellows made a tour of the station and on their return informed us that there was a menacing looking mountain called Black Combe at the end of one of the runways. Its proximity would be always on my mind during takeoffs and landings.

The weather at Millom

On the whole was quite mixed it was either freezing cold rainy, damp, cloudy and windy with occasional glimpses of sun - but I can't recall ever seeing the moon. Being at Millom in November and December I recall the bone-chilling dampness that crept into a huts on many nights when the fire in each of our stoves went out. I also remember going to bed many nights wearing long-johns, flannelette pyjamas, wooly vest, two blankets, thick socks and a greatcoat on top.

The main reason the stoves went out was the fact that the coal ration for each hut was minimal because the supply was so limited. In fact, because the supply was limited raiding forays were made to other huts when the occupants were at classes or flying. These raids were terminated when the occupants of said hut clued up and posted a guard to watch over their precious buckets of coal. On occasion even the station coal compound was raided. The ploy was to keep the guard busy by offering him Canadian cigarettes or by trying to learn the Italian language (usually by this stage of the war, the guard was an Italian prisoner of war)

We ate a considerable amount of a fish called Skate. We always thought that had it been properly cooked it may have been quite delicious.

I saw the movie national velvet with Liz Taylor at a movie house in Barrow-in-Furness I guess that was her first major picture at the age of 16. We were given a tour of the shipyard in Barrow-in-Furness and after seeing how hard the employees worked together with the noise heat dust and dirt etc I felt lucky to be a navigator.

My dad would send me parcels which used to include things like chocolate powdered milk and soup mixes. Often at bedtime we would make a delicious pot of soup and also steaming hot chocolate toddy. It was delicious wholesome, nourishing but above it all it warmed us through and through. On one day off we visited nearby Coniston were we were told that so Malcolm Campbell raced his speed boat in the 1930s on Coniston lake.

I recall the almost daily speed tests featuring the type E-6b navigation computer. By the time we completed the course everyone was a virtual Wizard and speed demon on this instrument and it proved to be a good thing too.

We loved the John Peel pub in Millom town and on many occasions the landlord would invite us into their living quarters. We would of course always pay for our beer but he and his wife would serve us a tray of delicious sandwiches and usually some special dessert. Millom is a friendly town with friendly people and I enjoyed my brief stay there.

Regarding a member of our hut who was killed in action. I recall a popular chap F/O Harold, Alfred Jones a Canadian from Toronto. He was killed on the 13/05/45 age just 22. He was flying from RAF Dishforth No1659 in a Halifax bomber which crashed into the North sea ten miles from Fife Ness in Scotland. F/O Jones is buried in the Sleepyhillock cemetery, Montrose Scotland. His name, along with that of 18,000 others may be found in a book called *They shall not grow old,* a book of remembrance dedicated to the men and women who lost their lives between September 1939 and August 1945 whilst wearing the uniform of the RCAF.

Harvey Jackson 1998

MR P. JORDAN – 1944

Prelude to promotion

It was dark, wet, and windy and very, very isolated. Nothing stirred and, although I knew that I was not entirely alone, it was not exactly comforting when a large shape appeared in my peripheral vision. I thought the parked aircraft were unlikely to move but then of course as a young, inexperienced airman of just 19 one was never quite sure about little known things in the middle of the night. Fortunately for my peace of mind, a sudden shaft of moonlight showed the clear outlines of a cow.

The night in question was my last after nearly 10 months at RAF Yatesbury. The 6 month course at No. 2 Radio School had been, extended by about 4 months for want of decisions about the future of Air Signallers in1944. Much of our extended sojourn had been occupied by airfield guard duties, Alternately as guard and guard commander, after qualifying and being promoted to sergeant (Aircrew sergeant as the non aircrew, regular camp NCO's were quick to remind us). No. 2 (O) AFU awaited and the next part of air signaller training.

An exhausting train journey through the following night being shunted in and out of numerable sidings was ultimately enlivened at first light by some cheery WVS ladies with some very welcome refreshments, on a station -platform, which announced itself as CARNFORTH. It was all a long time ago (before the same ladies were 'enroyaled' by becoming WRVS) and I don't remember too many other details of our arrival at RAF Millom except that my friend and I had been told to appear properly dressed.

We were both commissioned at the end of our main Yatesbury course but not allowed to wear our rank until arrival at our next unit. Millom, of course, was unaware of our status and we had no uniforms except a battledress on which we had put P/O badges of rank, so we moved into the Sergeants Mess with the rest of our course. I suppose this lasted for about a day before the CMC asked us to leave as soon as possible. We appeared to be homeless as we doubted the Officers Mess would have welcomed us with our air-men's kitbags emblazoned with 7 figure numbers and AC2 ranks

So, initiative or something, said a weekend pass was essential – fortunately it was Friday - and a train south to get some officers kit. We detrained at Liverpool (or was it Manchester), discovered the train was London bound (we both lived there), promptly re-boarded, and rattled through another night in slightly more comfort than the earlier journey. An early Saturday morning arrival gave time for frantic calls to parents to rendezvous at Moss Bros, expenditure of £103 (the officers uniform allowance

- a vast sum when compared to the £1 a week I'd been earning in a bank not so long before), a quick night stop at home, and back up north on Sunday to start the course the next day correctly accommodated and uniformed. By contrast the 4 week course was uneventful, although leaving me with a lasting impression of north country friendliness. The exact dates of my course were from the 26th of July 1944 to the 21st August 1944 and I believe that my flight commander was Flt/Lt Atkins. The pilots I flew with were F/Sgt Mitchell, F/Sgt Spencer, F/Sgt Gooch, Sgt Thomlinson and Sgt Whittaker. All my flying was done in the units Avro Ansons and I logged 17 hours 50 minutes of daytime flying plus 11 hours 35 minutes of night flying. I retired from the RAF at the rank of Squadron Leader.

Peter Jordan 1994

MR A. J. L. HICKOX – 1941

Myself and my friend John Archbold attended the Air Observer course at RAF Millom from March to August 1941. I recall that the writer and broadcaster, Godfrey Winn visited Millom on the 2nd of July to prepare an article on Air Observer Training for the Sunday Express newspaper. John Archbold and I, with GRP/CPT Wray as our pilot, flew him out to the Isle of Man to visit No.5 Air Observer School at RAF Jurby. The photograph which John and I signed for you was taken on that occasion, just prior to take-off. The other officer in the photograph is W/CDR Hadow who was Millom's Chief Instructor, and a strict disciplinarian! I became friends with one of the girls who worked in the NAAFI and we used to take walks down to the beach together. One evening whilst walking back round the perimeter track we bumped into Hadow, who gave me a tremendous rocket, saying that I should have been in my billet swotting! The sequel to this story was that whilst the top seven people on each course were commissioned, although I came fifth I was only made a Sergeant!

At the end of the course I volunteered to go on a delivery flight to Blackburn's at Brough with a pilot named F/Sgt Friend. We landed at RAF Church Fenton after mechanical problems and the aircraft was rendered unserviceable. As a result I was stuck there for the next four days, in an airman's billet with no change of clothes, when I eventually got back to Millom I found that I had missed my wings parade. I flew with a Polish P/Officer by the name of Spychala several times on Bombing and Gunnery details, all without mishap. However, on one occasion I remember that whilst taxiing out to take-off, the brakes on our Botha failed and we wound up, nose to nose with a Fairey Battle on one of the dispersal pans!

Both John Archbold and myself had elected to go onto Wellington Bombers on completion of our training at Millom and so off we went to the Operational Training Unit at RAF Harwell. On completion of our course there we delivered brand new Wellingtons Eastwards. When we arrived on Malta to be re-fuelled, to our surprise, the aircraft were taken off us. They wanted us to stay on the Island also, but my crew declined and after a couple of nights we flew on to Egypt as passengers. On arrival in Egypt we joined No.70 Squadron and after 40 operational flights we were shot down by a night-fighter. I bailed out safely but had a long walk back to base! Two of my crew were not so lucky and lost their lives. John Archbold did stay on Malta and joined No.40 Squadron, moved on to Eqypt and then to India. Whilst stationed in India, he had to ditch in the sea off Phittagong when the airfield refused to light up the airfield believing John's plane to be a Jap! This mistake cost them the lives of 3 aircrew and John spent a year in hospital and a further year off flying due to the injuries he sustained, he still has a gammy leg.

On my return to the UK I spent some months instructing at O.T.U. then went on to Pathfinder Mosquitoes for another 40 operational flights. At the end of that tour I was instructing at the Mossie Training Unit at Warboys, when who should come through on the course but John Archbold, prior to his second tour! So we had somewhat parallel careers. We did lose touch however and did not meet up again until two years ago.

"Bill" Hickox 1992

TOM JUPP

Author's Note:

The following story relates to the tragic and horrific loss of Anson N4869 and her crew on Gowdebarrow Crag Muncaster. As told in section one of this book, the RAF Millom team and myself carried out a series of small excavations at the crash site in the late summer of 1992. No signs of the tragedy remained visible on the fell-side and it is fitting, I think, that flowering shrubs cover the site in abundance. Due to this however, investigation of the site was difficult, but, with the blessings of Muncaster Estates, our work was completed in a single weekend.

The Death of F/Sgt Tom Jupp and his Crew whilst flying from RAF Millom 20th September 1942. Told to us by his Fiancée Mrs Peggy Fray (née Richards)

It was a fine autumn night and good flying weather when, at 23:11 hours on the 19th of September. 1942. Aircraft Anson Mark l Serial No. No.4869, with five airmen on board, took off from No.2. (Observer)Advanced Flying Unit, RAF Millom on a routine night flying navigational training exercise.

During the flight the usual messages were transmitted and at 01:00 the next morning, with a lowering cloud base, rain began to fall. At 01:04 another routine message was received at base, but thirty six minutes later, with rain still falling, at 01:40 hours on Sunday the 20th of September, 1942, the aircraft collided with the ground at high speed, by Gowderbarrow Crag, on Muncaster Fell, near Ravenglass, and completely disintegrated, with the loss of all five young men.

The sound of the impact was heard by a young boy in his farmhouse home a mile away across the valley, and later that morning his father, with others of the Home Guard, went up the fell side to aid the RAF recovery team, wreckage being scattered over a wide area.

The young pilot was buried in St. Luke's Churchyard at Haverigg; he had recently returned from home leave and his parents were too heartbroken to have his body taken back so soon. He was their only child, born as men were still returning from the war that was supposed to end all wars.

The last few days of his last leave had been spent at my home, for we planned to be married the following spring, but when that season came around, I saw it through different eyes. Partly in sorrow, and in protest, to, at the waste of young life occasioned by war I wrote;

> Spring has wiped old winter's tears away,
> The lanes are wearing wedding gowns of May.
> Streams flow, clear washed by April showers,
> In woods new leaves unfurl for lovers bowers.
> On fells blue harebells rustle in the breeze,
> And sheep with lambs are grazing on the leas.
> Curlews wheel and cry to nest in the ling,

The land is re-born, all nature does sing.
But my love in the Kirk yard is lying,
I am alone, my heart ever sighing –
Say they still - sweet lovers love the spring?
I was, after all, very young.

The scarred fell side on Muncaster is green again and trees have grown there, I am told, but should an alien piece of metal be seen there, as sometimes is remarked in writing of these wartime air accidents in Lakeland, please to remember those five young men and... tread softly.

In the early 1980's, when I was in contact with the Air Historical Branch of the Ministry of Defence, at Lacon House. London, in phoning there one day I was answered by Erie Turner, who was not usually in that particular office - he said it was a million-to-one chance that he should have been there when I phoned. It transpired that he had been a staff Wireless Operator at Millom, when Tom was there. They had only known one another for a few days, but he had been in the Guard of Honour at Tom's funeral. He was also a friend of 641453 Flight Sergeant H. Smith, Wireless Operator/Air Gunner, whose war grave is next to Tom's, on the left, who died on the 8th February, 1943, aged 21 years.

At the time we spoke. Erie Turner still paid occasional visits to his friend's last resting place, as did I, in visiting Tom's grave. It was a strange coincidence that he should have answered the phone that day, in London.

Weather report from Silloth MU (Cumberland) for the night of 19th-20th September, 1942. From old records now (1981) held by RAF Carlisle (Meteorological Office No.14 MU).

On the night of the 19th September 1942 at 18:00 hours ...the temperature was 550f. It was a nice, warm autumn evening; as to visibility, at midnight cloud extended between 4,000 and 9,000 feet, but it grew cloudier in the early hours of the 20th September.

It began to rain at 01:00 hours – the cloud base was 4,000 feet at that time. The temperature was 510 F, the wind was North East by East at Force 3, and the humidity was 91%.

At 01:40 hours on the 20th, the cloud base was still approximately 4,000 feet, but as it began to rain at 01:00 hours, the visibility would be cut down.

No.14 MU explained that although it was a reasonable flying night, the rain would cut down visibility and probably, since aircraft had not much to help with navigation in those days, it was possible that the aircraft crossed the coast at the wrong point and realizing this, they came down below the cloud base to try to find a landmark. They may have turned back to go seawards again to follow the coastline and in the turning, struck the crag on the south side of the fell, as they turned to fly out of the valley They would come down low, if they were trying to find a landmark in the rain, and they might have seen the fell looming up, and tried to climb too steeply, at too slow a rate of airspeed, which could cause the Aircraft to stall.

Author's Note:

In the wake of Tom's death, his parents were extremely supportive of Peggy. With the hope that it might bring her some small comfort, Tom's mother sent Peggy the above poem. Her story remains as fresh in my mind as the day she told it to me and I am sure that she would join me in dedicating this poem, to all those, both past and present, who have waited in vain for the return of a loved one.

I Shall Come Back
By Treveleyn-Smith

Do not lose heart, where silence Shadows hope
Gather more close your cloak of
Gallantry, and wear it ever proudly,
Confident, smiling, as when I left,
I shall come back.
Perhaps not quite as when that
Autumn down I held you closely In my arms,
And knew your eyes shut tight
Against the traitorous seas
Not thus, perchance, but yet –
I shall come back
It will suffice if even what is sent
Is service in another sphere
For me,
And you are left to tread
Remembered ways without my
Hand, but still –
I shall come back
The very all will be so filled With me,
That when you move or breathe
Our spirits each will be united
Inescapably
Together – two in one
I shall come back

MR PETER MESTON – 1942 – 1943

I arrived at Millom in early 1942 having been training navigators using Airspeed Oxfords at RAF Shawbury. Millom at this time, had just "phased out" their awful Blackburn Botha's and were flying the Mk1 Avro Ansons. I was posted to the unit as a Warrant Officer and became Chief Navigational Instructor with a free hand to establish the syllabus.

My wife came to Cumberland with me and lodged with Mr and Mrs Barnes at the Ship Inn in Millom town on Holborn Hill, they were wonderful hosts to us. I unfortunately, had to spend my nights in a badly built single brick hut on the airfield trying to keep warm as the wind from the Irish Sea forced its way through the gaps in the mortar! At this time Millom was receiving pupils from Canada, New Zealand, Australia and South Africa who had trained in conditions where visibility was unlimited, and who were to be taught to deal with less than ideal flying conditions. Where better to teach them!!

The Cumberland climate came as a nasty shock!! I frequently flew with crews and our exercises from Millom often took us out over the Scottish West Coast Islands. Once we spotted a German U boat sitting on the bottom of a large bay on the south side of Islay, no doubt feeling very secure and oblivious to the fact that he could be clearly seen from above. We reported our sighting but by the time a Coastal Command aircraft reached Islay the Germans had moved on.

In the early summer of 1942 a very high profile delegation from Canada arrived at RAF Millom. The group consisted on an Air Vice Marshall and three politicians. I was summoned by our Station Commander, given his Humber Estate car and told to conduct the delegation around the station and show them everything they wished to see. I assumed that they would want to be briefed on the training we were engaged upon, however, they showed no interest in that at all. Our first port of call was the stations Cook House and dining halls. At this time we had a superb Warrant Officer Caterer and the place was spotless and lunch in progress. I had no hesitation in inviting the group to take a meal but they declined and asked to be shown the "other cookhouse". I informed them that we did not have another cookhouse and upon doing so was virtually accused of lying to them! I called over our Warrant Officer cook and asked him if there had ever been another cookhouse. The Warrant Officer looked at me as though I was crackers and said "I have been here since the unit opened sir and as you well know, this is the only cookhouse". The situation became even more bizarre then when the delegation demanded to see the parade ground! I pointed out that we did not have parades and indeed did not have a parade ground. The atmosphere became very frigid then and their demand was pressed once more. My solution was to drive up the edge of the station and they could direct me up any roads they chose, after which, if a parade ground or additional cookhouse was found I would apologise unreservedly. Of course we found neither but I was flabbergasted when the Air Vice Marshall asked to inspect the bomb damage to the unit! I had to point out that we had never been bombed and asked finally "sir, what is this visit about please"? The delegation conferred among themselves for a moment then with a collective sigh, enlightened me. Apparently Canadians had written home describing the constant heavy bombing, the awful living conditions, foul food and the fact that they had been kept on the parade ground till they dropped! There had been so many of these complaints reported by distraught parents that the Canadian Government had sent this delegation to investigate. The delegation was finally embarrassed. Why the Canadians wrote home in this way remained a mystery to us all.

Whilst I was serving at Millom I managed to arrange a spell of attachment to an operational Lancaster Squadron at RAF Scampton. Though I was converted to fly twin engine aircraft I was not passed for the "heavies" however my obvious talents as an Instructional Navigator and my being a qualified Bomb Aimer / Air Gunner ensured me two operational flights, both with new crews. As I was not at that time qualified to operate the new, and highly secret navigational aid known as "GEE" I flew both missions as base gunner / bomb aimer. The target for my first "OP" was Saarbrucken and as we began our flight over the North Sea we discovered that our wonderful (and highly secret) navigational aid had in fact failed! Our navigator was not at all confident in continuing without this aid and so I pitched in to help using the time honoured method of "dead reckoning". I was absolutely confident that we were bang on track and right on time a big river came into view right where it should have been. The river bends looked correct, the large docks and town all checked out and I was happy that we had indeed found our target. We made our run into the target and released our bomb load. As we turned away we witnessed massive explosions which lit up the whole area as we turned for home. After landing and debriefing we all fell into our beds but my slumbers were disturbed at 9am when I was ordered to the briefing room to be confronted by an irate Operations Officer who demanded to know where I had bombed. Apparently a photo recce flight had shown no damage at all to Saarbrucken! Maps were produced and I then realised my mistake. Just short of Saarbucken was a small town called Saarkauten, the river bends were very similar and the dock areas and town were closely enough aligned with the town to be mistaken for our target. The main difference was the scale of the area but of course at night from 25,000 ft this was overlooked by myself, I was not a popular gent at all! I was to be let off the hook somewhat a short time after the event when intelligence reports from enemy territory spoke of a very successful raid on Saarkauten by a lone Lancaster. Apparently the Germans had been using the small town as a munitions dump believing that there was little chance of it being attached.

My second sortie was to raid Dusseldorf and again, all did not go according to plan. After a tense flight and as we approached the target area to begin our bomb rune, our rear gunner suddenly yelled "fighter"! Our pilot immediately threw the aircraft into a textbook evasive left handed corkscrew dive taking us nearly vertical in the process. We began our corkscrew at 25,000 ft and by the time we were able to pull out of it and achieve level flight we were down to 5,000 ft. The main raid was now in full swing, with heavy anti-aircraft fire and searchlights, two of which now had us illuminated in their beams. The raid was timed to take 20 to 25 minutes and with our payload it would have taken us that long to achieve bombing altitude and make a bomb run on our own. We had been given a marshalling yard as a secondary target and so decided to attack that. Picking up the railway line we followed it to our target and began to low level run releasing our bombs on a stick of one second intervals. Straight away our rear gunner reported huge explosions and we made our escape at low altitude. On return to base my dear friend the Operations Officer (a wingless wonder) insisted that we should have climbed back to our original altitude and bombed our primary target! Bless his cotton socks!! Vindication for our decision came swiftly when it was discovered that we had laid our stick of bombs almost perfectly along a munitions train (hence the massive explosions) and in doing so had caused extensive casualties to two German divisions parked in troop trains in the sidings. With my operational secondment at an end I soon afterwards returned to RAF Millom. My two operational flights could not have been more exciting and eventful though very difficult to recount without seeming to be a bit of a "line shooter"! In late 1943 I was posted to RAF Silloth to be converted onto the Hudson aircraft of Coastal Command.

I made many pals at Millom but frankly, due to the weather and the unit's remote location I was pleased to leave.

Peter Meston

MR R. MCGILL – 1944

I tried to join the RAF as an apprentice in 1939 but was unable to do so as I had scarlet fever at the time of the entrance exam. I left school in July 1939 and started work on a farm, on or near my 18th birthday in August 1941. I again tried to join the RAF, only to find I was in a reserved occupation and could only join by volunteering as aircrew. I volunteered as a navigator but was turned down and offered " Wireless Operator / Air Gunner" – after more trouble getting away from the farm I did eventually start training as a W.O.A/AG at Blackpool in March 1942. I qualified from RAF Modley, Hereford later that year and was posted to RAF West Drayton, near the present Heathrow Airport. From there in spring 1943 I returned to RAF Modley to complete my wireless operators training, before being posted to RAF Evanton (Inverness) where I passed out as a Sergeant Air Gunner in August 1943. Next came Radar School at Hooton Park in Cheshire before I was posted to RAF Haverford West (Pembrokeshire) crewing on Wellington Bombers which were engaged on anti-submarine patrols. I was posted from there to 179 squadron at RAF Predannick (Cornwall) but never got there due to an accident which resulted in me breaking my ankle. I remained at Haverford West, as a result of this, eventually taking part in the Normandy invasion as an Aircraft Observer on H.M.S. Azalea (a Flower Class Corvette), during which we took part in an attack on a U-boat off Lundy Island. It was from Haverford West that

I was posted to RAF Millom for refresher training before being returned to flying duties on Coastal Command.

I arrived at Millom in October 1944 and left the following month having completed my course. At the time I was there the unit was designated No.2 Observer Advanced Flying Unit giving training to navigators prior to them being posted to Operational Training Units. Avro Ansons made up the greater part of the stations aircraft strength and gave ground crew a continuous maintenance headache as they were being flown virtually around the clock and becoming very "tired"! I remember that after take-off and before landing it was the W.O.P./AG's job to go up front with the pilot and manually retract or let down the undercarriage by turning a crank handle. The number of turns needed to accomplish this task escapes me but I clearly recall that it was over 100!

The weather at Millom was rarely good and I remember being part of a crew searching the Irish Sea, fruitlessly, for two missing Fleet Air Arm Corsairs in the most foul weather conditions. Vivid memories remain too, of the industry around Millom town, in particular the Iron Ore mines. One often saw the tired miners, red with the ore trudging homeward. I am afraid I remember Millom as a gloomy area and I must confess that I always thought it a bad choice of location for an airfield due to the close proximity of the Lakeland mountain's, indeed, when flying our exercises, pilots would often point out crash sites on the fells. When my time at Millom came to an end, I was posted to RAF Turnberry (now a famous Scottish golf course) on to Warwick Air Sea Rescue Aircraft, then RAF Thornby (North Yorks), Reykjavik (Iceland), Ballykelly (Northern Ireland) with 279 and 281 Squadrons.

From Ballykelly, 281 Squadron moved to RAF Azores but I missed out as I was on leave and ended up at the less exotic posting of RAF Aldergrove (now Belfast Airport).

From Aldergrove I went back to Warwicks at RAF Kinloss in Scotland to train in preparation for a Far East posting, this never happened however due to the end of hostilities. Instead, I went to RAF Chivenor in Devon and on to Headquarters Coastal Command at Northwood (Middlesex) where I served in the organisation branch as a Warrant Officer until 1st of May 1947. Four days later (5th May) I put on a different uniform as a Customs Officer in Southampton Docks. My service in the Customs Preventive Service took me to most parts of the UK but I spent most of my time in Southampton Port, and Heathrow and Gatwick Airports before coming to Northampton in January 1971 to set up a Fraud Investigation unit and supervise the Customs staff at Luton and Stanstead Airports. My RAF connections did not end in 1947 as in 1958 I was commissioned in the Training Branch of the RAF Volunteer reserve as a Pilot Officer for duty with the Air Training Corps – serving initially as a Squadron Officer with Southampton Squadron, then with Maidenhead, Reigate, Redhill and Newbury Squadrons. I followed these by becoming a Wing Staff Officer based at RAF White Waltham (Berkshire). This ended when I moved from Heathrow to Northampton and joined No.5 Northampton Squadron as Adjutant – a post I continued to hold after my formal retirement as a FLT/Lieutenant in 1978. I eventually gave up this post to serve on the Squadron Committee.

As you can see, my association with the RAF has been a long and varied one!

Bob McGill 1992

RON MORGAN

A Young Boys War

Early in the War, The Dandy and The Beano soon lost their prime spots as items of Schoolboy bartering. Military cap badges, uniform buttons, shrapnel from the Blitz on Barrow and empty cartridge cases became the items of currency. Swapping became an obsession. In my school at Millom it had a fatal result. A group of class mates embarked on a Saturday afternoon expedition to recover spent bullets from the stop butts at Haverigg aerodrome. Spotted and challenged by an RAF guard they turned and ran. Straight into a minefield. Where one of their number lost his life.

For most of the War, the skies over Cumberland were filled with droning Avro Ansons from the airfields at Haverigg, Cark and Walney. Air Gunners, Navigators and Bomb Aimers were trained in the canvas and tubing aircraft as they trundled around the rim of the Irish Sea. In an era of primitive navigational aids when the weather clamped, aircraft were often hard pressed to make it back to their bases and many came to grief among the hills of Lakeland. It was from these wrecks that the best trophies were to be obtained and any self respecting schoolboy would be on his bike pedalling post haste for crash sites as soon as they became known.

My adventure was in 1945, and probably had its seeds in a wartime school dinner, more than likely cheese pie followed by prunes and custard. One of my Scout mates came with a tale of an Avro Anson that had crashed and burned out on Black Combe. The following Sunday was set aside for a trip to the wreck. For some reason that I have never been able to fathom the three of us who went were accompanied by a spinster aunt of 'a certain age': that ruled out bikes and so there was a six mile trek into the Whicham Valley. There on Black Combe Screes was the object of the journey, the tangled and blackened wreckage of what had once been one of the Royal Air Forces workhorses.

Despite the fact that we were dressed for an afternoon stroll and had no climbing gear or ropes we were soon near the top of the 1,500 foot scree. (Auntie stayed at the bottom!) To our delight there was the ultimate prize, two Browning .303 machine guns in what was left of the mid upper turret. Although lacking any tools we soon managed to free the guns from their mountings and to compound our delight, despite the fierce fire that had burned after the crash there was plenty of ammunition lying around. It was only when we got off the scree that we realised how heavy a machine gun was but we were not going to give up our trophies easily. There was the added complication that it was now dark and there was still the long walk home.

At home anxious parents were soon getting the inevitable reply, "But I thought that he was at your house." It was our good fortune that my mates Dad ran the local Auxiliary Fire Service and as we had said that we were going to Black Combe he took the fire engine out and set out to look for us. We were duly discovered tramping home. The black-out came to our aid as the dimmed headlights of the fire engine enabled us to smuggle out precious cargo onto the tender with it being seen.

I don't remember getting home. I suppose there was the predictable "telling off". What I do remember is tucking into bread and dripping when we got to my pals house. Never has any meal tasted so good! The guns were by this time suitably hidden as we planned our next move. Monday must have seemed the longest school day ever. Eventually 4 o'clock came and we hastened to our weapons.

The first thing that we did, aided by a pair of pliers and a gas ring was to find out how tracer ammunition worked. That resulted in our blowing out the kitchen window. More grief!

With all the skills of practised gun runners, one of the guns was then taken to my home. I lived in a mining hamlet, a few hundred yards from the sea shore and with nothing between the shore and Ireland. We soon found how to cock the gun and how to release the breach block. Saturday afternoon was to be the day when we opened the shooting gallery to end all shooting galleries! My Mother had gone shopping and the gun was rigged in my bedroom window. Soon bullets were whistling over the sea. Not surprisingly neighbours soon complained about the noise, and the smell of cordite took a bit of explaining away! Eventually the truth came out. What was the next step to be? Contacts with the Police or the RAF could have had unfortunate consequences. Eventually my brother who was in the RAF contacted an Air Gunner from Haverigg and he removed the breech block, the barrel and the return spring from the gun, and they were thrown off the local seas wall at high tide. What was left remained the prize of prizes, but it was eventually relegated to the back of a cupboard.

Many years later after I had married and had a family of my own, the remains of the gun became central to the camps and forts that my youngsters built. I also learned from my friend, Gilbert Rothery, of Workington the story behind my trophy. It was on January 2nd, 1945 that Anson LT 741 left Walney aerodrome for a live firing exercise with a target tug to the North West between the Isle of Man and the Cumberland coast. There was a crew of four on the Anson, the pilot, a gunnery instructor and two trainee gunners. Their rendezvous with the target was never made and in bad weather the Anson radioed that it was making its way back to Walney. That was its last message. When nothing further was: heard a sea and land search was put into operation, and after 8 days the burned out remains were found on Black Combe. The Combe had not been searched before as it lay to the north of the track of the aircraft which should have been flying south. In the wreckage were the bodies of three of the crew. The fourth member had been thrown clear and had rolled down the. 1,500 foot scree, and although suffering from terrible burns and a broken leg had attempted to crawl to help, before dying from exposure. The Anson had failed to clear Black Combe by some 50 feet or so and the irony was that with the War ending 5 months later, the trainee gunners would never have flown operationally had they survived.

Ron Morgan 1995

MAX MUNDY – 1941–1945

The funny side of my wartime experiences!

Being a Londoner and having served in the RAF as a LAC up in Millom camp from 1940 until 1945 I thought as it was 45 years ago that I was there it would be nice to see that old camp once again. Well being 79 years now to wait any longer to do that sentimental trip would be foolish. After all those years had passed me by I no sooner reached the old Millom station when I met up with many local people who actually remembered me so naturally the funny side of the Second World War for me became the subject of conversation.

The beautiful blackout

During the war the whole country was in total darkness at night to avoid the Germans finding places of importance to bomb and therefore Millom railway station was completely blacked out and we RAF lads loved that beautiful blackout for other more important reasons. On weekends the Millom train to Barrow was packed with us lads going to Barrow for a rest from the rigid camp duties. Most of us usually got on the train from the wrong side, but the right side from where the station porters couldn't see us getting on the train and strangely enough on arrival at Barrow most of us got off the wrong side, the right side for not being seen by the ticket collector or porters. British Railway therefore had carried 70% of us free of charge. Going back to camp at night was an easier task because of the Blackout. We would be on the train bound for Millom unseen and when we arrived at Millom the Beautiful Blackout came to our rescue. We would alight from the train and give the ticket collector our tickets and make a fast retreat and get lost in the blackout because the moment the ticket collector collected the last ticket and went into his well lit office he discovered he had no railway tickets only bus tickets, cigarette pictures and pieces of cardboard.

Camp routine on Christmas day was nil, it was the only day of the year when anything and everything would happen and the wrath of an Officer never occurred. The day began as usual with the flag being raised on the pole on the parade ground but the identity of the raiser that did this was never known, he was like the invisible man, well he had to be because the flag he raised was always a pair of WAAF black knickers. The WAAFS themselves throughout the year were subject to strong discipline so Christmas day officers of all ranks including the Group Captain had strange things happening to them. Trousers would go missing, their beds would for no reason fall apart and for Christmas presents they would find bottles of whisky outside their doors which turned out to be watered down tea. One WAAFOfficer woke up one

Christmas morning to find a Christmas present inside the bottom of her bed, she was woken up by its loud croaking.

There was one Warrant Officer on the camp that went beyond the bounds of duty and made the lives of a great many good lads terribly miserable and something had to happen and it did.

The Warrant Officer, no names no packdrill came back, or rather staggered back to camp from Millom worse for drink – and wanting to relieve himself entered his toilet and sat on the seat which had been half sawn through in the middle in the meantime. He had to go to the expense of a new uniform.

Another officer that never once missed out helping me out on camp shows and concerts was the camp Padré, a tall Canadian with a heart of gold and a never end of thirst. He put himself in charge of the liquid refreshment department for the cast and helpers, and he made his headquarters and stores underneath below the stage and he did an excellent job in seeing all the cast and helpers got their full share of liquid refreshment, and his own of course which somehow strangely made him stagger back to his billet when the shows were over.

Business as usual - we had a tailors shop on the camp mostly for necessary alterations to uniforms and repairs and the two airmen in charge were two Jewish lads from London and were happy lads and always helped out if we had an accident with our uniforms and didn't want to have to report to our Officers for fear of being on a charge. There were many of us on the camp that in Civvy Street liked our jackets with square shoulders but alas our uniform jackets issued to us were far from square shouldered, so being business like our two Jewish lads for a ten bob note made the difference, our shoulders were so square you could play snooker on them.

There was always a time during my "five" years there when the gloom over the Black Combe was nothing compared to the gloom that came over me. Rather I should say to most of the lads on the camp. Brought together by the war we came from different parts of Britain, Scottish lads, Lancashire, Lincolnshire, Londoners, you name it we were all there, twenty or more together in those same huts that still stand on the old RAF camp.; Close knit together as time passed comradeship took over and our dialects and thoughts made us all into Musketeers, but always within a few months that gloom would appear, one of the lads would get his marching orders to leave for another camp and in many cases to the other side of the world. It was something that you couldn't get used to and played havoc with the heartstrings, and then the whole process would begin again by other lads being posted and arriving at our camp. In my capacity as entertainer and in charge of the Camp Theatre I grew to know many Senior Officers on the camp including a doctor in charge of our hospital, actually he had been a baby specialist of Harley Street London and wore a monocle in one eye that was weak. He used to like to be involved with the shows I produced and one day although I just an ordinary airman he invited me to go shooting with him but it was the last and only time that I did so. His eyesight was very bad for he mistook some rumbling movement among some bushes and took aim for which he thought was a duck only to find he'd shot a cow in the behind, though his eyes were bad he ran faster than Seb Coe back to camp and I followed.

Whenever I hear that old American song "Don't fence me in", I am always reminded of the Canadian Pilots that we had at the camp at one time. One weekend when they were not allowed out of camp they decided they would have a Rodeo Show. There were no horses around near the camp and so they harnessed up the local cows in the fields and though camp personnel found it amusing the Group Captain didn't when the farmer pointed it out and complained!

Max Mundy 1992

Author's Note:

Max and I often discussed the Millom weather, which is frequently "disappointing" to say the least. Max suffered it as an airman, I endured it for 29 years as a Prison Officer. Max told me that he had come to terms with Millom's "climate" and offered me the following advice – it has been a help over the years...
When you Wake Up

When you wake up in the morning

and the sky is dull and grey

and it looks like rain don't complain

it has to be that way,

cos you can't have sunshine all the time

it would be nice I know,

but there again without the rain

not a thing would grow

and then the oceans and the rivers

all over the Universe

would all dry up and where would we be?

why, dying of hunger and thirst.

So...

When you wake up in the morning

And the sky is dull and grey

And it looks like rain if you must complain

Do it the proper way,
Just look in the mirror and say to yourself
What a Lousy Ruddy Day.

Max Mundy

<u>Author's Note:</u>

In early 1992, and prior to the lead up to my research project into the history of RAF Millom, two of the first ex-service men and women of the station I encountered were Max Mundy and his wife Rita, who was WAAF The couple had met at RAF Millom and still visited the area in order to stay with Mr Reg Hodgson and his wife, Reg had also served at Millom during the war as an LAC Max joined the RAF at the outbreak of war but was unable to fly in any capacity, due to a perforated eardrum. He was no stranger to the stage, having started acting at the age of eleven and so it is no surprise that his talents came back to the fore at Millom as the man in charge of station entertainments. With begged, stolen and borrowed materials, Max constructed stage and sets, scenery etc. And put on many well received Pantomimes and shows. Max was an inexhaustible source of jokes and anecdotes gathered during a lifetime in the entertainment business – but my favourite story concerns the now world famous singer Tom Jones. When Max left the RAF in the early 1950's he became a theatrical agent. One day he was approached by the manager of the then unknown Welsh Bricklayer – cum-singer who asked if Max could find Tom a bit of work? Max managed to get him on engagement at the Gresham Ballroom, singing for £30 a night. The Ballroom manager rang Max after a couple of nights and said "this singer is a load of rubbish"!
Two weeks later, Tom Jones appeared on Top of the Pops, and the rest as they say, is history!! Max himself made

his first real stage appearance in 1992 but told me that he knew he had made it, when he took a part in "Legend of the Werewolf" with Ron Moody and Peter Cushing, during filming breaks he took great pride in the chair provided with his name boldly printed on the back of it. Max remembered Peter Cushing as a very kind and thoughtful man who always had time to chat. Max was no stranger to TV screens in his later career, though he seemed destined more often than not, to be cast as a tramp of some sort, or someone down on their luck. Look out for Max in re-runs of, Grange Hill, Poldark, The Gentle Touch, Robins Nest, The Bill and London's Burning all great performances! I however, will always remember him better for the way in which he brought the old station alive for us again with his excellent memory and ready wit.

MR A.L. MELOCHE – 1944 R.C.A.F.

I was very interested indeed, to discover that the former No.2 O.A.F.U., RAF Millom, now has a museum!! My flying logbook indicates that I was there in training as a Navigator, from October the 21st 1944, to December the 31st 1944. I recall that the weather was our greatest concern. We flew when the birds didn't fly! It was said that Millom used to win the pennant for logging the greatest number of flying hours per month amongst the Advanced Flying Units.

Engine problems were also common with all the old Mark 1 Ansons. They had been around a long time and seen a considerable amount of work. Horizontal rain, cold winds – a fitting description of Millom, we always seemed chilled to the bone. I recall my pal, Jimmy McCusigs teeth chattering uncontrollably while having his soup. Jimmy was accustomed to cold winters on the North Shore of Lake Superior (Fort William, now Thunder Bay) in Ontario.

The problem for us Canadian boys was not the cold, but the damp which came with it. We had known 20-30-40 degrees below zero in dry cold, but this was horrible! In December it was so bad that we used to wear our inner flying suits to bed, with our greatcoats and anything else we could fine, thrown on top of our blankets and we were still cold! Each billet was allocated just enough coal for a bit of heat at bedtime, but! We had a good pal by the name of Maurice Anthoni (a Frenchman from Paris) who was most resourceful in acquiring extra coal for us. The Canadian boys reciprocated by donating items which came in our food parcels from home. 'Tony' as he was know, would collect these and, with the blessings of the Air Ministry, send them to his mother in Paris.

Our disappointment at the weather was surpassed only by our disappointment in the food. Brussel sprouts, Welsh rarebit, potatoes in a variety of forms, sawdust sausages and black bread. Sometimes on Sunday morning, a rubberised egg floating in grease. The highlights of station life were the occasional dances, at which we would consume copious amounts of Nutbrown Ale! After Millom, I was posted to Squires Gate, Lancs, for General Reconnaissance and a pre-O.T.U. course as a Navigator / Wireless Operator. This was followed by a posting to 123 O.T.U. East Fortune, near Edinburgh for Beaufighters. I was due to join 404 Squadron, which was a coastal command strike wing, (Beaufighters and Mosquitos) but it was at this point that the war came to an end. Following a short interval at Holding Units in Bircham Newton, Norfolk and Eastmoor, I joined 437 Squadron R.C.A.F. Transport Unit in Odiham, Herts. I flew in Norwest – Europe until the spring of 1946. Following that we flew our Dakatas back to Canada where I was "de-mobbed" as they say, at the rank of F/Officer. I was 22 years of age at this point and became a student until 1950. I studied for, and had, a career in education – 19 years in Secondary Schools, and 18 years as an Education Officer with the Ontario Ministry of Education, I am of course, now retired!

Leo Meloche 1996

MR R. MARSDEN – 1941 – 1943

I first came to RAF Millom as a Sgt WOP/AG (Grade 2) in April 1941. I remained on the staff at Millom in a training capacity until 1943. I actually contracted jaundice whilst at the unit and was admitted to the Military Hospital at Conishead Priory in Ulverston for a time.

Upon my discharge from hospital I was married on the 5th of June 1943 and a posting to 26 O.T.U. came very shortly afterwards. At the O.T.U. I was crewed up on Wellingtons, before moving on to 1651 Heavy Bomber Conversion Unit at Waterbeach, to begin training on the huge Sterling Bomber. My operational posting was to 'The Gold Coast Squadron' No.218 at Downham Market.

I completed my tour of operations with the squadron in July 1944, having survived 'The Battle of the Ruhr' and having been involved in the spoof attack on 'D' Day. I was commissioned in late 1943, and became an instructor at 1651 and 1653 conversion units during late 1944.

In 1945 I was re-crewed for a second operational tour (this time on Lancasters, 635 Squadron) on Far East duties; however, the dropping of the Atomic bombs brought an end to my flying career in July 1945. My RAF career ended in the Admin area as an Officer Commanding a recruit wing in Wiltshire in 1947, only a few miles from where I started my Wireless Operator Training at Yatesbury in 1940.

And so to my confession! It was an overcast August day

at RAF Millom. I was detailed Signal Officers duties, on the lookout for incoming aircraft. I carried a flare pistol, and if the runways were clear for landing I would flash the approaching aircraft a green flare. If the runways were obstructed, or some other event would make landing dangerous, I would fire up a red flare and the pilot would hold off landing until I gave him the necessary green. At around noon, and whilst happily dreaming my time away, I was suddenly aware of the sound of aero-engines approaching the station from out at sea. Out of the mist, and extremely low, came what I took to be a Blenheim seeking our runways. Knowing that all was clear, I fired up a green flare straight away for the fast closing aircraft. As I did so, the pilot banked slightly and I was horrified to see the black crosses on the underside of his wing! I had just given permission to land, to a Junkers 88!!

In a split second, all hell broke loose and I dived under the nearest vehicle for cover as the Junkers made a west/east pass with all machine guns and cannons blazing. The attack was so swift and so well executed that none of our defences managed to fire a shot and the Germans departed as swiftly as they had arrived. When I emerged from my cover I realised that I had, in fact, taken shelter under a fuel bowser! By an absolute miracle, no real damage was caused to the station and not one member of personnel were injured during the attack. I was frequently ribbed about my aircraft recognition skills thereafter! So far as I am aware, this is the one and only occasion that the Germans raided the station, we all felt that it had simply been an opportunist attack.

Ron Marsden 1994

ROBERT S. NIELSEN

We arrived at Millom at 8am on the 21st of March 1942

after an all night train journey from London. In spite of the shunting on and off the main tracks I slept very well everybody seemed pretty relaxed as we rode out from the town of Millom in the usual RAF tenders. The airfield was surrounded by barrage balloons, anti-aircraft guns and mountains... I hope we can keep clear of all three of them!

This is an advanced flying unit but we will be flying in Avro Ansons and that doesn't sound too advanced to me. They say we will work hard here and we won't get much time to go into town but if we do then a pub called the peel is the place to go. About two-thirds of our course are posted here plus some Canadians and Englishman.

Dear family,

I am writing to let you know that I have been posted. This is surprising considered we had only been in the personnel reception area for 4 weeks. Some of the lads have been there for 9 or 10 weeks and still don't look like getting out of the place.

We are now in our new home on the Northwest coast of England it is an AFU and is really a refresher course for most of us. I know that there will be many things I will be glad to have explained to me once more.

We are right on the coast here, the airfield is flanked by the sea on one side and mountains on the other. The mountains are all the high for England ranging from 1000 feet to over 3000 ft in elevation. The weather around here is inconsistent to say the least so we will get plenty of poor weather flying experience which will be helpful for later on.

The barracks are lousy cold and damp and I don't think the floor has been swept for 3 months at least. I believe the Australian course ahead of us as a protest against living conditions refused to make their beds and no power of persuasion would make them do otherwise.

We have to get up at 6:30am. Breakfast is from 6:30 till 7:30 and parade at 8.00. The food here could be better but it could be worse today we had sausages that were camouflaged I hazarded a guess that it was Yorkshire pudding for the one who served as dinner said 'how dare you insult the Yorkshire pudding'.

News from Australia is more cheerful today it seems that our aircraft are still bombing the Invasion fleet and MacArthur seems to be achieving results in the matter of organisation. I believe we will win the battle for Australia and the Pacific as I believe we will win the battle for Europe.

I just hope I will be taking part in the Pacific war one of these days.

Robert S. Nielsen 1998

MR E. NYE – 1942

After completing my early Navigator Training in Canada, I was posted in to RAF Millom in august 1942. Like my fellow course members, I had been fully trained in this respect, but was required to undergo a 21 day course at an Advanced Flying Unit to further polish my newly acquired skills. A maximum of 5 flights and 15 hours daylight flying, however, did little to achieve the aim of 'acclimatising' crew, trained in un-blacked-out Canada, to the vastly different conditions which prevailed in Wartime Europe. We had been given our 'O' Observers badges in Canada, but were not given our Sergeants Stripes until we were actually en route by ship for the UK.

I remember Millom as being very wet and hazy, with Black Combe appearing menacingly out of the gloom on take-off. Because of the weather, we seemed to be able to spend quite a lot of time in the public houses of Haverigg. This may well have something to do with the overall haziness associated with my time at the unit, and I do remember watching a snooker game upon my return from the village, where 3 cue balls rolled down the table to pot 3 blacks, all in perfect formation!

Not long after my arrival at the station, we were prevented from flying one day, by very overcast weather. It was afternoon, I believe when we heard the sound of an aircraft circling out at sea. Having been on anti-aircraft gunner in the outer London defences, on the flight path of the German attack on Coventry, I boastfully identified the hostile from the sound of its twin jumbo engines. The Senior Warrant Officer was stood within earshot of my remark and upbraided me for spreading alarm and despondency and identified the aircraft, as it emerged from the cloud base, as a Blenheim. The 'Blenheim' then proceeded to shoot up the field with cannon fire!, it was, of course, a Junkers 88! Do you know? I never received an apology from anyone! After Millom, off we all went to O.T.U. and crewing up for operations. My 'O' (Observer) badge was exchanged for the new 'N' (Navigator) badge and the 'O' sewn on to the battle dress which had just been introduced for flying. This badge remained in position until 5 years, 2 operational tours, 2 'V' Days and 1 De-mob later, when I removed it so as to wear the battle dress blouse for rough work in the garden and woodland. I then found underneath it a ha'penny piece, bearing the year of my birth, which my mother must have placed there when sewing it on, presumably as a good luck charm. It worked!!

Ernie Nye 1993

MR M.H. PRYCE, 1943 –1944

I was stationed at the unit whilst completing my Navigator Training, from December 14th 1943 until February the 8th 1944. We were granted a week's leave over the Christmas period and as a result, I don't think our course started until the New Year. I remember Millom as a cold, wet, foggy place, with our billet completely surrounded by water, and not enough fuel to heat the place properly.

My brief diary notes mention many people complaining about the food, and in my own case, about coming in from a night flying exercise to find that breakfast was three pieces of beetroot with melted cheese on top! By a stroke of luck, my cousin's husband, Avonwy Davis, was the newly appointed librarian in the town of Millom and I was able to visit them at their house on occasion.

I was posted from RAF Millom to No.22 O.T.U. at Wellesbourne Mountford. After crewing up and further training there, we went to No.1666 H.C.U. at Wombleton in Yorkshire and ended up on 432 Squadron, 6 Group, at Eastmoor, just north of the city of York. I was posted back to Canada to be an Navigation instructor and received my discharge in May 1945.

Morgan Pryce 1998

MR M. PITCHERS, 1944 – 1945

I was posted to RAF Millom after completing a Staff Pilot Training course at RAF Cark. At the back of the station lay the Lake District mountains, and at the front of it, the Irish Sea. Very close to the airfield stood the imposing fell of Black Combe. We were all very conscious of this menace and circuits were always flown away from it. As far as I can remember, none of us every hit it, other mountains yes, but never Black Combe.

Flying at the unit was often disrupted because of the rapidly changing weather, due, I expect, to the combination of sea and mountains. For the trainees who came to Millom, courses consisted of a mixture of ground instruction and practical flying. The flying part entailed navigational exercises with occasional sorties over the bombing range for the Bomb Aimers. Other special flights enabled the student navigators to practice using the Astro Sextant. A crew was made up of a Staff Pilot and a Staff Wireless Operator, the Navigator, a second wireless Operator, and Bomb Aimer being the students. The navigational exercises lasted about 3 to 3 1/2 hours and were usually routed around the Irish Sea. In ideal conditions, four of these exercises could be flown each day, two in daylight, and two at night. The staff aircrew flew shifts, a month of day flying and then a month of nights. The Ansons thus often clocked over 12 hours flying in a day. No wonder the turn-over of aircraft was so rapid. However, Millom being where it is, the weather often interfered with the programme, flying was cancelled all too frequently and it was not unusual to receive a recall or a diversion (by W/T) part of the way round the cross country because the weather was closing in rapidly. Diversions were often welcomed, particularly if it was early in the evening while the bar was still open at our destination. I can recall clearly such a diversion, to No.1 O.A.F.U. at Wigtown. We arrived at the height of a party in the Sergeants Mess. First of all we had to "sing for our supper", we did Nellie Dean, badly. Later I can remember that we played "cardinal Puff", but recall nothing much after that, it was a good do!!

We returned to base the next day, probably with fat heads. I can even tell you the date! It was the 25th – 26th of November 1944. I shall try and re-create a typical night exercise for you from memory. A briefing would be held in the early evening for the complete crews in the briefing room, which had been modelled as an operational one A raised platform was backed by a large air-chart of the Irish Sea and the surrounding country. On the chart a coloured string marked the proposed cross country route. A board listed the crews and the numbers of their allotted aircraft. The Briefing Officer talked through the exercise listing likely problems and special tasks such as bombing runs on an infra-red target. The target was an Infra-red beacon sited out in the wilds of Scotland, being Infra-red, the beacon was invisible to the naked eye. There were no landmarks for miles, so the bombing run relied wholly on Dead Reckoning Navigation. A camera fitted into the aircraft would be loaded with Infra-red sensitive film so that when the pupil Bomb Aimer pressed the bomb release button, the camera shutter was opened and recorded a trace from the I/R beacon (in theory). To my knowledge, no one ever found this target and we came to the conclusion that there was nothing there! There was another bombing target that we were supposed to attack, this was a very dimly illuminated triangle, sited, once again, out in the wilds. Small flash bombs were loaded for use on this one. I don't think that any of my crews ever found this target either.

There was a story circulating of one crew who spotted a dim light close to the target area. A bombing run was made, and concluded with "Bombs Away", the bomb accurately went through a house roof and blew an old lady out of bed. If this story is true, it is possibly the only direct hit ever made on a target by a No.2 A.F.U. pupil!!

Back to our pre flight briefing. The briefing continued with the Met Officer giving his best guess as to what weather we might run into enroute, together with wind direction, wind strength and any likely changes. The "colours of the day" would be given so that if challenged we could reply by firing a Flare pistol using the appropriate coloured pyrotechnic. The navigators were then left to mark the tracks on to their charts and work the courses to fly using Dead Reckoning. D/R Navigation is hardly ever used nowadays; even light aircraft can carry a portable satellite navigation gizmo which is far more accurate! Meanwhile, the aircraft would have been serviced and test flown by many spare pilots who were not on day exercise. All this would take an hour or so, and there was time to have a light meal before take-off, around 22:00 hours or earlier in winter. A typical route could be: From Millom to the beacon on the Island of Islay, then to Chicken Rock Lighthouse, south of the Isle of Man, returning then to Millom, a distance of about 290 nautical miles.

After landing, crews went through a de-briefing session in which their performance was assessed and anything of note mentioned. A quick cup of tea or coffee was followed by a second briefing and another cross country training flight over a different route. Landing was often made with the dawn just breaking. I recall, early one morning, flying back towards Millom from the Isle of Man at around 6,000 feet, "low flying" over the top of a cloud sheet, the sun came up as we watched and it was truly beautiful. The trailing W/T aerial had been dragging through the cloud, and when the W/Op wound it in, it was sheathed in ice. At least once a month there was a special bombing session put on for the Bomb Aimers. Our bombing ranges were at Askam and in the Duddon Estuary, quite close to Millom. In summer these exercises were pleasant, being able to fly in shirt sleeves in the warm greenhouse cockpit of the Anson. With each sortie taking about 1 ¼ hours we usually managed 3 in a day with breaks for a N.A.F.F.I. tea and wash between flights, all very civilised. Low flying was part of the O.A.F.U. course and I admit that I enjoyed the opportunity to indulge in "official" low flying as against the "other" sort. We had two specific low level routes that I can remember, one was south through Shropshire, where I am afraid we "put the wind up" a lot of farm animals. The other route was in Northern Ireland, somewhere not far from Loch Neigh. This area was very sparsely populated and seemed to be all marsh and moorland. There was one occasion when we must have been below 100 feet and coming over the top of a rise the noise of our engines scared a flock of birds and they rose in a great cloud in front of the aircraft. There were such a lot of them that it seemed there was more daylight below then than above so we flew even lower and luckily hit none.

I was reminded of a bird-strike that happened to another student while I was under pilot training in Canada flying Airspeed Oxfords. He brought his rather battered plane back after having been struck by a very large owl. The bird had first hit the top of the cockpit, breaking the frames and Perspex and from there had embedded itself right inside the tail fin. It was fortunate that it had not impacted on the centre of the windscreen. The only bird strike that I personally experienced was in a big four engine Stirling Bomber whilst coming in to land. Something rook sized hit the starboard inner engine cowling and dented it. What surprised me was the noise, it sounded like a gun shot. With so many Ansons milling around the Irish Sea at night we took the precaution of always flying with the aircraft navigation lights on. By that time in the war (1944), there was little likelihood of meeting hostile aircraft.

One event which really caught my attention happened when we were flying at night, just under the cloudbase at around 5000ft. Suddenly another aircraft, with lights on, emerged from the cloud right in front of me going in the opposite direction. He passed, about 30ft above us, so close that I could actually hear him, and that is surprising in itself! The whole event took place so quickly that I had no chance of taking any avoiding action. It's 50 years since that night and I can still recall the shock.

Towards the end of my stay at Millom I volunteered for Mountain Rescue duties. It's not that I was a keen hill walker, it just seemed a worthwhile thing at the time. I was only called out once with the team, to go to the aid of an Anson crew from Wigtown who had flown into the far flank of Black Combe, just above Bootle village. I have no idea how they came to be there, well below the fell summits probably a navigational error. The Anson had struck the ground at a slight angle and had slid along shedding bits everywhere. Two of the crew had fallen through the floor as it was torn out, one unfortunately was dead and the other badly injured. The pilot was trapped by the legs and had to be cut free while the W/Op walked away from it virtually unharmed. No helicopters then, we had to carry the injured down to the Humber Ambulance on stretchers. All of the injured aircrew made full recoveries in due course. There was however, a very tragic sequel to this rescue. In the Sick Bay, as the haversacks were being unpacked, someone picked up the Verey Signal Pistol, pointed it at one of the WAAF orderlies, who was laughing at the time, and not knowing that the pistol was still loaded, he pulled the trigger. The result was a terrible death for the poor young girl which cost a pall over the unit for some time afterwards.

On the 8th of September 1944 myself and my crew set off on a day exercise in rough weather. First of all the navigator became airsick and them, to cap it all, we were struck by lightning! There was a flash and an enormous bang. It burnt off the tailing aerial and produced a very strong smell from our W/T set. In addition to this the fabric covering of the fuselage along the aircraft spine was split for about 6 feet. Happily no one was hurt and there was no other damage. I curtailed the exercise and returned to base. On a later occasion I was in a Stirling when that was also struck by lightning, in daylight.

Apart from giving us a bad fright it did no damage at all. Clearly, not all lightning strikes on aircraft have serious consequences. I did experience an engine failure once, as we were on the last leg of a flight returning to base. The port engine started to run very roughly and I could see that we were leaving a slight smoke trail behind us. Closing the throttle reduced the vibration and I left it idling. The Ansons prop's were fixed pitch and could not be feathered. With the slight contribution from the sick engine I found that I could just maintain height and we eventually landed safely. I think that the story would have been different if the engine had stopped completely. Later I found that the trouble had been caused by a broken exhaust valve stem. This may have been a weakness in the Cheetah radial engines because I had exactly the same thing happen to me whilst climbing out of RAF Hendon in an Oxford. The Oxford, fortunately, had a rather better single engine performance than the Anson!

By 1945 the requirement for aircrew began to taper off and I was posted to No.9 O.A.F.U. at Llandwrog in North Wales. I must say that the weather there was even worse than at Millom. I found myself in a Nissen Hut about 100 yards from the sea. In the snow and gales we could actually see the Nissen Hut bending under the pressure of the wind. There was a two mile cycle ride if you wanted to take a bath, not many of us wanted one that badly! My last flight from RAF Llandwrog was the most eventful. It had started as a night cross country in bright moonlight. We had passed the last turning point at Squires Gate beacon (Blackpool Airport) when we received a recall to base. Squires Gate to Llandwrog is about 35 minutes at an Anson's cruising speed and long before we neared base I could see a cloud sheet covering the whole of the Menai Strait area. Knowing that area, it seemed reasonably safe to have a look under the cloud and it proved to have a base of about 400 feet. I decided to follow the Menai Straits as the water could be seen quite clearly. I switched on the landing light and turned it downwards so that I could better judge my height. By the time we got to Llandwrog the cloud had come down to about 200 feet and it was quite an exciting circuit trying to remember the position of the water tower, with at least four other pilots trying to land at the same time. By the time that we were back in the briefing room the cloud was on the deck and any late arrivals were diverted to Mona. The airfield at Mona on Anglesey is higher than Llandwrog by 230 feet and this difference could possibly have been the factor that killed a friend that night. He was one of the last to return and flew into the ground well short of the runway at Mona. I never heard the results of any enquiry, but, if he had forgotten to reset his altimeter, his approach would have been too low with the inevitable result. As flying tapered off at the unit following V.E. Day, I was posted to Transport Command where I served until my de-mob.

Mike Pitchers 1998

MR F.W. RAMSAY – 1942

At the beginning of 1942, Training Command were unable to get what were termed as "Screened Aircrew". This meant aircrew who had completed a tour of operations and were due to be rested. These crews were being kept at Operational Training Units etc which came under Bomber Command, so Training Command decided to train their own Staff Crews. In June 1942 I was one of 21 Wireless Operators who were posted in to RAF Millom. Being a Fleetwood lad this was a good posting for me as I was able to go home on my days off. Once we had passed our Air Operating Course at Millom we did a month's Gunnery Training at RAF Walney. I enjoyed this a great deal. We trained on the Boulton Paul Defiant Aircraft and after passing out with "Wings and Stripes" at the end of

July 1942 I returned to RAF Millom to join the stations staff.

I was married whilst serving at Millom on the 19th December 1942. With my aircrew leave and days off I spent a happy Christmas at home, but was feeling a bit fed up as I caught the last train back to Millom. I was even more fed up when I was told that I had been posted to RAF Wigtown with effect from the next morning! I was only at Wigtown two months when they opened a new station to train Staff Pilots at RAF Cark. I can honestly say that I enjoyed every minute of my stay at Cark. I was posted there as a Sgt and left as a Warrant Officer for an Operational Training Unit. From O.T.U. I was eventually crewed up and we were posted to RAF Luffenham for training on the four engine heavy Lancaster Bombers. As we finished our course, VE Day was declared, Bomber Command found themselves redundant and that was the last of my flying. I was posted to RAF Kirkham (now Kirkham Prison) for an equipment assistants course which I completed before being de-mobbed in March 1946.

Fred Ramsey 1992

MR C RICHARDSON – CARK 1944

I was only stationed at Cark from the 30th of July 1944 until the 29th of August. On the 4th of August 1944 I took off as Pilot with F/Sgt Nicholls, an Australian, to carry out a practice bombing of the target in Morecambe Bay. Upon reaching the target F/Sgt Nicholls got into the nose where the bombsight was located and I opened the bomb doors and watched the 'tell tales' emerge indicating that the bomb doors were open. We made our first run. Nicholls called out "bombs gone" and then, "sorry skipper I've not seen that one". We made another run with the same result.

I now suspected there was something wrong, aborted the

exercise, pulled the aircraft into a steep turn and headed back to base, landing 'on tiptoe'. On landing I got hold of an armament fitter and told him the tale. He promptly got under the aircraft and pulled open the doors. Much to my surprise nothing fell out and there were no 'hang ups'. Where were the missing bombs?

Unknown to me the chain drive which opened the bomb doors was broken but there was enough left on the sprocket to work the 'tell tales' without opening the doors. A few minutes later I was called to Flying Control to be told that two bombs had fallen on Carnforth! Fortunately they had fallen between two houses without doing any damage. It appears that when I made the steep turn centrifugal force had taken over and the bombs had sprung together again after the bombs had gone.

It cost me five shillings in the Red Cross box to forget the incident. I thought this was a bit unfair at the time since it was hardly my fault but I paid up without a murmur just to make a quick exit from Flying Control and forget the whole thing. There were never any repercussions for which I was grateful.

We then climbed into another Anson and completed the exercise. So it's very strange that I have come back to live so close to the scene of my escapade since I came from the North East of England originally and spent all my working life in Bolton, Lancashire.

You can be sure I have made no enquiries since coming to live in the Carnforth area!

Mr C Richardson - 2011

MR K. RICHARDSON, 1942 – 1945

I was a Fitter/Armourer at RAF Millom, from 1942 until the station was shut down. I have many fond memories of the unit and remember it as a very friendly and hard working station. We had some great entertainment nights and the odd visit from the E.N.S.A. troupes. During one of the latter I remember we were entertained by a singer called Vera Lennox who received wild applause and a standing ovation. My mate said to me, "I can't decide whether they are applauding her singing or the size of her chest!

I had always wanted to work an aircraft and so I had my dream job, the work however, was not without its dangers. Two of my fellow fitters were killed by propellers and we were such a close knit bunch, it was like losing a family member when it happened. The first casualty was an engine fitter who was starting the engine of an Anson with its crank handle. When the engine fired, he pulled out the handle and walked forward into the propeller. The second such horror happened to an armourer in a similar way.

On night flights, all Ansons carried two 4" parachute flares on the bomb carrier under the starboard wing. The armourer had just completed a final check on these and again, walked forwards instead of backwards with the same terrible result. It may sound a stupid mistake to make but a fast revolving propeller is nigh invisible and it was a reminder to us all that a lapse of concentration could be fatal. As a fitter / Armourer, it was my job to check and service the, bomb release gear, the bomb sight, the bomb racks, and of course to load the racks with 11½ lb practice bombs. On occasion it was also my job to remove bombs which were "hung up" (failed to release). I suppose I must have loaded up many hundreds of bombs without incident, until January the 3rd 1943, that was the day I dropped a clanger, or rather, a bomb! It was a very cold day, and I was checking the aircraft which had returned from bombing practice on the ranges. I cursed my luck when I found one with a bomb hung up on its port bomb rack. As I tried to put a safety pin back in the nose of the bomb to disarm it, l was struggling because my fingers were so cold as to have no feeling in them at all. I had to move the bomb slightly in order to insert the pin and as I did this, the bomb dropped and exploded, stunning me and covering me in smoke mixture. It took me a few seconds to realise that I had been quite badly hurt. I had two large gashes in my left calf and one near my right eye. Following the explosion, help came quickly. The ambulance and crash tender rolled up and I was in the station sick bay in less than 5 minutes where two Medical Officers stopped the bleeding stitched me up and made me comfortable – they were great. I spent the next 12 weeks in a military hospital in Ulverston and was discharged fit and well once more! When I returned to Millom and Armament Officer said "you are a lucky young man to be here at all"! "do you want your old job back"? Of course I did, and there were more hang ups to deal with, but, happily, all successfully.

The station always tried to field a team for any local sports which were taking place and we were invited to enter a tug of war team in the Cumberland Games. We trained long and hard with the intention of showing the local yokels how it should be done. We went up to Whitehaven on the great day and were completely humiliated by a team of Miners who were all built like superman. We may as well have been pulling against the Rock of Gibraltar for all the impression we made!

During my time at Millom I took part in a "Backers up" course. These courses were one week long and were held on camp with the idea of training ground staff to back up the RAF Regiment in case of an attack on the station. We were taught tactics and strategy, did exercises in defence, used rifle and sten gun on the range, and lastly, fired a Lewis gun at a target which moved around on rails in the sand dunes before throwing a live hand grenade into a pit and taking cover behind a protective parapet. Our instructor was a tough old Sergeant from the Border Regiment who stood no nonsense. On these exercises we each had to take a turn at being in command of the squad. One young lad took his turn and his first order was "would you hurry up please." The Sergeant went purple and hissed at him, "please? Please"? Then bawled, "You don't say bloody please lad! yer not leading a bloody group of bloody schoolgirls across a bloody road"! Needless to say, the rest of us found the incident highly amusing!

On many occasions we would play host to a variety of aircraft which had been forced to divert to our runways, usually due to the weather. Whilst on duty one evening I watched as a diverted Vickers Warwick Bomber came in to land on our east/west runway. The aircraft touched down almost halfway down the runway but to our surprise, no touch and go and circuit was attempted by the pilot. There was a screech as the brakes were slammed full on and we all held our breath as the bomber headed for the sand dunes on the airfield boundary. At the very last moment the pilot executed a severe turn off the runway, bending the undercarriage legs well out of line and bringing the Warwick to an untidy but safe stop. As we approached the aircraft, out stepped its pilot, a most attractive female member of the A.T.A. in her early thirties. She strode across to us, all the while muttering oaths and when we asked if she was OK she replied woefully, "yes thanks, but what a bloody awful landing"!

My memories include the mountain rescue team also. It was usual for an Armourer to go with the team in case there were any bombs, flares etc in the wreckage. I went on two occasions. The first time was into the mountains near Wastwater, searching for an aircraft reported crashed by a shepherd. We found nothing. The second was to the area between Foxfield and Broughton-in-Furness. There was a truck with an Engineer Officer and a couple of Fitters, plus the Ambulance with two Medical Orderlies sat in the front, and I sat on a bench in the back. We went up a country lane, turned on to a farm track in order to reach the crash site. The crashed aircraft was a Miles Magister and it was smashed to pieces. The pilot had been pulled out of the wreck by a couple of farmers, he was dead. He was a young Royal Navy pilot, and to me, he only looked to be in his early teens! His body was carried to the ambulance on a stretcher and covered carefully with a blanket. Once again I had to take my seat in the back with him as we made the journey to deliver his body to 10 AGS on Walney Island at Barrow-in-Furness. It was not a pleasant ride for me.

So, good times and bad! The good times all warmly remembered! My last anecdote is completely true, no matter how far fetched it might seem today. The young pilots at Millom were prone to a bit of unofficial "low flying" when they could get away with it, and I do mean low! I remember a sheepish looking pilot returning with a bent propeller tip and saying to me "I suppose I must have been flying a bit low"; I suppose he must have been eh?

Ken Richardson 1993

MR J. RUSSELL – 1941

I trained at RAF Millom as an Air Observer from the 29th of November 1941 until the 13th of September 1941. My memories of Millom are few. I recall our station C/O was GRP/CPT Wray and that we had our end of course "bash" at the Kings Arms at Broughton-in-Furness on the 10th of September, three days before our course officially ended. We flew from Millom in Botha's and Ansons. The Botha's were being phased out and were used mainly for Air Gunnery Training; the Ansons were used for the Navigational exercises.

My abiding memory of the station was arriving back over the airfield in an Anson after a cross country, the staff pilot, a F/Officer, no doubt bored with flying Ansons "round the houses", looped the loop without any warning to his crew whatsoever! Every item of gear which was not stowed away floated around the aircraft and we were surrounded by maps, instruments and all manner of items as we reached the apex of our loop. I have no idea what action was taken against the pilot but the very next day, a notice appeared in our crew room which said that aircraft over a certain weight should not be flown acrobatically! At the end of my course I was posted to No.40 O.T.U. at RAF Andover where I trained on Blenheims. I began operational flying on Bostons with 107 Squadron at Great Massingham, Norfolk, flying daylight operations with fighter escorts. In November 1942, 25 of us from the three Boston Squadrons in 2 groups were loaned to the U.S. Army Air Force, Troop Carrying Command, as they had no available navigators! We flew C.47 Dakota's to North Africa carrying U.S. Troops following the invasion (operation torch).

On returning to the UK I was commissioned and eventually was posted to a newly formed "special duties" Squadron in North Africa, flying one of its two Ventura Aircraft, the rest being Halifax Bombers. I finished the war as an instructor on Baltimores at an O.T.U. in Egypt. De-mobbed in 1947, I rejoined the RAF in 1951 and served in Bomber Command on various aircraft out in the Middle East before finding myself back on MK19 Anson's at RAF Andover on a communications Squadron.

I then spent four more years as a photographic

interpreter before retiring in 1969 as a Flt/Lt.

John Russell 1996

MRS A. RENTON, 1941 – 1942

Author's Note:

Almost all the RCAF material contained in this book was provided by Audrey. I first made contact with her in 1997 and she eventually attended one of our reunions with her husband Lawrence. In the past few years, Audrey has worked timelessly to contact, and gather stories from those who served at RAF Millom during the war years and to preserve their recollections for future generations.

Audrey was born and educated in England and served in the WAAF from 1949 until 1945. She married F/Officer Lawrence Renton, a Bomb/Aimer in the R.C.A.F. in 1944 and returned with him to Canada as a war bride at the end of the war. Audrey is the author of several historical stories for which she has twice won awards and at the time of writing is the historian for St Johns Anglican Church, Kars, the Public Relations Officer for her local Womens Institute and Volunteer Researcher/Writer for Rideau Township Archives. Active in community affairs since arriving in Canada, Audrey was awarded the commemorative medal for the 125th anniversary of the Confederation of Canada by the Governor General of Canada in 1993.

I served at RAF Millom as Corporal Audrey Wood, Physical Training Instructor, from 1941 to 1942. It is strange to think of RAF Millom as a Prison now, with prisoners warm behind double glazing, with central heating and colour TV's, we spent most of our time frozen!! I recall that as 1941 drew to a close, Nissen Huts began popping up as if by magic all over the station. This was to cope with the rapidly increasing numbers of

206

personnel but as a consequence, the WAAF were allocated one of these buildings.

It was about then that I was promoted to Cpl and was suckered into being Cpl in charge of the hut. I lived just inside the door in the left hand corner. At first glance the hut looked like a section of giant culvert pipe cut lengthwise down the middle. The floor was a slab of very rough concrete, no covering or mats whatever, not even painted. The ablutions were a couple of hundred yards away, we quickly solved the night time ablution problem that cold winter with empty 5lb jam tins pinched by the night waitresses from the Officers Mess!

In 1941 each member of the WAAF at Millom were sent a little blue cotton bag from the U.S.A. The bag was 11" x 8" and on it was a label which said "Ladies Garment Workers Union." Inside were – one toothbrush, one tube of toothpaste, one packet of needles and pins, one comb, one face cloth, one bar of scented soap and six plain white lavender bags or so we thought. We couldn't understand why in the world they would send lavender bags to England. My pal, Minnie McCaffery opened hers and much to our surprise they were tea bags which had taken on the smell of the lavender soap! None of us had ever seen tea bags before and we were quite intrigued, but of course we could not use them because of the taste of soap and lavender. There was a note in each bag from the American lady who sent them and I exchanged letters with her in due course.

One warm spring morning in 1942, I was awakened by someone crying softly a few beds down from me. It was very unusual for anybody to wake through the night as we worked such long hours plus all the extra duties, once we hit the sack we flaked out completely until the wakey-wakey call came over the tannoy at 6am. Creeping out of my bed, I felt my way in the darkness down to where the weeping was coming from and then gently bent over the pretty little fair haired girl. Unfortunately I do not remember her first name as we always went by our surname in those days, but I do remember it was A.C.W. Mills. For some reason or other, over the many years I have thought about this incident and actually spoken of it to my family often. It was a sad story and looking back, the picture I see now is that of a nineteen year old trying to comfort and understand the pain and loneliness of another young girl uprooted and possibly confused in an unfamiliar and strange setting. Sitting on her bed with my arm around her, she told me why she was crying. Before the outbreak of war, she had been a young married homemaker on one of the Channel Islands. When they were occupied by the Germans she was forced to leave very quickly and leave all her belongings behind. I'm not certain as unfortunately time dulls the memory, but I think her husband was serving in the British Army. She whispered to me "it's not the first time I have cried, but usually nobody hears me. It always seems worse at night and I keep thinking about our little house. What's happened to it, what state it's in, who is living in it now and will things ever be the same again"? It was difficult for me to be reassuring in any way, shape or form, because we were in a total state of war and it seemed nonsensical in 1942 to make any plans for more than a couple of days hence. We talked in whispers for some time and then I crawled back to my bunk to lay there and ponder her predicament before falling asleep. Hopefully things did turn out well for the young Channel Islanders, but that was part of airforce life, we lost touch one with the other and seldom saw or heard the outcome of anything.

Audrey Renton 1997

MR E.G. THALE – 1944

I trained at RAF Millom in early 1944 when the station was designated No,.2 O.A.F.U. my memories of Millom are few as most of our flying was done at night. The exercises consisted of dashing about over the Irish Sea, trying to locate an infra-red beacon on Chicken Rock (off the tip of the Isle of Man), then back to Cark in Cartmel to drop our load of 11lb flash bombs before landing back at Millom. Most of us were earmarked for Bomber Command upon completion of our course and I was posted to 625 Squadron at RAF Kelstern in Lincolnshire. It was here that I met the man who had been RAF Millom's first Station Commander, Group Captain A.Wray when he took over command of our squadron.

Author's Note:

Eric has provided us with a very vivid pen portrait of Arthur Wray which appears later in this part of my book. It is a set of very clear memories of a remarkable man who's leadership skills and compassion for this men earned him the fond nick name "Father Wray".

I completed my Operational Flying safely and rose to the rank of Warrant Officer on the 13th of March 1946 before my discharge. My flying then became commercial and for pleasure, I used to drop in on Millom's runways in a little Auster after the place became a Prison, great fun!!

Author's Note:

What follows are Eric's reflections during a visit to his old station at Kelstern in the early 1990's. Of the many operational flights he made with 625 Squadron aboard their Lancaster Bombers, this one which raided Dresden remains the most discussed by historians today. This is how the raid is remembered by someone who actually took part in it, you will read an account written with a clarity that will take you to the target and back should you let it.

DRESDEN, I WAS THERE
BY ERIC THALE

A gentle breeze barely disturbing the leaves on a nearby tree – complete silence broken only by the distant sound of a skylark high overhead singing its heart out.

They say "you should never go back". Things look smaller - places look different- it will be a total disappointment.

Why am I here?
Pondering on this question I look upwards in search of the elusive skylark when I catch a glimpse of something out of the corner of my eye. Before I can turn my head that "something" materialises as a Tornado aircraft about to curve upwards at an unbelievable angle, afterburners literally hurling it skywards. Micro seconds later the silence that had reigned is shattered by the roar of two engines pushing the aircraft to 30,000 ft. or more in less than a minute. Where is the skylark now I wonder?

The explosion of sound answers the question "why am I here?" Nearly fifty years ago the spot where I'm standing was the Station Headquarters of Royal Air Force Kelstern, an airfield carved out of agricultural land high up on the Lincolnshire wolds and part of the country's war machine. The airfield became the home of 625 Squadron, one of many Squadrons of Bomber Command. The Squadron flew Lancaster aircraft crewed by seven young and sometimes very young men. Men? - the government of the day graciously allowed us to fight for our country but considered us too young to vote for it. How strange?

The Tornado's earth shattering roar is now no more than a distant rumble as my thoughts go back to another roar, not as noisy as the recent one but noisy enough.

Twenty-two Lancasters are wending their way around the perimeter track, engines at idle power with perhaps an occasional more throaty roar as the odd engine is opened up to increase the air flow through the radiators to keep the glycol temperature down. The date and time stand out remarkably clear after all this time. February 13th 1945. The day began with the usual operational Squadron routine. Crews walking or cycling from their dispersed Nissen hut sites to the Mess for breakfast then out to their aircraft to check their equipment, or practise parachute and dinghy drills. The navigators, bomb aimers, wireless operators and flight engineers using their GEE or H2S trainers while the less energetic sat in the Mess reading the papers, writing letters home or reading intelligence reports at the intelligence officer's hut.

The weather was cloudy with continuous rain and moderate visibility, the ever optimistic "Met" man suggesting an improvement to fair conditions after lunch.

By mid-morning the ground crews had a rumour going that "Ops" was on later. They always knew long before the crews were briefed. It was fairly obvious that when orders went out to them to tank up the aircraft to a certain capacity their fertile minds were way ahead of the ball game.

Today was no exception; all aircraft were being fuelled to capacity - 2154 gallons. A long trip to somewhere lay ahead. The fuel figure given to the ground crews had been part of a signal called Form "B". This was the official order emanating from Bomber Command Headquarters detailing the forthcoming operation. This particular Form "B" was serial Numbering Task 1762.

About 11.00 Hrs. the crews were officially alerted to the fact that ''Ops" was on and the Battle Order now pinned to the notice board was scanned with interest. The navigators and bomb aimers pre flight meal would be at

15.15 Hrs followed by briefing at 16.00Hrs. They always had their meal before the rest of the crews because of the necessity to get their charts and flight plans completed. The rest of the crews would have their meal at 16.15 Hrs. with the main briefing taking place at 17.00 Hrs when the full details of Form "B" would be divulged. With 2 to 3 hours to idle away before briefing time - coupled with the unofficial knowledge of the fuel load and its very long flight implications most crews on the Battle Order retire to their beds to snatch a few hours sleep.

The main briefing took place in a large blacked out Nissen hut. It had to be large to accommodate 154 crew members and about two dozen other people; Met Officers, Navigation, Bombing. Signals, Engineer and Gunnery Leaders, Air Traffic controllers and last but not least the Squadron and Station Commanders.

As the crews arrive at the briefing room door their names are checked against the Battle Order by a security policeman ensuring that no one entered that room who was not directly involved with the coming operation. The Briefing room furniture consisted of long rows of benches facing a curtained off end wall and a slightly raised platform enabling the Briefing officers to be seen and heard by all.

With everyone checked in, the noise of subdued chatter and nervous coughing came to an abrupt silence as the Squadron Commander called everyone to Attention as the Station Commander strode towards the end of the room. This ceremony of accepting his rank and status was almost instantly dismissed by his "Be seated gentlemen" A nice gesture on his behalf as he was old enough to be a father to most of us under 20's. The briefing commenced with the Squadron Commander pulling back the curtain revealing the large topographical map of the UK and the Continent of Europe. This map indicated all the UK airfields, danger areas, German defences, Radar sites and all the other enemy facilities that could shorten our life span. All this was taken in at a glance. We had seen it before except for one feature and that was a long length of pink tape that ran across the map from our Base in a series of Dog legs from left to right - in fact a very long way right, to our target for tonight 'Dresden'.

Before any of the detailed briefing had commenced agile minds had already worked out that we would be over enemy occupied Europe for nearly eight hours. Whilst this rapid mental exercise had been going on it was accompanied by muttering from all and sundry that varied from the polite to impolite. The speculation was brought to a halt by the Squadron Commander saying simply "Your target for tonight is Dresden" and then calling on the Intelligence Officer.

The Intelligence officer – a Flying Officer not much older than we, stands up grasping a cut down billiard cue and strides onto the platform to tell us all. He starts by giving us an update on the war situation and the reason for the attack on this city. Apparently the Allies had been pondering for some time on a plan for a series of very heavy raids on East German cities with a view to causing such confusion and consternation that the hard stretched German war machine and civil administration would break down and the war would end. The name given to this plan was "Operation Thunderclap" and Dresden was going to be the first city to get "clobbered". He continues – "Your task on this operation is to destroy built up areas and associated industries and rail facilities". "As the Russian front is only 70 miles east of Dresden your attack tonight will delay German reinforcements heading that way as Dresden is now a vital point in the communications and supply route to the eastern front".

For some reason I had half drifted in my own thoughts

at this point, probably still mesmerised by the long length of pink tape pinned to the wall map. This was my 17th operation with at least another 13 more to achieve before a rest. 13 times 8 hours over enemy territory is a long time to get shot at. I recalled from a previous briefing when the Intelligence officer had for some reason mentioned that the RAF raids had caused the Germans to deploy more than a million 88's from the army to defend their cities thereby reducing the threat to the Allied armoured divisions. At this point I began to visualise the 88's pointing skywards at us - no, I mean ME!

Back to the briefing. "As you can see the route to the target looks quite complex and you are seeing only half of it. Tonight's attack will be in two waves. 5 Group will open the attack with 254 aircraft including their own Markers and Master Bomber to get the fires going, with a time on target of 22.15 Hrs. Their marking point will be this sports stadium". He indicates the point on the Target Map. "3, 4, and 6 Groups will be supporting them with diversionary attacks on Bohlen, Magdeburg, Bonn and Nuremburg timed to confuse the German fighter controllers as to what will be the main target. 1 hour and 45 minutes later we will attack the same target going in and out by a different route as indicated by the tape. Our marking and aiming point is south of the River and will be marked by 8 Group Pathfinders. They will also provide the Master Bomber who will use the callsign "King Cole" his deputy will be "King Cole 2", the Main Force call sign will be "Strongman". Listen out for him at H-15 Hrs. H Hour will be 01.30hrs. We in 1 Group will be putting up 500 aircraft in 5 waves of 3 minutes each so there will be a heavy concentration of aircraft over the target. The Air Traffic Controller will allocate the aircraft to the appropriate wave. The delay between 5 Group and us will ensure that all emergency services that are situated outside Dresden will probably have been called in to support those already there so our attack will knock those out as well. The route and tactics for tonight's operation are extremely good and should confound the enemy defence system to a degree that will prevent them from realising where the main attack will occur. The main threat from the enemy tonight will be Flak, his fighter aircraft should be chasing the "Window" feint force in the earlier stages and by the time we get into the picture they will be running out of fuel and therefore landing. All aircraft will carry 500 bundles of "Window" with an additional 24 bundles of ordinary type to be used if engaged by heavy predicted Flak. The Bomb Aimers have already been briefed on the position and rate of 'Windowing". "Any questions? No one posed a question.

The Squadron Commander now invites the Navigation Leader to say his piece.

"The Navigators already have the route so for the benefit of the rest of you I'll go over the tracks with the aid of this map. All Group aircraft will depart Bases on route for Reading to be there at 8-10,000ft. Continuing at that height as far as 01 30 East on track. Maintain this height to 06.00 East on track then climb to bombing height 16-20,000ft by 09 05 East. We will be at 20,000ft - top of the pile! Maintain this height through the target and as far as 05 East on the return journey, then lose height but keeping above cloud to cross the Continental coast out at 6-10,000ft. Maintain this height to the English coast at Orfordness then lose height gradually to Base". "This is a very deep penetration therefore your fuel will be tight so stay on track". "8 aircraft from each Base will be detailed to act as wind finders". "Our crews have been notified at the navigation briefing" "These crews will radio their found winds to Bomber Command HQ'. "You will note from the map that our route takes us very close to some heavily defended areas; Navigators please alert your crew as you approach these area". "As the Intelligence officer stated - the attack will take place in two waves with 5 Group operating ahead of us". "We hope to take advantage of this fact and the weather situation that the "Met" man will brief you about; together with the other diversion attacks to outwit the German defences to a degree that will prevent him from assessing the prime target until it will be too late for him to concentrate his night fighter force".

"A frontal belt of weather will allow 5 Group to fly between Dusseldorf and Cologne and thence North of Kassel and Leipzig to Dresden". "A "Mandrel" radar jamming screen will operate North and South of longitude 06 East from 20. 05hrs. until 21. 10hrs. when 5 Group aircraft will penetrate it and proceed North East towards Düsseldorf". "At the same time the Halifax aircraft of 4 and 6 Groups will also penetrate the jamming screen to cross the Rhine just North of Koblenz and South of Kassel on route to the synthetic oil refinery at Bohlen" "100 Group Special Duties aircraft also alter course South East and commence "Windowing" to give the enemy the idea that the main target could be Frankfurt, Mainz, Darmstadt or Mannheim". "As the weather will be better in this area it will enable the Luftwaffe night fighters to get airborne in an endeavour to intercept a mythical main force". "Meanwhile 5 Group will be free of night fighters because their Northern route win be over the weather that will keep the enemy grounded". "However, just in case any of them do get airborne our Light Night Striking Mosquitoes will be patrolling their rendezvous beacons and airfields waiting for them".

"Mosquitoes will also be attacking Magdeburg and Nuremburg at the time of 5 Groups opening attack on Dresden". "S Group will withdraw on a Southerly route and will be covered by the approach of our second attack". "Hopefully by now the weather front will have moved further East and the plan for this stage of the night's work will be the feint with a "Window" force Northward from Luxembourg to the Rhine". "Then to a fine from Cologne to Koblenz and for us to proceed - not through the Frankfurt gap but across the Mainz - Mannheim defended belt. Relying on cloud cover to defeat the searchlights and Flak, and on the exhaustion of the enemy night fighter's fuel after three hours activity against the first attack"."One last point". It is vitally important that accurate time keeping is observed and crews are not to set course from the rendezvous position 06 East before their concentration time". "Frequent time checks must be made before reaching this point and particularly at Reading and position 02' East."

"Are there any Question? Someone pipes up "What if ad this cloud cover does not materialise?" The Nav. Leader has no reply!

After a short pause the Navigation leader steps down to be replaced by the Bombing Leader who starts his briefing.

"Tonight's attack is a fire raiser as our bomb load indicates". "All aircraft will have a 4,000 lb. "Cookie" and the rest of the load will be incendiaries". "The bombing method tonight will be controlled "Newhaven" ground marking with emergency "Wanganui" sky marking if there is cloud cover". "Pathfindcr force of 8 Group will open the attack with long sticks of illuminating flares at H-6." "The aiming point will then be marked with large salvoes of mixed Red and Green T.1s. and will be kept marked with Red T.Is.". "If the aiming point is not marked visually the target area will be marked with Green T. Is in the early part of the attack".

"If ground marking is obscured by cloud, the release

point will be marked with sky marking flares Red/Green stars igniting at 15,00Oft".

"The Master Bomber or his Deputy will be giving aiming instructions to the main force who will listen out from H-15 minutes". "We will aim our bombs in the following order of preference".

On Master Bombers' instructions

Centre of mixed Red/Green T.I.s

Centre of Red T. I's

Centre of Green T. I's

Centre of Skymarking flares Red/Green stars on an exact heading of 069' T 073 M."

"In the event of the enemy lighting decoy fires - these will immediately be indicated by Yellow T.I.s but there should be no doubt of the real target as 5 Group will have the fires going jolly well by the time we get there". "There will be a large concentration of aircraft over the target in a short space of time, please ensure that your load is not going to drop on the fellows below you if you can see them in time". "All aircraft are fitted with cameras and also H2S cameras". "Lets get some good aiming point photographs tonight" "When you get to your aircraft check the photo flash in the flare chute is correctly toggled, we don't want any going off inside the aircraft". "On the run up to the target would the Wireless operators go back to the "Cookie" position and stand by to release manually in the event of a malfunction of the normal release mechanism". "Also when the bomb doors are closed after bombing would the Bomb Aimers shine the Aldis lamp up the bomb bay to check for any hang ups". "If there are drop them live over Germany, we don't want them brought back, we've got plenty". "Finally I must emphasise that in the event of bombing on "Wanganui" sky markers please ensure your heading is 069' True (073' Magnetic) "."That's all - any questions?"

The Signals Leader now takes up his position on the platform.

"Wireless Operators check your watches with the Navigator and monitor the Command radio broadcasts at H+20 and H+40 minutes. If Group intercept any radio transmissions from the German fighter defence organisation their frequency will be sent to you on the Command Broadcasts". "On receipt of any such message all aircraft will tune their transmitters to those frequencies and using the carbon microphones proceed to jam until the next Group Broadcast is due". "There will be no break in the jamming because the Group Broadcast will be timed for different Squadrons". "There will be complete radio and radar silence including the "Airborne Cigar" jamming by 101 Squadron aircraft until 06' East on the outward journey". "The wind finder aircraft will transmit their findings to Group using the Bomber Code - please ensure you have the correct code for the period". "Also check you have the appropriate Signal cartridges and double check before firing them". "When you get to your aircraft ensure the detonator charge for the IFF is set on the right position so that it will self destruct if the situation demands it". "As we are all now aware this is a very deep penetration of enemy airspace so the Navigators will probably run out of "Gee" range long before the target but you may be able to extend the range of reception when the signals begin to fade by coupling the "Gee" aerial to the trailing aerial and cranking out an extra length". "The desired length will be a matter of trial and error".

"When outside the H2S restricted area - that is East of 06' East use the "Fishpond" radar and keep the Gunners informed of anything suspicious below your aircraft". "Check you have your intercom, extension lead to hand when you go back to the "Cookie" manual release position and don't forget to take your portable oxygen bottle with you". "Some of you in the past have gone back in the belief that you could make do without it and you are now all aware of the result"

"100 Special duties Group will be out in force tonight providing the "Mandrel" radar jamming to cover our approach". If 10 1 Squadron with their German speaking Wireless operators will be creating their usual mayhem and our "Y" service here in the UK will be jamming the German night fighter rendezvous beacons so all in all this combined distraction will be to our advantage". Finally cheek the dinghy radio is in its stowage and remember the radio silence times if you have to use it". There were no questions.

The Gunnery Leader now stood up to address the crews.

"There will be no moon tonight, maximum visibility will be about 300 yards away from the target area so team work between the Mid Upper and Rear Gunners will be essential for a successful and continuous search". "The Wireless Operator will keep you informed of anything below the aircraft and pilots will be rolling the aircraft to widen your field of search". "Keep your reflector gun sights as dim as you can". "Bright gun sights reduce your night vision". "Your ammunition now has a reduced number of tracer rounds so if you do have to fire - good deflection shooting is required". "The target area will be very bright with a visibility of a mile so be extra vigilant there". "Also the Navigators will announce any course alteration and at those points be on the look out for the other aircraft that might be turning early or late - this is the time when a collision is very likely". "That's all".

Last of all the Engineer Leader addresses us.

"As all the other Leaders have impressed on you we are going a long way tonight and fuel management will be very important". "Keep an accurate log of all engine parameters, and assist the pilot with engine handling if any form of emergency occurs". "During taxiing for take off keep an eye on the glycol temperatures and do something about any rise as soon as you see it happening ... ... X Flight might have this problem tonight as they will have the longest taxying distance". "Thank you.

The Squadron Commander now calls on the 'Met'. Officer who produces a detailed weather map covering our intended nights' flight.

"The frontal system that gave us rain and low cloud this morning is now clear of all Bases so the first part of your route tonight will be clear to about 03' East which will be the position of the frontal system when you arrive there". "Tops of the cloud should be about 16 - 18,000ft. with the freezing level at 3,000ft." "Icing will be moderate to heavy in any Cu. type clouds". "From this position to 12' East there will be large areas of broken clouds with tops 12 18,000ft." "The cloud will then disperse entirely and clear conditions should prevail to the target area". "To the East of the target area the cloud tops will be about 8,000ft and hopefully it will remain to the East" "For the return journey the picture will be similar except for an easterly drift of the front". "From the Continental coast to our Bases the weather will be clear". "The Navigators have been briefed on the wind velocities, but remember to expect a wind change as the front is traversed". "Wind finder aircraft please send back your found winds to Group so that they can be averaged out and repeated to all aircraft on the Group broadcasts". 'All Bases will have good weather for your return"

Finally the Squadron Commander calls on the Air

Traffic Control Officer who starts his briefing.

"Gentlemen we will be using the long runway tonight therefore aircraft from 'C' Flight will be first off their dispersal followed by U, and 'A Flight will be last". "There will of course be no radio contact". "You will start your engines when you see the Green Very light fired from the Control Tower and start taxiing to the take off position in the progression I mentioned earlier".

"Bomb Aimers in the nose of the aircraft can assist the pilots by swinging the Aldis Lamp beam to illuminate the edge of the perimeter tracks on some of the sharp turns". "Be extremely careful not to get a wheel on the grass as the ground is very soft and you will bog down". 'Any aircraft having last minute problems - flash a red Aldis at the Control Tower with the aircraft letter and we will get a maintenance team to you immediately". "If trouble occurs during taxiing, get off the taxiway immediately by pulling into a vacated dispersal and again, flash your aircraft letter to the Control Tower". "Do not impede the aircraft behind you as we have a very tight departure schedule. I shall be planning one aircraft departure every minute" "When you become number one, taxi onto the runway alongside the Caravan; when you get a Green from the Runway Controller start your take off immediately". "Both Binbrook and Ludford Magna are operating with us so there will be about 100 aircraft departing in an area of about 6 miles so I emphasise time keeping is important".

"If any emergency occurs after take-off which necessitates a return we don't want you trying to land back here while departures are in progress, so push off out to sea and jettison your bombs in the jettison area if possible", "If an early return is likely at a later stage of the flight and you think you can make it safely with the bombs on board, please advise us of that fact".

"You can keep your navigation lights on for taxiing,

take off and initial part of the route until 06' East on the outward journey then switch them off after that"

"On return in the event of enemy intruder activity in the area all aircraft are to fly west for 10 minutes and then South West until recalled or diverted". "There will be 5 Waves of aircraft over the target tonight - your times and wave are listed on the board to the left of the map".

At this point the Briefing from the specialists was over. The Squadron Commander stands to speak - "Well chaps that concludes the evenings' briefing, the tactics are well planned so let's do a good job". "Before you leave the Briefing room please empty your pockets of all personal belongings and put them in the envelopes before you pick up your Escape Wallets". Don't forget, if you fall into enemy hands you only give them your Service number, Rank and Name - nothing else". (What he really means is if you get shot down!!)

The Station Commander now stands up and as we did for his entrance we also stand up to hear his parting voice say "Good Luck men"

The Briefing Room suddenly becomes a noisy place as crews get to their feet, start talking to each other and begin queuing up to sign for their Escape Wallets that are then tucked into their Battle Dress tops. From the Briefing Room the crews proceed to the locker room which is another large Nissen hut next door. Here, they don their variations of flying kit. The Gunners don their very bulky electrically heated suits and flying boots while the rest of the crew generally make do with their white roll neck sweaters, flying boots and helmets- the latter checked for correct functioning of the oxygen mask on the test rig. Finally the parachute harnesses are clipped on and carefully adjusted to a tight fit as anything less can inflict a lot of damage to the wearer if he has to jump. At an adjacent counter little blonde Diana and her mate

Fionna are handing out the parachutes. Both these girls are held in high esteem by the crews who are well aware that their skill in packing and caring for the 'chutes' might mean life or death. The usual forced light banter prevails, "Will it work?" a quick reply "If it doesn't bring it back, you can have another one free".

As the final preparations are going on, the 3 ton trucks that are the crew transports have arrived to take us to the aircraft dispersal pens some of which are 3 miles away. The drivers are all WAAFs, who a short while ago had been driving tractors towing bomb trolleys from the bomb dump to the aircraft. Quiet efficiency and a shy caring for the crews that they transport around the airfield become very obvious as we get of the truck - our driver says "I'll be waiting for you lot when you return".

At the dispersal our aircraft 'Raggedy Anne' stands prepared with the huge 33ft long bomb doors open displaying the load. Our ground crew, Lofty the engine's man, Jim the airframe fitter, electricians, radio mechanics and armourers stand by to help us up the short ladder on the starboard side of the aircraft. However, before entering we go through a ritual carried out before every trip. We all pee against the tailwheel. Jim our airframe's fitter doesn't go much on this at all, we know that, but he has never said so. Come to think of it, it was not so much a ritual but the fact that once we were on board and on our way it was going to be a long time before we had another chance. We do have a chemical Elsan toilet on board - right at the rear of the aircraft but no one has ever felt that they could grope their way back there in total darkness with an oxygen bottle clutched in one hand and hope to get to the front end of the aircraft in 5 minutes.

The ritual completed we all scramble aboard carrying our parachutes, Nav. bags and all the other bits and pieces that may be required during the long flight ahead. We climb over the main spar having checked various pieces of equipment as we move up the fuselage. The huge photo flash - as lethal as a bomb, is firmly in the flare chute with its arming cable secured, the IFF detonator 'Ready to Destruct' switch is correctly set and the roof escape hatch is tested and secured. The Nitrogen bottle on the starboard side of the fuselage - positioned so that we bang our heads on it as we clamber over the main spar - is registering FULL. The contents we hope will blanket the fuel in the tanks with a fire retarding gas should we be unfortunate enough to get Flak damage in those areas. Apart from an intercom. check between all crew members we remain fairly silent, going about our individual checks in order to pick up any unserviceability early enough to get it rectified before the 'Start engines' signal is given.

At this stage of the proceedings most crews have a variety of thoughts going through their minds as eyes will now be on the Control Tower. Will the cartridge be Red for a 'Scrub' or Green for a 'Go'? Both these signals will have tremendous implications for all people. A 'Scrub' to a crew who might be on their last trip before a rest or leave would be a state of speechless annoyance to say the least, while a 'Green' would relieve the tension and clear their thoughts for the job ahead. Either ways this last hour always becomes a period of tension to all seven crew members in every aircraft every time 'Ops' are ON. This tension is broken as a Green Very cartridge lights up the sky as it soars above and away from the Control Tower and in every aircraft the past silence and individual thoughts are replaced by the urgent demands of the pre-start up drills that require close attention. The start signal also alerts the ground crew who have already connected the starting trolley and completed a last minute external check. Pilot and Flight Engineer chant and action their start drills;

The starboard inner is started with a hesitant whine, an unsteady crackle accompanied by a puff of smoke from the exhaust stacks and then a steady familiar throb as the 'Merlin' engine settles down to its ground idle RPM allowing the brake pressure to build up and powering the nose turret. Finally all engines are running, bomb doors closed, landing lights switched on and we are ready to taxi away from dispersal as soon as the aircraft in the next pen starts to move.

Ahead of us the 'C' Flight aircraft are almost at the take off point, with B' Flight and then us rapidly catching them up. One aircraft ahead leaves the taxiway and turns into a now empty dispersal area allowing the other Lancasters to pass. He obviously has a problem and already we notice a team of ground crew heading in his direction to solve whatever problem they might have.

The first aircraft is on the runway and in the dimly lit caravan we see the runway controller flashing a green light from his Aldis lamp. In the fight of the aircraft's' landing lamps the propeller speed can be seen to increase to a blur as take off power is applied. we notice too, a small group of off duty airmen and WAAFs standing alongside the caravan waving a friendly goodbye. These people are always there to see us off regardless of the time of day or night. It gives us great comfort to know that we are cared for.

This scene is being repeated at another 13 airfield of our Group and at another 18 airfield of the other Groups participating in tonight's operation. Soon the roar of the departing aircraft will end and the airfield will become very quiet. The ground crews going back to their huts; the duty air traffic people and intelligence staff having little to do but await the return of the aircraft will probably spend the time reading or catching up on their meals that were interrupted by our departure. In contrast, the sky to the

South of Lincolnshire is gradually becoming very busy and noisy as all the squadrons converge on track to the first turning point at Reading. Aircraft that appears to be ahead of time trying to reduce speed, pulling back on the power and hanging on the 'props', others flying a dog leg track, while inevitably some clot will do an orbit scaring the hell out of everyone who sees him coming at them head on. All this is happening in total darkness so any sightings are split second affairs, but although we seldom see another aircraft, their presence is felt as we wallow through their slipstream.

The time is now 22.20hrs and for 5 Group ahead of us, the moment of truth will have passed - they were due on target 5 minutes ago. Have all the tactical predictions described at Briefing worked out? Did the frontal cloud over the heavily defended areas really materialise? Did the German night fighter controller send his aircraft in the direction of the spoof 'Window' force? We hope all went well but we are not to know. Thirty minutes before - just as our Group was getting airborne, a small force of 62 Mosquitoes was attacking Magdeburg approaching this target on a heading that could have taken them to Berlin. At the same moment as the 5 Group opening attack on Dresden, 4 and 6 Groups with their 326 Halifax aircraft will be attacking the oil refinery at Bohlen creating yet another dilemma for the enemy. These tactics we know will succeed, and just as an insurance our low level intruder aircraft will be over the German airfields of Kassel and Guttersloh, aided by an'Oboe'bombing raid on Dortmund

While all this activity has been happening our second attacking force is progressing along the pre-ordained flight plan track, climbing in an Easterly direction toward the next check point at 50' North 03' East to be there at 12 - 14,000ft. 'Gee' reception is good, navigation is accurate, confirmed by heavy Flak activity from defended areas that we are well aware of either side of track. Attaining 14,000ft. most aircraft are bouncing around in and out of the cloud tops that are causing light icing to collect on the windscreens and wing leading edges. The Mid Upper Gunner reports that what little icing there is on his turret quickly disappears as he rotates the turret. The Wireless Operator reports slight precipitation static on his receiver but not enough to blot out the powerful transmissions of Group HQ's SW8B transmitter. At the moment all is well.

The Mandrel' radar jamming force will have moved to their new position to cover our approach at 06' East timed to be there at 23.25hrs. when we will have achieved our bombing height. As we burst through the radar jamming screen we switch on our H2S radar to assist us in position finding, switch off the navigation lights just in case there are enemy aircraft around and everyone in the crew becomes doubly alert. The special 'Window' force accompanying us break away heading North East in the direction of Cologne, Dusseldorf and Koblenz.

We achieve our bombing height, above cloud most of the time, but there are occasional tops that bounce us around. Ahead we pick up Darmstadt on our radar that gives us a good position and a check on the windspeed. Farther ahead is a well- known night fighter airfield of Kitzingen so the Gunners keep their turrets revolving in a ceaseless search whilst the wireless Operator keeps a watch on his! Fishpond' radar for anything suspicious below the aircraft. We pass the likely trouble spot then alter course North East towards Leipzig - this alteration again intended to deceive the Germans that Leipzig is the main target. However, 50 miles South West of that city we alter course for the real target Dresden that is now just 40 minutes away.

As promised by the 'Met' man, the cloud starts to break

up and soon we notice a faint glow appearing in the sky ahead of us. We still have 20 minutes to run for our ETA on target. Is that glow ahead coming from Dresden? We switch the radio on and hear the Master Bomber and his Deputy giving a time check and discussing the Marking method that will be used. From their discussion we gather that the visibility is excellent and what little cloud there is, will not affect the ground marking method for bombing. By now the sky is getting visibly lighter and we see aircraft all around us causing the Gunners to advise on possible collisions. At H-6 minutes, just when the Pathfinder Illuminators should be dropping their flares the Master Bomber calls to them that they are not needed. The fires raging below provide all the illumination we are going to need. The Master Bomber calls the Illuminators on the radio saying 'Go Home 'Go Home'. At H-2 we are 15 miles from the target endeavouring to get on to a heading that will reduce last minute corrections on the bombing run when ahead of us we see the first Markers going down, a mixture of Red/Green target indicators. The fires that are burning below us don't seem to be generating much smoke although the whole area is just one sea of flames. Puzzling for a moment then the reason becomes very apparent. The fires are burning with such intensity that they are generating their own winds - probably gale force, which carried the smoke away at low level and kept the target almost clear. Unfortunately these fires also quickly swallowed up the Markers within seconds. The Master Bomber realised this and ordered the Main Force to bomb visually with the radio command becoming., X ing Cole' to 'Strong man' bomb visually , bomb visually, there will be no Markers. Ahead of us the first wave of aircraft is dropping their loads and we see aircraft below us silhouetted against the background of fires. As the 4,000lb. 'Cookies' explodes a shock wave ring momentarily appears in the fire to be swallowed up again in an instant.

We commence our own bombing run at 01.33hrs. exactly on time. It is very turbulent now. Could it be caused by the tremendous heat generated below us or is this turbulence due to the slipstreams of aircraft ahead of us? The Bomb Aimer calls for the bomb doors to be opened causing a cold draught and an increase in noise level. Shortly the whole reason for this journey into the night sky will have been achieved. The bombing run is a time of intense concentration for everyone. The Gunners are searching the sky for any sign of fighters who would have an easy time attacking us as we are committed to straight and level flight until our cargo is despatched. The Bomb Aimer is watching the target slowly slide down the hair line graticule of the Mk.14 bomb sight giving Left Left or Right corrections as required - probably thinking - "Have I got the selector properly set on the 'Mickey Mouse"? or is the wind setting correct on the bomb site - or is the camera running". They all are of course. The Wireless Operator is crouched behind the main spar by the 'Cookie' manual release standing by to trip if necessary. The odd puffs of Ack Ack are few and far between. Little or no Flak for a change. "Left Left a touch - Steady - Bombs away" a slight pause then Bomb doors closed". As 12,000lb of bombs leave the aircraft the tendency to 'balloon' and surge forward is immediately checked and a steady course is maintained while the camera continues to run hopefully going to provide us with confirmation of a good bombing run. The Navigator warns of the next change of course in 2 minutes causing the Gunners an even more watchful search as aircraft ahead of us turn slightly early and cross our path. With the decreased weight we can now reduce power slightly on the engines thereby reducing fuel consumption. We still have a long way to go. At this lighter weight we are also in a better position to defend ourselves if a night fighter appears. At the lighter weight our 'Corkscrew` manoeuvres' would test the skill of any attacker to stay with us.

Ahead of us the sky is now dark again and seemingly we are on our own but we know there are other Lancasters close by as we occasionally bounce around in their slipstream. A comfort to know that we are in the bomber stream and therefore on track. The Bomb Aimer has confirmed that we have no bombs hanging about in the bomb bay, we are still in one piece and every minute takes us closer to home. The high pitched tension we all have approaching and over the target has decreased a little but not to a degree of complacency. We become aware of the minor irritations again; oxygen masks chafing on our faces, some of the warm air from the mask escaping around the bridge of the nose and then almost freezing on our eye brows and eye lashes. The need to wriggle in our seats in an endeavour to be more comfortable and lastly a wish that we were all back on the ground again. This latter wish is not really important because we are alive and every minute, including this one, is to be appreciated.

150 miles from Dresden - now well behind us- the Rear Gunner reports that the glow from the fires is still visible. We feel that it was a very successful attack with little or no opposition so far. Abeam of Nuremburg we note a great deal of heavy Flak, is someone off track and getting the treatment? or are the Germans putting up a deterrent barrage just in case they think it's their turn? Once again tension and alertness increase because we are near Schwabishch Hall that is one of the Luftwaffe fighter bases, the hornets nest of fighters that we hope win not get involved with us. We want to clear this area as quickly as possible; the desire to increase speed to achieve this is great but we know that if we do we will be eating into

our meagre petrol supply remaining, so we control our impulses and fly steadily on. Just South of Stuttgart we alter course to almost due West with the knowledge that soon we will be over the ground battle front and even if a night fighter skirmish occurs during which we had to bale out we would be in allied hands. This is probably wishful thinking - it does not really happen like that but it passes a few minutes.

The Navigator reports 'Gee' reception is now returning, confirming our position and enabling us to maintain track and stay in the bomber stream that increases our defence capability and safety.

Approaching 050 East we gradually pull the power back but maintain speed by lowering the nose and commence our descent - now in clear conditions and heading NNE to Orfordness with 1 hour to go. Although we are now over allied occupied territory the Gunners and indeed the rest of the crew too, are very alert and will remain so until we are on the ground at Base. The German long range night fighters - the Me 410's and Ju 88's have a nasty habit of infiltrating the returning bomber stream to follow us back to our airfields and into the landing circuits. When our aircraft are in the landing configuration - flaps and wheels down, the intruders then come up from behind, open up with their cannon and shoot us down. It has happened in the past when crews and particularly the Gunners were lulled into the false impression that with their airfield below them - all was well and they were home. A sudden blast of cannon fire soon disillusioned them in their last seconds of life. Eternal vigilance is the price of safety.

We cross the Continental coast still in a gradual descent then pass Orfordness with the comforting thought that nearby is a Master Diversion airfield at Woodbridge. This airfield is one of three airfields that can cater for any aircraft emergency envisaged - even a shortage of fuel.

We check our own remaining fuel at this point - just in case. There is not a lot left but we will make it and so we fly on across the Wash until ahead of us we pick out the River Humber on our H2S radar. Radio Contact is established with Base and we join the circuit following the cardioid shape of the 'Drem' lights that will lead us into the funnel and hence line us up with the runway. The landing or I should say 'Arrival' is a Wheeler' causing the odd ribald remark from the tail end but nobody worries - we are back. 17 trips completed, 13 to go.

We taxi into our dispersal pen helped by the signals from our ground team, then go through the shut down checks including opening the bomb doors before we stop our engines. This last action helps the ground team because it would take 15 minutes to hand pump them open. With all engines stopped we sit there a while, taking off our helmets and masks just listening to the silence noting the first hint of dawn giving colour to the South East sky as we exit the aircraft. The ground team are eager to hear of any problems either with us or the aircraft but we have none - at least we thought so until Lofty our engine's man states "You have 7 holes in the starboard wing". That's news to us, I wonder where we collected them, anyway they are not very big.

We clamber aboard our truck - welcomed by our WAAF driver and just as we begin the drive to the Interrogation room, note that the petrol bowsers are already filling the aircraft tanks another one tonight?

After the long night's actions we are beginning to realise how fatigued we are, but there are still things to be done. At the Briefing room the Intelligence officer wants a complete run down on the whole trip. Naturally the most important point being 'Was the attack a success?'. The answer to that one was a definite "Yes". "Was the aiming point visible?" 'What markers did you aim at?" 'Was the Flak heavy?" 'What night fighter activity was observed"? "Do you think a return visit to this target will be necessary?" (Is he kidding?) The various Leaders then want their information. 'What were the navigation aids used and were they up to requirement?" 'Were they being jammed by the enemy?""Was the weather prediction accurate?""Did the cameras function correctly?" (We will have the answer to that one shortly - the films are being developed now) While all this interrogation is going on, the Squadron Commander, Base Commander, the Padre and some helpful WAAFs are passing us cups of tea or coffee laced with rum and generally being helpful.

Eventually de-briefing is completed. Wearily we stagger to the locker room to hang up our kit and hand over our parachutes before making the next important decision. Shall we go to the Mess for breakfast or go straight to bed? To some crews the decision on this point was made the night before. As aircrew we are entitled to an egg with our breakfast after an Operation. However, most people reckon that if they get 'Clobbered' by the Germans they will have lost their egg too, so they have it on their pre departure meal before the Operation.

Seven fatigued airmen walk slowly and silently down the road to their Nissen hut in the distance. No noise, the trees are still, but way overhead a skylark starts its song.

Eric Thale 1992

MR NIGEL TRENDELL, 1943 – 1944

I remember my time at RAF Millom with fondness, not least of all because as a "local" it was a posting very close to home for me for a while. Prior to joining the RAF I lived with my parents in Windermere. I have very vivid memories of Char fishing on the lake with my father and moving inshore in order to clear the way for the huge Sunderland Flying Boats to take off. These very impressive aircraft were, of course, built at the Shorts aircraft factory at Whitecross Bay though little remains on the site today to remind us of the fact.

After my initial training and having gone through the selection process, I considered myself very lucky indeed to be posted to RAF Cark near Flookburgh to train as a Staff Pilot. My course only lasted a few weeks during which time I was trained in both day and night flying. We were flying the MK1 Avro Anson aircraft and were to be posted to Air Observer schools on completion of our course to assist in the training of navigators.

I remember the very long, straight road which led to RAF Cark and my rather 'smug' feeling that I was a 'local' amongst my fellow course mates, many of whom were from Canada, New Zealand and Australia. Before commencing the actual course cross country flights we were sent up in the Ansons to get the feel of the aircraft and also to familiarise ourselves with the local flying area. I took advantage of this to set course for Windermere where I would execute some steep turns at low level over my home, and always my mother would dash out and furiously wave a tea towel.

For entertainment in the evenings we would catch transport into Grange-over-Sands, or the train to Morecambe for a rather more adventurous "night on the tiles"! On successful completion of my course at Cark I was posted to No.2 Observer Advanced Flying Unit at RAF Millom. I was to spend twelve very busy and enjoyable months at Millom surrounded by the familiar countryside and flying trainee navigators and Wireless Operators around the Irish Sea both by day and night. Many of these students had been trained in Canada, Australia or South Africa in weather that provided good flying conditions. Our job was to acclimatise them to the turbulence and bad visibility they would encounter upon flying operationally over Europe.

A typical exercise route from Millom would be out to the lighthouse on the Southern tip of the Isle of Man, then South to Port Lynas on the Isle of Anglesey, followed by a Northern heading back to Millom through the industrial haze of Liverpool bay and passing Blackpool tower, which was always a good landmark!! Our routine would be broken on occasions when we flew bombing practice with students over the Duddon Estuary. Out on the sands was a target upon which we used to drop 11 ½ lbs practice smoke bombs.

At Millom both students and staff were required to undergo what was termed an "escape and evasion" exercise. This rather strange procedure was supposed to be helpful training if one was shot down in enemy territory. We would be taken out in coaches with the windows blacked out and deposited in some remote corner of the Lake District with only five shillings in our pockets. We were then required to make our way back to Millom as quickly as possible under the circumstances and using whatever transport might be available. The Home Guard and Police were alerted to try and stop us and to take us prisoner. I would straight away head for home in Windermere, spend a comfortable night in my own bed and return by train the next day to Millom via Carnforth. That day would be spent in the mess, waiting for all the stragglers to make their way back to base.

I was qualified to instruct on light aircraft and as a result I was allowed to borrow the Station Commander's Miles Magister on occasions. This was a small aircraft with a single engine and open cockpit which made it great fun to fly. I used to take huge delight in disrupting cricket matches up the coast at St Bees School, where I was a pupil just before the war, by zooming around just above the player's heads! Owing to the weather and the proximity of the Lakeland Mountains there were quite a few fatal flying accidents whilst I was at Millom. In due course, a dedicated Mountain Rescue unit was established at Millom and was of course, one of the fore-runners of the much loved and respected RAF Mountain Rescue Service we know today. During my time at the station however, the task was carried out on a "volunteer basis" though aircrew were discouraged from taking part for psychological reasons which are pretty obvious as the task was frequently a grisly and upsetting one. On one occasion however I assisted in a search and rescue operation which involved cruising Ullswater Lake in an amphibious D.U.K.W. vehicle, trying to locate the crew of a heavy bomber which had crashed nearby after the crew bailed out over the lakes. Our search was in vain as all the crew had landed safely on dry land and were in due course all located.

Most of the Wireless Operator and Navigator instructors were at Millom being "rested" following a tour of operations and they used to unwind in no uncertain manner!! The Millom pubs were always packed out and if night flying was cancelled then it was taken as an excuse for the most hair-raising parties in the respective messes! One escapade we used to get up to was really quite outrageous.

On a Saturday afternoon, one of our Ansons would be flying north up the Lancashire coast and returning to base following a daytime cross country exercise. They would deviate slightly and join the RAF Squires Gate circuit at Blackpool. The pilot would then rapidly switch one engine' magneto switches on and off. This would cause surging and misfiring on that engine, a condition that would sound quite alarming to those on the ground. Having made an emergency landing they would find that most of the civilian servicing crew had gone off duty until

Monday morning leaving only a small handling party for visiting aircraft. After helping push their aircraft into a hangar, the crew would then make their way to the Squires Gate RAF Mess to spend two nights enjoying the delights of Wartime Blackpool. On Monday morning, having tested and "run up" the engines, it would be found that they had miraculously recovered! The Anson would then return across Morecambe Bay to Millom with a slightly "hung-over" crew.

After Millom my adventures were many and varied, including a post war conversion onto Jet Aircraft which allowed me to fly the Vampire among others. In 1950 however I was seconded to a V.I.P. Squadron at RAF Hendon, North London. One glorious summer's day I was detailed to fly a party of Officers from the Air ministry up to RAF Silloth for an inspection. I was flying us at 6,000 feet and as we approached the Lake District from the Eastern tip of Morecambe Bay we could see the whole area spread out before us. I could pick out all the lakes and small tarns I knew so well and as I eased back the throttles over Derwentwater to slowly lose height towards Cockermouth and Silloth, I marvelled at the sheer beauty of Skiddaw and Bassenthwaite just off my starboard side. These days' passenger airlines are routed above the clouds and weather, but back in 1950 our RAF Flights were carried out under visual Flight Rules (VFR) so that one was free to admire the beauty of the country passing below. I have enjoyed my flying years immensely, but I digress! Millom? Yes, I remember it well!!

Nigel Trendell 1996

MR ROLAND WILLIAMSON – 1942

I was stationed at RAF Millom in Cumberland (No.2 O.A.F.U.) from January 1942 until November 1942 as a Wireless Operator instructor following a completed operational tour with Bomber Command.

During the latter part of January we had a good number of heavy snow showers which prevented us from flying for several days. On the 24th of January it was decided that an Anson be flown up in order to check the weather at altitude. With Sgt Hale as pilot and myself as Wireless Operator we took off, and after making a circuit in quite foul conditions, made our landing approach! It transpired however, that due to the weather and almost nil visibility, we had misjudged our height and as a result we made an untimely and very untidy arrival on the stations coal dump!! Sgt Hale was unhurt – however I suffered a minor head injury and was sent to Blackpool to be seen by a specialist. Having been examined it was decided that I should remain there for a week, and I was billeted in a civilian guest house. At first I was not at all happy about this state of affairs but after a week I had settled in very well indeed and had decided that this was in fact a very cushy number!! At my next appointment I informed my specialist that I did not feel at all well and managed to wangle a total of seven weeks of pure bliss before it was decided that I was well enough to return to Millom.

After 51 years, I am afraid recollections of the station are rather fragmented, however, I remember volunteering to help search for an officer who had gone off on a solo climbing trip to the Coniston Fells. I cannot recall his name but I believe that the search took us two or three days before he was found dead having fallen from a crag on Wetherlam Mountain. I remember too that organised sport was popular at Millom; Football, Tennis, Rugby etc. were all encouraged, though if one was not a "sporty type" it was decreed that you were required to climb Black Combe. This was not optional and our Station Commander would take up an Anson and perform circuits of the fell to make sure we all did so!

On the subject of sport it may be of interest to know that one of the staff pilots who served with us at Millom was a chap called Ken Wolstenholme, who of course went on to become a famous sports reporter and will always be remembered for his famous "they think it's all over!, it is now"! Following England's winning goal in the 1966 World Cup.

I flew a total of 282 hours at RAF Millom, mostly with Sgt Butcher who, after leaving Millom, was killed tragically, he was a good pal as I have said, I arrived at Millom having completed one tour of operations and when I was posted out it was to join Bomber Command for a second one.

On completion of my second tour I was transferred to Transport Command and continued flying until 1953. Whilst at Millom I became very good friends with a chap called Bill Gracie, who like myself was a Wireless Operator / Air Gunner. We parted at Millom but met up once again in the rather warmer setting of Cairo!! The year was 1945, and Bill, like myself, was serving at 216 Group HQ there. We shared a flat until my wife joined me in 1946 and we stay in touch to this day with many a laugh shared at our many and varied adventures over the years.

Roland Williamson 1993

MR CLAUDE WILLIAMS – 1944

In 1944 I spent some time at RAF Millom as a Bomb Aimer under training. This would entail flying both day and night time exercises. We would fly all our details in Millom's well used and a little tired, MK1 Avro Ansons.

On April the 12th 1944 I was part of a crew briefed to carry out a night bombing exercise on an infra red target over in Northern Ireland. We were to cross the Irish Coast and then track across Loch Neigh to Dungannon. The crew normally consisted of a trainee Navigator, a Bomb Aimer and a Wireless Operator plus pilot. On this flight we had an extra member, a Staff Flight Lieutenant Pilot, accompanying our skipper, who was a Flight Sergeant. The Officer occupied the co-pilots seat where I usually sat. We took off from Millom in the late evening and after completing our exercise, turned East for the Irish Sea and our return flight back to base. A short while after doing so we noticed the smell of something burning and the aircraft began to fill with smoke. The bomb doors were opened and the smoke quickly cleared but soon afterwards there was a flash from the starboard engine as it seized completely. Ansons have been known to fly OK on one-engine but our pilot told the co-pilot we were losing height at 200 feet a minute. The Navigator confirmed that we were over the sea and our pilot, after conferring with the co-pilot, decided to ditch. He told me to chop off the cabin door. Using the emergency axe I was able to do so and our exit was made clear. The crew all took up emergency brace positions. As mine was occupied by the co-pilot I crouched behind a bulkhead and hoped for the best. The pilot made his approach for a belly landing in the dark, there was a sound like several car horns blaring at once as the "wheels up alarm" sounded and the aircraft hit the sea with a huge bang. I was flung out of the door and into the water, which rushed into my open topped flying boots, pulling me downwards. I managed to kick them off and climb onto the aircrafts wing. The Anson was floating beautifully. It had been a superb crash landing in total darkness and awful conditions, the time was 30 minutes after midnight. The emergency dinghy was passed out and it inflated perfectly. We all climbed into the dinghy which was still attached to the aircraft. After about 15 minutes the nose of the Anson dipped heavily so our pilot cut the rope with the curved knife provided and we paddled away from the submerging aircraft. After firing a cluster of distress flares we decided amongst ourselves to keep the next until daylight when we might possibly spot passing shipping. Waves kept splashing into our dinghy and so we pulled over the cover to get some shelter. We were all sea sick from time to time but fortunately the waves were not huge. At about 4.05am our Wireless Operator suddenly shouted "buoy"! During the war years, buoys were used to store emergency rations etc for those adrift at sea and so we were quite excited at the prospect. What our Wireless Operator had spotted, however, was a ship which seemed to be bearing down on us at great speed! We were caught in the swell from the bow and propelled some fifty yards away. We blew furiously on our whistles and shouted as loud as we could. A searchlight was switched on and it scanned the water. We were spotted and paddled with all our might, eventually reaching the side of the ship. A rope was lowered and without ceremony, we were hauled on deck. How thankful we were to have encountered the SS Sheringham, a British Coaster, it was 4.20am. We were given dry clothing, a pullover and trousers, hot buttered toast and warm drinks. We arrived in Belfast at about 6.30am, where an RAF Medical Officer came on board and we were taken by ambulance to a Belfast hospital where we remained for two days before being flown back to RAF Millom in an Anson, this time without mishap!! I believe the Anson which we were forced to ditch that night was N5139 and our pilot was PLT/Sgt Usherwood. The most sincere tribute must be paid to our pilot, who, in the most difficult circumstances, pulled off such a brilliant forced landing on water in the dead of night.

Claude Williams 1997

AIR COMMODORE ARTHUR WRAY, DSO, MC, DFC, AFC.

A PEN PORTRAIT OF MILLOM'S FIRST COMMANDING OFFICER BY ERIC THALE

From the cramped cockpit of his glider, Arthur Wray looked down at the Lincolnshire farmland, scarred by the decaying runways of bomber bases he had once known so well. It was late one May afternoon in 1972, and he had already been airborne for five long exhausting hours. Now the weather was worsening, and so was the pain from his old leg injury. Wray was tempted to give up his bid to complete the 186 mile cross country flight that would help him earn the international "Gold C" badge, a coveted distinction in the gliding world.

Then through the haze ahead he spotted the flashing airfield beacon of RAF Binbrook, and knew his goal was within reach. At the unprecedented age of 75, Air Commodore Arthur Wray, had won a victory achieved by relatively few glider pilots. To add to his triumph, he had ended the flight at his wartime headquarters - a legendary airman returning from the sky.

I wished I had been at the welcome party Binbrook gave him that evening, not only to add my congratulations but to recall with him a very different flight we made together nearly 30 years earlier.

It was March 15, 1944. I was a young sergeant pilot with only seven hours flying time on Lancasters, posted a week earlier with my crew to 100 Squadron at Waltham, a windswept airfield near Grimsby, and one of three bomber stations making up 12 Base under Wray's command. That morning we had been told "You're flying on your first operation tonight with the Base Commander."

We were standing nervously round our Lancaster "J" Jig, when he drove up, a stocky figure with iron-grey hair and a blaze of medal ribbons on his battledress. Arthur Wray was then 47: we were all 20, and my first impression, as he limped across the tarmac was that he was so old. None of us seven sergeants had even seen such a senior officer before. But this one had a warm, friendly smile and relaxed manner that put us at ease. We took to him at once.

The target that night was Stuttgart, one of Germany's most viciously defended cities, and nearly 900 heavy bombers would be sent on the raid. For a crew as green as ours it was a daunting prospect; but Arthur Wray appeared totally unconcerned. When I walked with him around "J" Jig to inspect the aircraft before take-off, he chatted away as cheerfully as though we were going on a joy-ride.

We had been flying for an hour, with the Air Commodore at the controls, when one of the gunners spotted the dark shadow of a Lancaster sliding beneath us, crossing our path. A few moments later, another crossed above. Wray immediately suspected that we were straying from the bomber stream.

As we flew on alone, it transpired that the navigator had misread the flight plan and given the wrong course. "Now I can't get a fix, Sir," he reported. "Our radar's being jammed." "All right," said Wray mildly, "Work out a course by dead reckoning." There was a long silence, then: "Sorry, Sir but we're lost. We'll have to turn back". With a crisp "turn back, be damned", the Air Commodore helped us plot an approximate course, and we flew on across Germany towards Stuttgart.

We arrived 15 minutes late to find ourselves the only Lancaster over the city, and began our bombing run through an intense barrage of Flak. But Wray was dissatisfied with our approach. To impress on us the need for accuracy, he coolly circled back over Stuttgart and began a second run through the Flak.

To me those few minutes seemed interminable, but Wray set an example in the heat of action which no training school could hope to match. Bombs gone, we turned away with searchlights probing for us, and he gave me another invaluable lesson flinging "J' Jig around the sky in gut wrenching "corkscrew" evasive manoeuvres which would help defend us against searchlights and night fighters.

As we neared the coast of England after eight hours in the air, he said: "I'm a bit tired. You'd better take over now." In the Lancaster's cramped cockpit it was a real struggle for Arthur Wray, with his lame leg, to leave his seat. I realised for the first time that if we had been hit he would have been trapped with no hope of bailing out and admired all the more his courage in choosing to fly with a raw crew.

By the time we landed back at Waltham that night, I had decided that Air Commodore Wray was the most remarkable man I had ever known.

I was not alone. For so many of us who flew with Bomber Command in the Second World War, "Father Wray" was unforgettable. Repeatedly risking his own life to shepherd novice bomber crews half his age through their baptism of fire, he increased immeasurably our chances of returning from raids. Beyond doubt, I owed to him my own survival.

Born in 1896, Arthur Wray was the son of a pioneer missionary in Central Africa. Sent to school in England, he left in mid-term at 18 to join the army shortly after World War One broke out, and after passing out at Sandhurst, transferred to the Royal Flying Corps. In April

1917, with only two months' flying training and 30 hours' solo, he was posted to France.

There was no time for teaching new pilots the finer points of air fighting. Three days to learn to handle a Nieuport Scout and practice firing at a ground target, and Second Lieutenant Wray was flying over the lines. But luck was with him at the start. After his first combat he recorded laconically in his log book: "Eight Albatrosses engaged. Three of them crashed. Two of our own missing. Got one Hun down."

The average expectation of life for a flier in 1917 was less than three weeks. Arthur Wray had survived for exactly a month when on May 28 he dived to attack a German reconnaissance aircraft, he then felt what he later likened to a kick from a horse on his knee. A bullet had fractured his thigh and shot off the left knee-cap, which was found in his flying boot.

Surgeons gave him a choice. Either the knee joint could be repaired so that he would be able to walk relatively normally, but with a leg probably too stiff to pilot a 'plane - or without surgery it would retain a degree of flexibility that should make flying possible, but leave him lame for life. Wray chose to fly. Awarded the Military Cross for conspicuous gallantry, he endured a long convalescence and in April 1918 triumphantly noted "First flip for ten months. OK."

After the war he flew Bristol Fighters in India, earning the Distinguished Flying Cross for his exploits on punitive strikes against tribesmen raiding the camel caravans which came from Afghanistan through the Khyber Pass, then returned to England to become a bombing and gunnery specialist, and a star of the annual RAF Display at Hendon.

By the early thirties, Wray was commanding 407 Fleet

Fighter Flight, based at Lee-on-the-Solent, where his pilots, most at least ten years his junior, gave him the nick-name by which he became known throughout the RAF "Father".

Among them was Rodney Clarkson, who in 1933 died in a road accident. Wray flew up to his funeral at St. Paul's Walden in the Hertfordshire countryside, found the nearest airfield fogbound, and put his aircraft down in a tiny pasture near the church. After the service he met for the first time Rodney Clarkson's sister. Margaret; the following year they were married in the same church.

In 1935 Arthur Wray was given command of the crack 43 Squadron, its elegant Hawker Fury biplanes the first 200 mph fighters. Then, as an armaments expert, he moved to Fighter Command HQ and, after the outbreak of war in 1939, to bombing schools in Wales and Cumberland.

By 1941 he was station commander of RAF Hemswell in Lincolnshire, in charge of three Polish Squadrons. Station commanders were expected to fly a desk rather than a bomber; as a concession, they could seek permission from higher authority for one operational flight a month. But Wray, now 45 and walking with a stick, cared less for red tape than for his exiled young fliers. He knew they often went through a psychological crisis after their first few operations over Germany had shown them the grim odds, and carefully watched for signs. Before a raid on Bremen he noticed the edginess of one particular crew, and was not surprised when soon after takeoff their Wellington turned back.

The pilot blamed a faulty magneto, but when Wray checked the engines himself, he could find nothing wrong. Pausing only to collect his parachute, he recharged the crew's morale by flying them to the target and back.

It was one of many occasions when he earned from

headquarters a reprimand for failing to ask permission, and from the Poles their deep respect. They were devoted to a man twice their age who deliberately shared the hazards they faced, and at briefings managed to find a few words of fractured Polish to wish them God speed. Aircrew cheered him to the echo on the evening when he read them a fighting speech by Winston Churchill which he had translated phonetically into their own language.

"He was the finest kind of Englishman" remembers a Polish pilot. "Humane, straightforward, and very brave". As the London Gazette said when in April 1942 he won a Bar to his DFC after the Wellingtons attacked Essen, in the Ruhr: "His gallantry and exceptional leadership have set a most inspiring example". The Poles themselves recognised it by awarding him their highest honour, the Virtuti Militari.

In May 1943 Arthur Wray became an Air Commodore and commander of 12 Base, comprising Binbrook, Waltham and Kelstern. Now he was responsible for 80 Lancasters from his headquarters at Binbrook, the home of 460 Squadron Royal Australian Air Force

It was almost unheard of for a Base commander let alone one of his age to fly on operations. But Wray was soon off on his first mission with 460 Squadron, attacking Hamburg as part of a force of 740 bombers in one of the most devastating raids of the war. It brought him yet another decoration, the DSO, and a warm approval of the Australians.

By early 1944, when I arrived at Waltham, the RAF was losing about 265 heavy bombers a month, and nearly 2,000 men, with experienced crews the most vulnerable.

We were among the lucky ones, for during a raid on Stuttgart, Arthur Wray gave us the priceless gift of confidence, and throughout our time with 100 Squadron he kept a fatherly eye on us. For each of our next six operations, he drove over from Binbrook to stand by the runway and see us off. When we landed back at Waltham after our thirty-first raid, which marked the

end of our "tour" and a brief respite from the war, a beaming Air Commodore was waiting with a crate of beer in his car to join us for a celebration.

Soon afterwards, he and a friend who commanded a nearby station both decided they would go with their Squadrons on a major daylight raid. A few hours before take-off, Wray's permission to fly was cancelled. His friend was shot down. Word spread that Father Wray had been summoned to Bomber Command and read the riot act: "You know too much to risk being captured. NO MORE OPERATIONAL FLYING."

With the end of the war he was retired from the RAF at 50, and settled with his wife and three children at Pitney, in Somerset where he spent the next decade struggling to run a small farm. Eventually he gave up what had become a losing battle and turned to helping ex-servicemen through local branches of the Royal Air Forces Association and the Royal British Legion, earning the reputation of "always wanting to do something for somebody else."

The one thing he missed was flying. But there was no way an RAF pension could meet the cost of hiring powered aircraft. Then, in 1961, he discovered the Devon and Somerset Gliding Club, at Dunkeswell near Exeter.

At 65 he took off for the first time in 15 years, and became enchanted with silent flight. He had piloted everything from Sopwith Camels to Spitfires - but this, he said was the finest flying of all. He would come down in a state of incredulous wonder that he had actually been able to climb without an engine, using only sun powered thermals - "all for free!"

His bubbling enthusiasm had a great impact on the club and the young pilots he went out of his way to encourage. From the moment the hangar doors were rolled open he would be there in battered tweed hat and corduroys, sharing in the often strenuous work needed to get gliders launched - leaning heavily on his stick but refusing to admit that he couldn't do as much as others: "I'm as fit as anyone else!"

In 1964 he became one of the oldest pilots to earn the international "Silver C" badge, the mark of a qualified soaring pilot. It was a great achievement, but Wray soon found another challenge: the far more taxing "Gold C" and in particular its requirement for a 300 kilometre (186 mile) cross-country flight. Summer after summer he set out to cover the distance, but ran out of thermals and had to put down in a field, often limping miles in search of a telephone to call the club.

Then at last came that epic flight to Binbrook. It was a fitting climax to 40 years of flying. He bowed to medical advice, and sadly conceded that perhaps at 75 it was time to stop. But aviation had been Arthur Wray's life, and he would still hop into his car and chase a hot air balloon seen drifting over his garden, still make the long drive to the Farnborough International Air Show and watch with the critical eye of one who had once himself thrilled huge crowds.

When he died in April 1982 three generations of airmen remembered him with real affection. To those of us who were fortunate enough to fly with him, his indomitable spirit disproved the RAF adage: "There are old pilots, and bold pilots, but no old bold pilots." Father Wray was both.

ERIC THALE 1997

MR DAVID WATERS, 1942 – 1944

Authors Introduction:

I first made contact with Dave Waters in 1992 during my early efforts to contact ex RAF Millom personnel. Dave and I very quickly became good pals and quite aside from the huge amount of information and photographs he eagerly provided for my project, he introduced me to several of his old comrades who have also become dear friends over the years. My wife and I holidayed on more than one occasion with Dave, his wife Vera and their kind family, enjoying their company and Dave's infectious and mischievous sense of humour. On the occasion of the first RAF / Millom reunion, it was David who made the opening speech at my request, and he never forgave me for putting him on the spot! In the closing years of his long and fruitful life Dave did not enjoy the best of heath, but bore it all with a good humour and fortitude one could only hope to emulate. On the 15th of April 2003 following a brief stay in hospital, Dave passed away, and on the 24th of April took his revenge upon me. I was honoured to be asked by Dave's family to read a eulogy at his funeral service. As I stood very nervously in St Cuthbert's Church, Hull, and did so, I hoped that Dave, with his generous good nature would consider us quits! This is the story of David's flying career from its start to its violent though very fortunate conclusion.

The memoir of my flying with the RAF
1939 – 1945

I commenced flying with the RAF Volunteer Reserves in early 1939. However I must confess that I was a very ordinary average pilot. I was certainly no hero, but I did seem to have more than the average gift of luck.

I first decided that I would like to fly with the RAF in 1938 following Chamberlains visit to Germany to sign the so-called peace treaty with Adolph Hitler. We used to see a lot of the cinema news reels. As my father had been on the Somme in 1916, I must confess I was not very enthusiastic about joining the army. I did have some friends who had already started flying at Brough and they suggested I join them. I was 18 years old and working in the offices of J. Ranks Ltd. flour and provender millers in Clarence Street, Hull.

I applied to join the RAF at Newland House on the Beverley Road in Hull which was the RAFVR Town Centre. Following the interview I was rejected as a pilot as they said there were no vacancies but suggested I apply as a Navigator, I refused but was informed that if any pilot vacancies came up they would let me know.

Sometime later I was sent an application form requesting various information on my education, background and also asking for references. Later I was sent a railway warrant for me to attend a medical board and interview at RAF Hendon, North London. A few weeks after this test I was told to report to the Town Centre in Hull to be measured for my uniform and swear my allegiance, it was a good scheme as we joined as sergeants and got paid for attendance.

It was early in 1939 when I was told to report to Brough to start flying training. Most of this took place in the evenings and at weekends, quite apart from the two weeks summer camp which our employers were encouraged to allow.

There was quite a lot of theory which we did at the Town Centre every week and it was a treat to go to Brough to start flying in the Blackburn B2s. The advanced pupils were flying the Hawker Harts and Hinds. I remember so well the first evening 5th of May 1939 that I was told to report for my first flying lesson. It was a perfect early summers evening. I was introduced to my instructor F/Lt Allison who showed me over the biplane B2 L6892. He carefully explained what the different controls were for and how to fit and use a parachute. He then told me to hop in and sit beside him and after strapping in we taxied slowly across the field downwind looking at the wind sock. We then turned into wind after looking all round for other aircraft Allison opened the throttle and as the aircraft gathered speed I noticed the nose dip forwards and the tail lifted, we bounced along gathering speed and we were soon airborne.

We climbed to about 1000ft it was a wonderful sensation for me as I had never flown before. Allison then told me to take hold of the controls and feel how responsive they were. You push the control column forward and the nose dips, you pull it back and it rises. You push the rudder pedal to the left and it skids to the left. The same with the right foot, if you use the aileron which is also controlled by the column at the same time as the rudder, you bank instead of skidding. His advice was to treat an aeroplane as though you would a horse, which I always found good advice.

What a wonderful view an airman has as the River Humber looked like a silver ribbon and the fields no larger than pocket handkerchiefs.

On the first trip he took me over Swanland where I lived with my parents. The houses looked like dolls houses and the people so small. I could see my family waving. After about 25 minutes flying which I enjoyed so much we circled the airfield and came in to land.

My instructor told me to come for further lessons and on Sunday had a further three. By then I was doing approaches and landings, different turns and stalls with and without the use of engine and basic flying exercises.

The following weekend was taken up and shown how to spin and recover, I can't say I enjoyed that very much, but later realised how very important that exercise was. I had 16 lessons in the first three weeks and completed a total of 9hrs 50mins. By now I was doing circuits and landings and was taxiing round for another when my instructor undid his straps and said I was on my own. I was quite shattered at the time especially when I heard one of my friends from Ranks yell out "he's going solo get the fire engine and ambulance out". However I completed it thinking all the time my instructor was with me telling me what to do. I was quite pleased when I did a good three point landing and the instructor said everything went well.

It was a great summer for me in 1939 as my instruction improved and my solo trips got longer, flying to Bridlington Flamborough and over the Yorkshire Moors. I also flew over the West Riding area. I particularly enjoyed the map reading exercises. On one of these trips Sqd/Ldr Stockbridge told me to fly him to an old disused airfield called Sherburn-in Elmet I don't think it had been used since the First World War as it was then being farmed. We landed right behind a farmer and his team of horses. The Squadron Leader was meeting some officials from the Air Ministry who were surveying the site to ascertain whether to re-open it as an airfield.

I completed a full two weeks camp in August so increasing my flying hours on B2s to 56.

By the end of August 1939 things were looking

decidedly bleak with Germany and I found it quite a job to concentrate on my job at Ranks.On the third of September we listened to Chamberlain inform the Nation that we were now at war with Germany. On the following day all the VRs congregated at Newland House, in uniform wondering where we would be posted. This seemed to go on all day, day after day with nothing happening. After several weeks groups started to receive their postings mostly to Initial Training Wings, most of these being at seaside resorts on the south coast. My own posting came on the 30th October. We had to go by train to Bexhill-On-Sea in Sussex. One of our party missed the train, and chased us to Doncaster in a taxi, he joined the train when it stopped at Doncaster Station and told us that the taxi fare had cost him £5 which was a lot of money in those days as my own wages at Ranks was £1-17-6d per week and I had been with them almost four years!

When we arrived at Bexhill there were large numbers of Volunteer Reserves, Auxiliaries and members of the University Air Squadrons. Our group was billeted in the Sackville Hotel which had been stripped to the boards. We had trestle tables, bench seats and wooden chairs and were given three pall'iasses each. There were three or four men to each room, and the beds were as hard as boards. We had to be on parade at 6-30 am in vests and shorts and did PT. until you nearly dropped, a corporal took us and persistently shouted and bawled at us.

Breakfast was at Eight o'clock if you could eat it, and the COs parade at Nine o'clock. We often got bawled at on that especially when someone had shinned up the flag pole right over the Sackville Hotel and hung a jerry on it.

We had route marches often on the double and many a time doubled all the way to Hastings and back. We often met a large contingent of RAF Volunteer Reserves from No3 ITW Hastings, they had Len Harvey the heavy weight boxer as their instructor, so maybe we were lucky.

After an hour's dinner it was usually sand bag filling on the front and then lectures and occasionally instructive film shows. After the evening meal you did not feel like doing very much other than writing letters, listening to the radio and going to bed. We stayed there for just over four weeks before being informed we were being moved to an advanced flying unit. We had a farewell party and chucked most of the NCOs in the sea as we thought they needed cooling off a bit.

I and several other Hull pilots were posted to No 2 S.F.T.S. at Brize Norton in Oxford. We arrived there on the 3rd December. It was a relief to move into the sergeants' mess with its much improved food and accommodation. I remember that first night as they were flying North American Harvards, the prop noise from the aircraft was ear splitting and it went on all night.

I was told that I would be flying Harvards and those that did not fly single engine aircraft flew twin engine Oxfords. We had a lot of studying to do as we had to get our wings whilst there.

On the 12th December I was introduced to my instructor who gave me my first flight in a Harvard, it seemed a mass of instruments and controls compared with the B2 and I wondered if I would ever fly one. But soon found they were nice to fly and not noisy for the crew inside the cockpit. It did seem strange sitting on your own in front and your instructor was in the rear he communicated to you with phones.

I think what concerned me the most about these machines was the very strong smell of petrol, retracting the undercarriage and the apparent fast landing speed. We soon knew that we were doing advanced flying as we had to spin, do all types of acrobatics, flying blind with a hood on. Altitude tests and emergency landings with and without the engine. At the same time swat for the coming wings exam. You also had practical flying tests undertaken by very strict examiners. If you did not come up to their standard one was taken off flying. You also had to do two or three hours per week on the Link Trainer.

I went solo on the Harvards on the 8th of January after 8 hours dual. On the 23rd February I started night flying and did several circuits and landings with my instructor which was pretty scary as the flare path was very dim owing to the war time restrictions. On my second night trip we did three circuits and landings and then he got out and told me to do three on my own.

One of the pilots in the flight was called Stanley Lock, we saw a lot of each other as we were both billeted in the same block. He told me his family were farmers. He had a great sense of humour but was often getting into trouble by our instructor and was even threatened with being taken off flying, especially when he took the GPO telephone wires down with his undercarriage on the aerodrome perimeter when he came into land one day. In 1940 Stanley was flying in the Battle of Britain and was decorated several times, I understood he shot down about 20 enemy planes before he was shot down himself. He is on record as being one of the top scorers in that famous battle.

Early in March we sat for our wings examination. I was shattered when the results came through and discovered that I had failed on navigation. Several others had failed but they let us sit it again in a few weeks time. I got my wings on the 18th March, and had them stitched on my uniform in minutes. During the following two months we had very intense flying exercises both by day and night. These included drogue towing, gliding and night landings without a flare path using the aircraft lights only.

On the 8th May our flight was moved to a bombing and gunnery school at Penross in North Wales. When we arrived we were dismayed to find the pubs were shut on Sundays and even the local people did not approve of us flying on the Sabbath. I think they forgot to tell Hitler.

We did all types of gunnery and bombing exercises which included high level, dive bombing and low level on all different types of approach. I enjoyed these exercises as we used the 11 lb. smoke bombs and you could always see your accuracy. We stayed there for about ten days before returning to Brize Norton.

Soon after getting back I was moved to No 12 O.T.U. at RAF Benson to start operational training on Fairy Battles. This aircraft was a large single engine (Rolls Merlin) Bomber - Reconnaissance plane carrying the pilot and a Wop/Ag [Wireless operator air gunner], it proved a very unpopular machine in battle causing many casualties.

When we first arrived at Benson we were involved in trouble as the NCOs would not allow us in the sergeants mess, we had to eat in a hut some distance away, the food being sent to us from the sergeants mess. This was not on, as the meals were always cold. One day the duty officer received a plate of dinner when he asked if there were any complaints. The sender was immediately put on a charge so we all decided to go sick. As we were doing very intensive flying and there had already been one fatal accident the Medical Officer immediately grounded us all. All hell broke loose and soon the news reached the Air Ministry. We were all in the sergeant's mess that night!

We had to do a lot of very tight formation flying and very low level below tree top flying. The formations were so tight that often one touched the tail of the one your wing was in. I was trained to spray poison gas as I suppose they thought it may be used. We had special gas cylinders fitted and had all the protective clothing. We also had to go into the gas chambers with the different gases in. On these exercises there were sections on Salisbury Plains that we had to spray with different coloured dyes. On one of these trips some officials were watching us and when I did my run the valve stuck causing the spectators to get the full spray I was not very popular.

Almost at the end of this course I had an accident which put me in hospital and saved me from going to the pool in France and onto operations with the BEF. The Battles were now being used to strafe German troops as they crossed France and the casualties were horrendous.

I consider myself lucky as I was leading a formation of Battles at tree top height when suddenly there was a bang as a connecting rod smashed through the crankcase of the Rolls engine in my aircraft, allowing the hot Glycol to pour into the cockpit. I was smothered and did not remember anything as I lost consciousness and struck some trees and crashed. My gunner who fortunately was not hurt pulled me out and apparently ran with me as he thought the plane would catch fire. I was taken to the RAF hospital at Halton and was still there during the evacuation of Dunkirk.

While I was in this hospital I saw the true horrors of war as many very badly injured crews were coming in from France. One pilot had all of his limbs off. They had a type of basket pram and you could see young wives pushing their husbands round the grounds, most of them had no legs and the burns were dreadful.

When I was discharged I returned to Benson for a short while and then posted to Abingdon No 10 OTU for a short conversion on Whitley bombers. I moved there with another pilot from Hull called Walter Ward. We were first given tuition in an Avro Anson as we had not previously flown twin engine machines. We both spent the most part of a day doing circuits and landings and general flying.

The following day I was taken up in a Whitley, it seemed enormous compared to the types I had flown. I had five trips that day with different pilots and the following day went solo. After flying for some time I landed and was told to take it to the

Dispersal point. As I was being marshalled through a narrow space I followed instructions to swing round and the tail plane knocked down a post and damaged an elevator I was not blamed for this mishap.

We stayed at Abingdon for five weeks and did a lot of flying on types which included the later Whitley 5s fitted with Rolls Merlin engines. On the 8th of August Sgt Ward and myself were posted to 77 Squadron at Driffield. The Whitleys for squadron were operated and dispersed at Cottom and Cowlam. This did not seem a very large field for Whitleys particularly when they were fully laden as it was in a hollow and quite narrow. There was a wood at one end, however we were shortly to appreciate keeping our bombers there. The Whitleys based at Driffield apart from our own being serviced, belonged to 102 Squadron.

I mostly did local flying for the first couple of weeks getting familiar with the Whitleys and local geography.

On the 15th August at about 1.30pm I was in the sergeants mess with Walter Ward, we were listening to the radio having just had our lunch, when the air raid sirens went which we both ignored as we had been informed there would be a rehearsal after lunch. Almost immediately there was a deafening row outside. We both jumped up realising it was the real thing and rushed to the entrance. It was a squadron of JU88s they were bombing and machine gunning anyone in sight. We ran out looking for a shelter, someone yelled to us to get down which we did just as a 750 kilo bomb dropped in front of us. When we got up there was a huge crater in the place we would have been had we kept running. We were told afterwards that we escaped as we were so close and the blast went over our heads. Unfortunately a young girl WAAF who was in front of us appeared to lose her shoe and as she bent down was killed.

We eventually dived into a shelter and the next one to us received a direct hit. The damage done was extensive as 102 squadron lost 10 Whitleys, there were about 16 killed and the drome was badly damaged. The Duke of Gloucester visited us that evening just as our CO was having roll call. These JU88 bombers were from a Dutch base they were KG30 Aldler Geschwader latest aircraft.

We were told that Spitfires from 616 squadron and Hurricanes from 73 squadron had intercepted the JU88s and shot seven down and that three had crash landed.

Two or three nights later a lone German plane came over and destroyed our last hanger and hit the sergeant's mess which had survived the day raid. A bomb fell on the car park, and damaged many cars and a motorcycle I had bought new just before the war. At the time I was in my bunk fast asleep when the first bomb dropped and my windows were blown out. I cut my feet when I jumped out of bed. I managed to get to a shelter with some more staff it was pitch black and we could hear the German plane who appeared to be doing some very accurate bombing. We could also hear a constant ticking which was nerve racking as we all assumed it was a time bomb. We dare not get out of the shelter until someone came and told us it was all clear. The ticking was caused by the windscreen wipers that had started on the damaged cars. The bombing on this raid was so accurate on such a dark night that our CO suspected a fifth column member was possibly signalling near the airfield and he informed the guard to shoot any light on sight.

Fortunately none of our aircraft had been damaged at Cottam. Shortly after these raids the two squadrons were evacuated to Linton-On-Ouse, 77 squadron was dispersed to a field at Tolthorpe.

I did my first bombing raid on the 13th September 1940, and a further five before the

month end. One of these was a raid to Berlin and as we were taxiing out to take off the main wheels sank into the soft ground and could not move. It was pouring with rain Tolthorpe was waterlogged. We tried to get out with our engines and all the time we sank further down. The control tower told us to switch off and they would send a tractor.

While we were waiting outside the aircraft a Whitley from Linton crashed taking off and exploded as it was fully laden. Our crew had climbed out waiting for the assistance apart from the rear gunner who did not know what was happening. He truly thought we were airborne and when the engines stopped and the machine from Linton blew up near us, he called us on the intercom and got no reply as we were not in and so he thought we had abandoned the aircraft and left him. We saw the turret rotate and the two doors open and he bailed out straight into the mud covered in his parachute. We saw the funny side of it later but I don't think he did.

Eventually tractors pulled us out but as we were too late for Berlin we were told to bomb a secondary target. We flew over a German airfield in Holland who were night flying they must have thought we were one of their machines as they gave us a green to land as we made our very low approach F/Lt Burbridge (who was the captain) told me to go down in the bomb bay. I dropped everything we had and the explosion nearly brought us to grief. The aerodrome lights were quickly extinguished and as the guns opened up we flew straight back to base.

For our trips to Italy from Linton we had to fly south

to Newmarket racecourse to bomb up and refuel for the long journey. The Italians were very surprised as they did not think that we could reach them, in fact on the first raids they had no black outs everything was lit up for us what a shock they must have had. On one of these Italian raids we were caught by search lights over northern France. The guns opened up and soon got the range, we were badly hit and caught fire when a shell burst right by the port engine. We managed to get it out with internal nacelle extinguishers. We were lucky to get out of range but with only one engine functioning we had to jettison our bombs, and everything that was loose in order to maintain height. We turned back for home expecting we might have to ditch in the sea as our height was now falling. However we just managed to reach the Kent coast and forced landed near Manston.

Whilst we were at Linton-on-Ouse The Battle of Britain started in earnest and Bomber Command were involved in an intensive campaign of bombing the Channel ports as the Germans had been massing a concentration of invasion barges and many squadrons made many return visits. We were assisted with the Home Fleet and approaching these ports was a sight to see as the big guns of the fleet opened up, and the fires on these docks inflicted by the combined forces.

We had good luck signals flashed to us from the cruisers as we made our run in to the targets. Sadly my great friend Walter Ward was reported missing on a raid over Germany I was very concerned as I knew he had suffered severe shell shock from the bombing incident at Driffield. I had the awful job of informing his wife who I also knew very well. Pre-war Walter was employed by the Distillery Co Saltend.

In the October of 1940 our two squadrons moved to the new airfield of Topcliffe near Thirsk. Whilst at

Topcliffe the squadron started to receive the large four engine Sterling bombers. However I was not one of those converted to fly them.

In late December I was posted to the testing and experimental unit at Boscombe Down in Wiltshire with a few other crews. We were attached to the Bomber Development Unit which was being formed by the request of the Prime Minister Churchill. We flew Wellington bombers and the long and short nosed Blenheims. We flew in the most atrocious weather and flying conditions. Our flight commander was Squadron Leader Tomlin. He was known for his lucky escape whilst flying Whitleys with the B.E.F. in France. He made a forced landing and when he saw German troops running towards them realised he was on the wrong side of the lines and made a very rapid exit.

Whilst I was at Boscombe I was told to fly into London to pick up one of our bomber crews who had bailed out over the city and were at Hendon. I took a Blenheim and was given a route down a narrow corridor to Hendon by the London defence as the balloons were all up.

I landed at the drome all right and when the crew got in we were like sardines. My take off into wind was towards a hill and houses. By the time I got half way across the field I could not get the tail up owing to the excess weight, by then it was too dangerous to abort the take off, so I broke through the wire barriers on the throttles to get an extra 9 lbs boost to the engines. We took off like a rocket but I had no other choice. This extra thrust is only permitted in an emergency as the engines have to be stripped or changed after such stress. We arrived back safely and there was no problem with the landing.

I stayed at Boscombe Down until late January when I was posted to No. 11 O.T.U. Bassingbourne in Cambridge to fly Avro Ansons. This job entailed flying both wireless operators and navigators on navigational exercises.

On one of these trips I was flying on an exercise that passed quite close to London. It was a night trip and the weather was very poor, drizzling with rain making visibility bad. Unfortunately we just crossed the London defence and I was surprised when searchlights caught me and the guns opened up. We were hit with shrapnel but not badly I managed to break away and return to base. I took a very dim view the following night much to the amusement of the crews present when we listened to the news on the radio and the newscaster informed the nation that one enemy aircraft had approached London from the North and was driven off with gunfire.

One night I was on the circuit of the airfield at Bassingbourne waiting for permission to come in to land when I noticed that a plane landing in front of me was doing an unusual type of approach. Although it was very dark I could see he was going to miss the runway, and when he did land he appeared to cross over it. I thought there must be something wrong as that would damage his undercarriage.

I landed just after him and on taxiing to the dispersal I tried to find out why he had done that. At the time there was quite a commotion round the plane and I was surprised to be told it was a JU88 that had been apparently bombing London and the pilot was trying to make out that he thought he had landed in France and wanted refuelling. I thought that seemed a likely story the crew offered no resistance and it was quite a good prize for us as he had only damaged one of the compression legs.

I was curious to examine one of these German bombers and climbed in to have a look around, but I think the crew must have been very sick at both ends from the putrid smell so I did not bother, possibly one of our fighters had been after them.

I was in London soon after one of the heavy bombing raids, the poor Londoners were getting bombed so consistently. I was in my little sports car with a couple of other pilots from Bassingbourne. The buildings still on fire were terrible to see it looked as though the whole city was ablaze, there was rubble all over. We drove right through the West End to Ealing, we appreciated the super fire and rescue services we had.

I did have an amusing incident during one of these raids which I thought was funny but possibly no one else did. I had a date with a nurse and we had been to a show and she had to get back to her hospital in Harrow. The sirens blew and a raid had started so I went to Paddington Station with her and told her I would travel with her to Harrow and see her safely to the Nurses Home before returning to my unit. We caught the dimly lit train and opposite us was one other passenger, a middle aged crabby man. The train seemed to move in fits and starts due to the heavy bombing raid. After we had travelled for about half an hour the train stopped and the man opposite opened the carriage door and said this was his station and suddenly vanished, it was quite a fall to the track as I helped him back in he was swearing and cursing the railway company for switching platforms. He opened the opposite side door and stepped out again and vanished. Again I helped him back, fortunately he was not hurt but I saw the funny side of it and couldn't stop laughing, much to the embarrassment of my companion. We eventually got to his station and Harrow and I returned to my unit.

One thing that comes to my mind is that whenever we had occasion to use any form of public transport in most of the cities, particularly in London, and many of the shows during this time of the war, it was very difficult to pay for these services. We were whisked into shows, and conductors on the transports nearly always missed us even the taxis did not charge.

Coming up to Hull from the South I often came so far in my car and thumbed the rest owing to petrol rationing. The heavy transport drivers used to take us in their cafes for a meal and many a time I had 10 Gallon coupons given to me. What a wonderful Nation of people we had in Britain during those dark days of wartime.

Early in March 1941 I was transferred to No 18 0.T.U. Bramcote, a Polish Air Crew unit. Several RAF crews were sent there to assist them in getting the Poles to know our way of flying, getting acquainted with this country and using the equipment. Most of these men could not speak a word of English when we arrived at this unit which made life quite difficult. My job was to fly these crews on all types of exercises both during night and daylight hours. We flew Anson aircraft and put many flying hours in.

These Poles were very anxious to join a squadron (many went to Lyndholme near Bawtry) and told us of their terrible experiences when the Germans and Russians invaded their country they certainly wanted to settle the score.

When I was there I was a duty pilot (airfield control pilot) on the night Coventry got its second very heavy raid. My duty was to control the movement of aircraft by Aldis signal lamp and to lay the goose neck flare path for landing and taking off. On this particular night we had a squadron of Hurricane fighters using the drome for refuelling and rearming, they were coming in and going out all night long. Coventry which was quite close to the drome was being very heavily bombed. I was anxious that the Germans should not see my flare path and bomb the airfield. Several Poles went out looking for Germans who may have been shot down, the consequences if they found any was quite obvious.

On the 4th October after lunch I had taken off with a full crew for a long exercise I climbed to about 2000ft and was turning towards the drome from Coventry direction when there was a splintering crash and the plane became violently unstable. I struggled with the controls to try and get it on an even keel and thought that I had struck a balloon over Coventry. The aircraft was pitching so violently that all the crew except one decided to bale out. I automatically switched both engines off and turned the petrol tanks off. I could not and dare not try to bank as the aircraft was so unstable. I gradually lost height and by keeping the machine on a dead straight course I managed to belly land in a field of cows. I could not get out of the door as it had been jammed by one of the crews intercom cords as he jumped out, so I went through the emergency exit in the roof. The other member of the crew was lying on the floor gripping one of the spars which I could not persuade him to release.

When I climbed out I was amazed and shocked to see that half the tail plane and one elevator had disappeared. I went over to a nearby farm and asked the farmer's wife if I could notify my base and inform them of what had happened.

When I got through they told me they had seen what had happened and that an ambulance was on its way to collect me. They told me that another diving Anson apparently could not avoid me and had struck my tail plane, unfortunately this aircraft was badly damaged and could not recover from the dive, the crew were killed. The pilot of that machine was a very close friend, I was absolutely shattered.

My own crew were all picked up OK but very shocked. The doctor got one of the crew from my plane in a very bad state of shock. None of the farmer's cows were touched but I must have frightened them. This was a very tragic experience and a lesson for me. The RAF would have taken a very dim view had they known that I had flown without a parachute. I would have probably been reprimanded but fortunately a friend placed a spare one in the ambulance, and when I got out in front of the senior officers I was carrying it. I must admit I never flew without one again.

I think most of us went through a phase that it won't happen to me and when it does it gives you a jolt. I had to fly almost immediately after this accident to regain my confidence, and then I was sent on a short leave until the inquest.

My next move was to No2 O.A.F.U. at Millom on the West Cumbrian Coast. When I first arrived I was quite taken aback with the Black Combe a 2000ft mountain almost on the circuit. The airfield went right up to the sand dunes on the shore which was mined. We had an Alsatian mascot called Danny and soon after I arrived on the unit he became over exuberant and ran into the minefield, and that was the end of poor Danny

My wireless operator F/Sgt Archie Lang came with me from Bramcote to Millom and we soon got down to a lot of flying. We had a large intake of Canadian navigators who had not sufficient night exercises so night flying was a priority. We did long trips across the Irish Sea to certain turning points from up the Cumberland Coast to the Western Isles, over to Ireland, back to the Isle of Man. Chicken Rock and the Point of Aire were familiar turning Points then down to Wales and the Bristol Channel and return. We also did trips into the Atlantic from Southern Ireland and from the Western Isles. I used to think these long sea trips were most rewarding as they kept the navigators busy all the time. We did many exercises across the British Isles as well and on moonlight nights could do a certain amount of map reading, but we predominately did the sea trips. I often saw the Queens leaving Liverpool for the United States, they were lone voyagers.

Occasionally we flew over convoys assembling for the Atlantic crossing. In the winter when the seas were rough as they pitched into the rollers you could see their screws threshing. They were very brave men as the U boat packs were causing havoc at this time. I was very glad to be in the air.

I was flying over the Irish Sea on an exercise one afternoon in an Anson when the starboard engine started to run very hot, followed by a large drop in oil pressure. As it was running very rough I switched it off and feathered the propeller. I had a full crew and was having difficulty maintaining height on the one engine. I decided to make for the nearest airfield, a Fleet Air Arm unit at Campbletown on the Mull of Kintyre. I landed in the early evening and the engineer examined it and informed me that it would require an engine change, I contacted Millom and asked if we could be collected. But it was too late so we had to stay the night. It was a depressing place compared to our own unit and we were all pleased to see an Anson landing just after lunch the next day that had come to collect us.

Some weeks later we had a signal from Campbletown to inform us the aircraft was ready for collection. I was informed that as I had put it there I could collect it, so I was duly flown to Campbletown. I decided to stay for lunch and then fly back. The Naval pilots were doing arrest landings in Seafires, I assumed they were using on the carriers.

I went to the hanger to collect the aircraft and started the engines, but on trying the starboard engine I realised they had changed the wrong engine. When I rang my base for another collection their comments were unprintable. I never saw that aircraft again and as far as I know it could still be there.

One night I was in the flight office with Frank Tizard, he was the only other pilot from Hull, we were getting ready for a long night exercise. Frank incidentally was a member of the regular Air Force and he also flew in a Whitley squadron in France. On this night he told me he felt dog tired. I told him to get off before me so that he would be back first. It was a pitch black night when I taxied out behind him. He took off and I followed. I completed the trip and when I landed I was asked if I had heard anything from Frank as they had not made any radio contact with base. I was worried particularly when I was told an aircraft had struck a flare on takeoff and did not really think that was such a hazard as the goose necks were not very big. I decided to have my machine refuelled and said I would go over the course again as it was now daylight Archie Lang said he would come with me. We did a comprehensive search over the whole course but did not see any sign of them. We returned to base very despondent and tired out. It was some weeks before we knew what had happened.

One day during a very low tide a crew saw some wreckage of a plane about half a mile out to sea from the airfield, and we found it was Frank Tizard's Anson they must have struck the gooseneck and dived into the sea.

I was sent on two or three interesting courses whilst I was at Millom, the first one was to Banbury to Armstrongs the makers of the Cheetah engines.

I soon found out the weather can get very rough over the Lake District, and noticed that this was more prevalent in the late winter and early spring. On one night exercise in April 1943 we were flying on a Northerly course of the Cumbria coast, the weather was very rough with very heavy showers and a gale force wind blowing, When we saw a fairly large water spout a mile or so off

271

St. Bees Head. I was very surprised as I did not expect them to appear as far north as this. Shortly after seeing this we turned due east over the Lakes to the Cumbrian Mountains our height about 4000ft when suddenly the aircraft started to fall like a stone we lost about 1000ft. I knew I was in a thermal current and was helpless, when we hit the bottom the crew were flung across the cabin. The battery was ripped out and also the radio and all the Navigators equipment went flying. We then started to rise and went up to 4500ft as though in a lift and being flung out at the top it was quite a sensation. I returned to base as I was worried that it could have done some structural damage to the aircraft. I had often caught thermals before but never one as fierce as that.

We had to fly in very bad weather and heavy snow storms did not stop us. If the runways were blocked with snow, lots of the aerodrome staff were given shovels to assist the snow ploughs, it was always a big operation but we had to fly.

During 1942-3 we were encouraged to eat large amounts of carrots as we were told this would improve our night vision. I think it was quite a national practice. I don't know who thought that one up and if anyone benefited, it certainly didn't help me. One day I was in the mess just after lunch. It was drizzling with rain and the clouds were down to the ground, when a Flying Fortress flew very low overhead. It was one being flown in from the United States. It flew into the fells just near the drome and blew up. What a tragic end for those men after such a long trip.

Several times when I had my leave I used to bring one or two of my colleagues from the Dominions home with me to Swanland. They were usually Australian, Canadian and New Zealand pilots. My parents enjoyed their company and we used to have terrific parties my sister organised. Her husband was also a pilot he had been instructing in Canada and at this time was flying Catalinas from Gibraltar. He was later converted to Short Sunderlands and went out to the Far East.

While we were at Millom one of these Australian friends, who used to come home with me, had a remarkable escape with his crew. His name was F/0 Arthur Watson, they were on a night exercise over Scotland when the aircraft came to a halt. He told us it was not violent and nobody was thrown about or injured in any way. When it stopped everything was deathly quiet but no one dare move as the aircraft rocked and it was pitch black and in the clouds.

Apparently they had struck the top of a mountain that was dead flat at its summit. It had ripped both propellers off and scraped along the belly of the aircraft and come to rest at the end of the plateau. If they had been a few feet higher they would have missed but if lower would have been killed. When they could see where they were they were petrified and were brought down by a mountain rescue team.

My flight commander managed to get hold of an army DUKW and had a Cheetah aero engine fitted on it with the prop in a wire cage facing forward and we used to take it on the beach and go in the sea, it was all good fun but we had designed it for the purpose of Air-Sea-Rescue in case any other aircraft were ditched in the sea, but I don't know if it was ever used for that task.

The sea by the airfield was a bit dicey as I learnt to my peril. One evening I decided to go for a swim and had been in the water for about ten minutes when I got caught in a current from the Duddon estuary. I was swept out to sea like a cork. I remember being taught not to panic when in difficulty but I could see the coast diminishing in size at an alarming rate and I must admit I panicked and went under. Very fortunately for me someone saw me from a boat and got me out just as I was on my last legs.

I never went in again unless there were several others in and never out of my depth.

I flew on several searches for aircraft that had been reported missing mostly these had flown into the Lakeland and Scottish mountains. Another notorious black spot was Snaefell on the Isle of Man. I was sent on an air sea rescue course and later went on a blind approach course using radio beams. I flew Oxfords on these exercises. We had to land completely hooded. Previously I had done what was called the Lorenze beam course when I was at Boscombe Down, which was one of the first blind approaches used in this country.

Most of the large airfields had a unit test pilot and as the one we had at Millom was leaving I was offered his job. It meant that I would leave the flights and was attached to the engineering department under the chief technical officer. I took this job as we had a flight of Westland

Lysanders and had the yearning for single engine aircraft again. I also flew the commanding officers Magister. I had flown about 2000 hours when I was offered the job.

As the unit test pilot I was able to take many of the personnel for flights. I remember a young WAAF asking me if I would take her up as she had never flown. I told her to draw a parachute and I would take her for a flight in a Lysander. I told her which one to go to and went to sign the form 700 which had to be completed before every flight. Whilst I was away she tried to climb into the cockpit with the assistance of the ground crew and slipped, she had a ring on her finger and it took her finger right off. After that I made a ruling that I would not take anyone up if they wore rings.

One afternoon I took an Anson on an engine and airframe test after a major service, and it was perfect. I passed it on to the flights and a crew took it on a navigational exercise. Within 20 minutes it blew up killing all the crew right over the town of Whitehaven. As it was suspected that the fabric had split all the Anson aircraft were grounded for inspection. I took another on test and while I was doing the airframe test an engine cowling blew off and cut a big hole in the wing. I saw the fabric tearing and decided to belly land on the drome as it took so long to wind the wheels down. I landed it all right without doing very much damage.

I was fortunate that I got on very well with my commanding officer. He offered me promotion and asked me if I would like the job of personal pilot to the group Air Vice Marshal but I was not keen. He then told me that the Central Gunnery School at Catfoss wanted a unit test pilot and as it was so near home and they were flying Spitfires, Beaufighters, Mosquitoes, Masters, Martinettes and Wellingtons and also Percival Proctors. I thought it would be good experience for me. He put my name for the job and I got it.

I came over to Catfoss on the 5th May 1944 and then my troubles started. When I first arrived I was not well received as they were all fighter pilots including the CO, and I was a rank outsider. When I went into Brandesburton Hall which was the officers mess I was hung on the harness pegs in the main hall by the back of my pants and had pints of beer chucked over me. I had my ties cut off at the knot, and my footprints were put on the ceiling whilst my feet were still in my shoes. They certainly gave me some stick but I could take it.

Most of these escapades I took in good spirit and then got on with my job. My senior officer was Wing Commander Scholey and he gave me my own office and staff.

I very soon took to the Spitfire and was expected to fly in weather that no one else would fly in and often did the early morning weather test in shocking weather to find the cloud ceiling and wind conditions. It was a very gradual process but I slowly gained the confidence expected of me. I think of all the types of war plane I'd flown the Spitfire was the perfect gem, it was easy to fly and had no vices. I flew the very early models to the Mark XVI with the Rolls Griffon engine.

When I was incorporating the airframe test I did what was called an Ailoron Upfloat test which meant flying at a minimum speed of 400 mph and measure the amount of lift on the ailorons at these speeds. There was a scale mark on the side which you could see from the cockpit. After finishing this manoeuvre it was almost second nature to fly into an upward roll. I can only remember two anxious moments in Spitfires. One was when a tyre burst, and the other was in an early model when the undercarriage got stuck when lowering it for landing. It was suggested I take it up to a suitable height and then turn it over on its back and whilst you are hanging upside down supported only by your straps then use the lever. The weight of the undercarriage was taken off the locks and you could then release the locks. It was quite tricky but it worked but while being in this inverted position some spanners hit the hood, they must have been left in the well by the riggers.

One day I was taking a Master up for a test with a fitter as passenger. We were waiting just by the intersection of the runways for a Mustang to land, I was watching him coming in and when he touched down he bounced and swung towards me. As an aeroplane is not quickly responsive to the throttle I yelled to my passenger to get out. I undid my straps and leapt out of the cockpit complete with parachute and ran like hell! (in the control tower they said they had never seen a pilot in full gear run so fast), and reckoned I did a four minute mile. I looked round just as the Mustang hit my machine they were both completely wrecked. The fitter was still getting out when he was flung clear.

Fortunately neither my fitter nor the other pilot was hurt but the pilot was court marshalled for wrecking a United States fighter and our own Master as he apparently had no business to be flying the Mustang and had asked an American pilot if he could have a go.

One afternoon I was the only one flying due to runway repairs when a high ranking army officer came into the camp with his staff and asked if they could be taken to Manby. He was told by the Station Commander that as I was the only one flying they could ask me if I would take them during one of my tests.

Unfortunately he had a staff officer who was not very polite in his request and gave me a lot of advice that I did not need or take kindly to.

However as I was testing a Wellington I agreed to take them. I landed them at Manby and the Captain had another go at me telling me exactly what time I was to return. I explained that I had several machines to test and would collect them as soon as I could. This did not appear to suit the Captain and I started to get annoyed.

I collected them as promised the Colonel sat beside me and his staff went into the back. I then took off and flew over the mouth of the Humber telling the Colonel I was going to complete an airframe test. I put the Wellington in every manoeuvre I could and was astonished to see how my passenger enjoyed it especially when he saw that his staff were sick.

When I landed the Captain reported me to my CO who laughed especially when the Colonel said he had enjoyed it and explained that I had a job to do.

A few days later we had the most awesome thing over Catfoss. The runways were still under repair and a

Wellington (not one of ours) circled very low over the field with smoke pouring out of an engine. It caught fire and very soon was a mass of flames, it turned and flew right over the hanger. It was terrible to see as there was nothing we could do to help them and they were much too low to jump out. It crashed on the perimeter and exploded. It made me feel sick there were five crew in it, and they just didn't have a hope of survival.

I had a close escape in a Wellington one day when I wasn't even airbourne. I had the chocks in front of the wheels and was running the engines up for a pre-flight test check, and had the starboard engine on full throttle when there was bang and the revs suddenly dropped. I looked at the engine and noticed that the main propellor shaft was white hot so I immediately throttled back and switched the engine off. I got up and told my crew that there, was a fault and they were looking very pale as I was amazed to see inches behind me where I was sitting in the cockpit. The fuselage was cut almost in half. Apparently a Martinet that had been towing a drogue must have had some winch trouble, as it fell on the Wellington and the hawser wrapped round the shaft and did so much damage. The comprehensive training I had on the Lorenze Beam at Boscombe Down, the course I did at the blind approach school at RAF Station Watchfield. In addition to all the time I put in on the Link trainer (mostly under the tuition of the well known Austrian glider pilot Mr R. Kromfeld). All this training was certainly to my advantage. Also in conjunction with this training, and the appalling weather conditions we flew in at Boscombe and the navigational exercises at Millom, must have given me a lot of confidence under severe stress.

On the 7th January we had a signal to take 10 Spitfires down to a place near Birmingham where we had to land in a field which was quite long but narrow. A Wellington would return us to Catfoss. All the pilots were volunteers on this job as it had to be done late in the afternoon.

When we set off the weather was pouring with rain making visibility very poor indeed. I soon ran into some very violent storms with the rain pelting down, I estimated a course and had to fly blind most of the journey. Occasionally I could see ground and was able to pinpoint my position. When I arrived near Birmingham the weather improved and I soon found the field and landed. There were some officials waiting to receive us who told me I was the first to arrive. I waited for about half an hour and as no one else arrived I rung through to Catfoss to be told that some had returned to base and the others had landed at other dromes, I was the only one to get through but they expected the Wellington which was coming from the South would pick me up. It eventually arrived and the pilot was surprised that I was his only passenger.

We took off and soon ran into the weather that had caused all the trouble. I was sitting with the navigator and as we approached the Humber the aircraft appeared to be flying at a dangerous angle so I went to the pilot who said he suspected his giros were faulty which was affecting the turn and bank instrument. I did not believe this and as I considered that he was flying by the seat of his pants which can be very dangerous. I asked him if I could take over which he willingly agreed. I soon got the plane stable and flew low over the Humber after breaking cloud and landed at Catfoss. We were both well aware that I was not supposed to do this and could have got myself into trouble, but to hell with protocol it was my neck.

This same Pilot did a very stupid thing later on when he tried to slow roll a Wellington (I believe he had been drinking) which could have easily killed himself. Before attempting this manoeuvre he was seen and did considerable damage to the machine.

He was court martialled and put under arrest and I was one of the officers detailed to escort him until his court martial. He was discharged from the service.

I was involved in a couple of Court Martials. In the second one I was asked to defend a pilot who had struck the sea and damaged the aircraft. His charge being endangering his crew and wilfully damaging one of his Majesty's aircraft. He was an NCO and lost his rank and got 90 days in the glasshouse. I don't know why they asked me to defend them as I was hopeless when it came to arguing with a Kings Counsellor who always did the prosecutions.

On the 10th of June W/Cdr Scholey who was the chief technical officer asked me if I would fly him to Llandwrog with two of his staff where they would be staying overnight. I would not take any flying crew as he wanted me to stay with them. They were engineering officers and the W/C was my boss.

I decided to take a Wellington as we had one ready for a routine test. The weather on the day was shocking it was very dull with drizzle and the cloud was down to about 200ft. I was a bit concerned as I had no radio operator I took off and soon was in the thick cloud with driving rain. I decided to climb to 3500ft and steer a course for Blackpool. We had flown for about 4-5 minutes and the weather was getting worse all the time the rain was heavier and I could see static glows round the two props it was also much darker. I flew a bit longer hoping to be over the Irish Sea so I could descend and break cloud as I was not sure where I was.

I knew if I was a bit off course to my port side I could be near Welsh hills and on my starboard was the Lake District and if I flew too long could reach the Isle of

Man. I must admit I was getting in a sweat as none of my passengers could assist me, I had seen so many aircraft that had flown into the mountains which made me feel a lot worse. I flew on for a little longer and then decided to reduce height, visibility being absolutely nil. I came down to 3000ft then 2000ft, then 1000ft and still could see nothing. I was getting very worried and only hoped I was over the sea. I reduced height to 800ft 600 and still nothing, I put the nose down and at 400ft I at last broke cloud and I was bang over the centre of Liverpool, it must have been a shock for the people in the city as I came right down to just above the buildings. Fortunately for me as the weather was so bad the balloon barrage was hauled down. We flew straight towards the bay along the coastline to Rhyle, Colwyn Bay flying at about 50ft then to Llandudno and down the Menai Straight. It was still pouring with rain when I landed at Llandrwrog. When I got out I felt like kissing the ground, but my W/Cdr took me for a welcome drink. I did tell him, if the weather did not improve I was all for going back by train.

Sometime after this trip I was having a meal in the mess and someone said they fancied kippers and I thought what a good idea! In fact we all agreed that Manx kippers were the best so I rounded up a few volunteers and took a Wellington and flew to Jurby in the Isle of Man and we got a van to fill up with crates at Peel, and had them loaded on the Wellington and we came back to Catfoss.

The CO would not have been very pleased if he had known about this, and when I was asked when the Kipper Kite was next going for further collection, I had to shut them up.

In mid 1945 we were using mostly Spitfire IX which I had been collecting from Brize Norton and also Cosford. These were now Maintenance Units and were our collecting points for replacement aircraft.

On the 4th of July I was asked if I would go to Cosford and bring back to the gunnery school one of the latest Mk XVI Spitfires with the Griffon engine. It was a delight to fly although when I took off the pitot head cover was still on (which was my own fault) and consequently I had no air speed indication, but who cared it handled as expected like a dream. I enjoyed my 40 minutes including the acrobatics as I flew over Catfoss on my return. The Commanding officer was in the control tower when I came in with several pilots who I am sure were waiting to have a go. I don't think I disappointed them.

We had one pilot at Catfoss that used to handle Spitfires in a way that was quite remarkable, and did many things that I was not prepared to try. One of these was to retract the undercarriage as soon as airbourne, hold the nose down to gather speed then go into a slow roll at the end of the runway, it was most impressive to witness and he did it often. I personally preferred more height.

My wing commander told me later that this same pilot had done the same manoeuvre in a Typhoon and it went wrong and was killed instantly I think it proved you cannot take liberties like that and always get away with it.

I was now flying the Mosquito being one of the fastest approach aircraft for landing I had flown as you came over the perimeter at about 140 mph but one soon got used to it. I also liked flying the Beaufighter you had a very good panorama from the pilot's position right up in front. The two Bristol engines were very powerful and it was important you set all your trimmers correctly before take off, otherwise it was difficult to hold. I was told if an engine cut on take off with full power it was virtually impossible to hold.

I was sent to the Rolls factory in Derby for a handling and engine course. It was very instructive and they showed us the big improvements in the Rolls Aero engines that had been developed due to the war. There were several of the Imperial airways pilots on this course.

On two or three occasions in August I was asked to take certain Spitfires down to Portsmouth that were being taken out of service and had to be broken up. They always seemed to fly beautifully on this their last journey. One day I think an error must have been made I was told to take one down and as it was almost new I queried it but was told to take it.

I took off and circled Catfoss and set my watch and opened it up to almost full throttle and steered for Portsmouth. I arrived in just over 35 minutes which wasn't bad for over 40 years ago. I used to wait for a Wellington to pick me up and bring me back to Catfoss.

One evening during mid Summer a message came to Catfoss that a high ranking WAAF Officer who was in Scarborough wanted to get down to Reading and could we fly her I was asked to do this and as the only plane available was a Martinet. She came to the camp with all her entourage and I wondered how on earth she was going to get in the back of a Martinet which was quite a climb. There were many helpers and the senior staff had come to see her off. She donned her parachute and helmet and was helped in.

It was a glorious evening and I decided not to fly above 1000ft so she could enjoy the scenery on route. I had a mirror and could see the rear passenger and noticed she did not open her eyes during the whole trip. When I landed at Reading there was a deputation waiting for her and I asked if she had enjoyed the trip and she said it was super (I wonder if it was her first trip) I was invited to stay for a meal but declined as I wanted to get back to Hull.

Later that summer I had arranged to go on a couple of week's holiday to Bude in Cornwall with a nursing sister whom I had known for some years. She had been twice engaged to pilots I had known and both had been killed.

When I was at Millom I was taken ill with appendicitis and sent to a hospital near Ulverston. She was in charge of the ward I was on. I met her previously when I was with 77 Squadron and she came to collect her fiancées belongings who had been reported missing on operations.

While I was having my operation she introduced me to her fiancée who was flying at Cark close by and it seemed incredible but he was killed in a flying accident whilst I was still on her ward. I felt so sorry for her.

I arranged to go away after I had completed my tests in the afternoon. In the morning when I got into my office they told me that I had only one Master, 2 Mosquitoes, and 1 Wellington to fly. I completed these four tests and at about 4 o'clock handed my parachute in and got in my car to go home. When I got half way across the airfield a sergeant fitter ran in front of me and stopped me and asked if I would test a Miles Master that they had been doing some major repairs on. As the flights had been complaining about a vibration in flight. I grumbled a bit but told him to draw me a parachute and I would do it.

He explained they had done some major work as it had consistently been rejected by the flights. When I arrived at the hanger several young ATC cadets asked me for a flight as I often took some up on routine tests, as most of the other pilots were unable to do so. However due to the nature of this test I decided to take the fitter along with me.

After the routine pre-flight check I took off and noticed a vibration which obviously was not cured. I talked to the fitter who was in the rear cockpit and told him to tighten his straps as I intended to climb to 5000ft and find out what the trouble was. When I reached this height I started giving the machine maximum stress as I suspected the airframe. These machines were very good for acrobatics and that is what we were doing. When I got near Fraisthorpe I did five or six rolls when there was a bang and the vibration immediately got very violent. Immediately I switched off the engine and feathered the prop which made very little difference. I hoped my passenger would jump out but when I saw him in the rear mirror he looked dreadful. I managed to keep it on an even keel and called through to base that I was in trouble.

The Group Captain at RAF Lisset was in the control tower as a squadron of Lancasters were taking off. He answered my distress call and said I could try for a landing on his airfield.

I steered for Lisset and as I had reasonable control and good gliding speed, I decided to hand pump the undercarriage down and attempt a landing. The green undercarriage lights came on which meant they were locked down. I had turned the petrol tanks off and my gliding speed was 130 mph well over the stalling speed. We glided to about 600 ft when all of a sudden the plane turned over and dived straight into the ground. I just remember a splintering crash.

The Group Captain of Lisset who saw us hit the ground said there was no hope for us as the machine did three somersaults as it was breaking up. He saw the engine fly up into a field about a quarter of a mile away.

The fitter was in another field with all his ribs broken. I was upside down still in my cockpit, when a German prisoner of war working in the field tried to get me out. I remember some of the incident including my back hurting like the devil and a desperate need for a cigarette, which was silly as petrol was all over the place which fortunately for me did not fire.

The ambulance and doctor soon arrived and he injected

me and told me one of my eyes had been knocked out of its socket. He put it back in for me. I was taken to Driffield hospital and had stitches in a gash over my eye. The throttle had gashed my wrist, and I had a broken leg. I could not move my legs and it was not until the RAF got a surgeon from Liverpool to come and see me that I knew my spine was damaged.

I was transferred to the RAF hospital at Northallerton where the pressure was relieved and I was told that my 1st and 2nd lumbar was crushed. This had made me one inch shorter. I was put in plaster cast for three months and transferred to Hazelrig Hall at Loughborough which was an RAF rehabilitation hospital.

It was a wonderful unit at Loughborough and when I saw the appalling injuries and burns of some of the inmates I wondered why I was there. I was put in the spinal injury section where we were given exercises by Raich Carter who was then playing for Derby County. I used to pull his leg and ask him to come to Hull City when it started again and he said he wouldn't!

I did see my fitter when he was at Northallerton and he used to come and see me in a wheel chair he appeared to be progressing satisfactory.

The RAF took a series of photographs of the wreckage of the Master and gave it a full two page cover in the Tee Emm November Issue which was an official RAF monthly magazine. They emphasized that we survived the crash only because we had our harnesses fastened so tightly.

My service release came through whilst I was still in hospital, as the war had now ended my unit was moved to Leconfield where I was discharged. I had been offered flying jobs soon after I left but decided I had had enough.

When I was in hospital at Loughborough I made many friends who were recovering from severe burns and injuries. One of these friends was Ken Pipe a New Zealand navigator. He came home and stayed with us for a few days and made many friends. I recall a little of what he did tell me of how he received his injuries which were extensive.

He was the navigator in a Lancaster bomber over Cologne when it received a direct bit and exploded he thought a shell had hit the bomb bay. He was the only survivor and fell about 15000 ft without a parachute he struck the top of a high fir tree that broke his fall. He said it was snowing heavily at the time and the tree certainly saved his life. Although he was badly injured he found a hut and sheltered in it. He was discovered the next morning by a girl and handed over to the police who did not believe his story. The Gestapo came and took him offering him medical treatment only if he told the truth, which is what he did. Ken was burnt with cigarettes, he had his nails pulled out and he told me they gave him the heat treatment. This meant being put in a refrigeration room and left shivering for long periods and then being put in a very hot room for similar time, back and forth until he was a complete wreck. He had a damaged spine from his fall. Eventually he was sent to a prison camp without any medical treatment, he had to march with the other prisoners when the Russians approached the camp, he knew if he didn't he would be shot.

He was eventually released by the Americans and sent immediately to hospital. He went home soon after the war but unfortunately never got over his experience, He died soon after he got to New Zealand. He said he would have liked to come back for a holiday which we all hoped he would.

David Waters 1992

CORPORAL FITTER DONALD EARL WRATHALL RAF MILLOM 1942 –1945

Thoughts on my late father by daughter Philippa.

When I was asked to pen a closing contribution to this book I was daunted by the prospect to say the very least – also, I was acutely aware of the fact that all the anecdotal material had been gathered at first hand by the author and that what I would be writing would be based upon childhood memories and research undertaken with the help of various agencies. Our family knew little of my Dad's RAF service as tragedy took him from us whilst we were very young. What we have subsequently discovered has made us immensely proud. I was born in the beautiful Lakeland valley of Kentmere, the youngest of five children. Much to the chagrin of my brothers and sisters I was known affectionately as "baby". I remember my father as a very tall, kind and soft spoken man who very rarely raised his voice and who would carry me high upon his shoulders at the first sign of fatigue on my part (real or contrived!) Dad loved vintage cars and I can remember him piling as many of the local children as he could get, into one of them and taking us all to the cinema in Stavely near Kendal to see the film of Sir Edmund Hillary's epic first ascent of Everest.

My only other really vivid memory is of Dad being struck in the face by our generator's starting handle and needing stitches to his face. In those days you made your own electricity in the valley or did without. My memories of Dad are few but very precious as he lost his life in an awful traffic accident when I was only seven years old, my Dad was only thirty nine at the time. My mother, Jane was involved in the accident and was to spend many weeks in hospital before she was well enough to return to the valley. As the years passed we spoke little of Dad's RAF service though we knew that he had served for a lengthy period at RAF Millom.

During this time Dad had made several friends with local people in the Silecroft area and I can recall being taken camping there, both before and after his death. My Dad was always a keen fell walker and adored the mountains but I am told that when he returned from his RAF Service he was extremely well versed in the skills necessary for mountain rescue. It is a fact furthermore, that he housed the local mountain rescue teams equipment in one of his barns and was active with them up to the point of his death.

Now I must apologise for taking a quantum leap to the year 2002 when Mum and I became aware that the RAF Millom museum had been established by the author of this book, Prison Officer John Nixon. It was in the Autumn of this year that we attended our first RAF Millom reunion and discovered that the airfield had been the birthplace of the RAF Mountain Rescue Service. When we began to understand how the rescue teams were formed and eventually officially given recognition, we started to ponder the possibility of my Dad's involvement. In 2004, by pure chance I met the author again and with his help began to research my Dad's service history and also to visit several of the wartime crash sites mentioned in this book for the purpose of taking photographs. Each visit was a sobering experience and I was left in every instance with a feeling of profound admiration for all Millom's Mountain Rescue Teams achieved, and indeed strove so hard to achieve.

Having read first-hand accounts of rescues and attempted rescues it is not difficult to imagine the awful scenes they must have been witness to and it speaks volumes of their dedication.

In order to conclusively establish Dad's involvement

with Millom's Mountain rescue unit I applied to the RAF for a copy of his service record. I was granted a copy and upon examination it gave me a clearer picture of Dad's service history. My father enlisted at Padgate on the 12th of September 1940 and began his "Square Bashing" in the seaside town of Blackpool on the 24th of October 1940. From there he was posted to No.6 School of target towing where he would have been taught all about the maintenance of the equipment used in the towing of aerial targets. These would be towed behind one aircraft whilst a pupil Air Gunner in another aircraft used the target for practice. On the 22nd of May 1941 Dad was posted to No.77 Squadron in Yorkshire to gain experience working on and maintaining twin engine aircraft before being posted to No.7 School of Target towing on the 29th of May 1941. A spell with No.150 Squadron followed until the 16th of April 1942 when he was posted to No.2 O.A.F.U. RAF Millom in Cumberland.

And so to the main question, was Dad involved in Millom's Mountain Rescue activities? Yes he was, on the very bottom of page one of his service record is a small note which reads "S/M Rescue" meaning Sea and Mountain Rescue. I think it is significant also that he was awarded a good conduct badge on the 23rd of October 1943, the time at which the RAF Mountain Rescue units were beginning to receive official recognition. It seems likely that as a local man with knowledge of the fells my father would have been active with Millom's rescue teams from his arrival up to the stations closure. When Millom ceased to operate all Mountain Rescue duties were transferred to RAF Cark and my father's record shows that he was to be posted there also. The posting however is scored through and cancelled written above it, why must remain a mystery. From this point on Dad really got around! No.96 Squadron, No.10 AGS (Walney),

RAF Conningsy, RAF Switon Moreley, RAF Sturgate and finally being discharged from the RAF on the 10th of January 1946. I speak for all my family when I say how immensely proud we are that my father was indeed one of the founder members of a service which has come to be admired the world over.

Never do I see a yellow Sea King Helicopter or an RAF Rescue Landrover without thinking of my Dad and his mates who, with the most basic equipment and frequently in the most awful conditions would do their utmost to locate and recover their stricken comrades. Through my association with the author I have been granted a glimpse of what life must have been like for my father and those who served with him at Millom. I would like to dedicate my contribution and the closing of this book to the men and women of RAF Millom each and every one. And to the RAF rescue teams of today who carry forward the wonderful and valuable work and standards set by those stalwart men and women over seventy years ago.

Philippa Nixon (née Wrathall) 2014. (yes... I married the author!)

F/LT G.F. PARKINSON

A very long way to Cark

I was serving in the army in 1942 when I obtained a transfer to the RAF for aircrew training. I had a long rail journey, as I was there in command of a small truck detachment in Elgin, Morayshire. So, my first connection was to Inverness and then an overnight train to London. Here the RAF recruits were housed in 'luxury flats' on the edge of Regents Park. The flats of course had never been used, so we used straw filled palliasses for beds.

The sleeping quarters were sited here because the Park grounds and buildings were utilised for parade and kitting out.

I exchanged my khaki for RAF blue and very comfortable poplin shirts. There was some basic 'square bashing', but I was excused as I had passed out from a drill sergeant's course in the army! The weather in August was very hot and humid. I was very pleased to 'skip' pounding the pavements.

We were soon moved to Torbay, where all the large hotels were housing RAF. This posting embraced our Initial Training. I shared a room with another pupil. We all had white "flashes" in the front of our forage caps. An apocryphal joke is as follows:

A Warrant Officer spotted an aircrew pupil with his white flash; "Come here son, what are you?"

"A pupil pilot, Sir,"

"I don't care if you are Pontius Pilot, get yer b****y haircut!"

The course was relatively easy to absorb, and the 'square-bashing' took place on Paignton promenade. The drill sergeant let me take over on some occasions and warned me to "go easy", this is not the army!

Two unexpected sessions were most interesting. One was clay pigeon shooting to illustrate very forcefully how the shooter had to 'lead' the aim in front of the disc - the same skill required in turret firing from an aircraft. The other surprise was a few trips from Torquay harbour to Brixton in pre-war 'pleasure' motor launches. Three or four pupils, plus the local skipper on board used a navigation sea chart inside the cabin. We took compass bearings on shore landmarks and established a moderately accurate plot of our voyage. With some degree of exactness we gave heading instructions to the skipper. We soon realised the fairly calm sea had hidden currents. (In the air, the problem is knowing the wind speed and direction).

I became pally with the drill Sgt who gave me some valuable tips. He suggested it was useful to be one of the top three course pupils as this would have a bearing on the selected country. He was of the opinion that the best choice was S.Africa as there were no freezing winters and more variety of topography. He also moved me in a room to share with 'Paddy'. I soon realised the reason. Paddy was an 'elderly' recruit, about thirty five years and a highly educated Dubliner - an ex college rugby star, a qualified lawyer and a 'five star' raconteur. He was excused all drill and sea trips (he was prone to seasickness). He was the star of the mess where many evenings he would be a super 'stand-up' comic and finish the evening with lead and chorus singing obscene 'rugby songs!' The latter were quite new to my relatively puritan upbringing!

The end of the course came near to the end of Christmas. We had a week's leave and had to report to Blackpool prior to embarkation. I opted for S Africa, which was granted. Blackpool's famous Winter Gardens and ballroom was cleverly utilised to issue tropical clothing. The Quartermaster Sergeant in charge bellowed the hackneyed advice, "If anything fits, bring it back and we'll change it!" I was surprised to have in the wardrobe, a large almost Victorian style pith sun helmet. The same Q/Sgt noting my astonishment said, "When you set sail, chuck the b****r overboard!"

For the few days in Blackpool, we were housed and fed in third rate Boarding Houses. This was a new experience for me, as coming from a fairly wealthy family I had only knowledge of hotel accommodation! From this unwelcome 'brief encounter', we had a short train journey to Liverpool dock where we boarded a troopship; an old ship, about 15,000 tons, oil fired boilers, and a large mess deck, where at 22:00 hours we slung our hammocks for a sleep.

The chilly, damp, January weather made the vision of the Liver building and Custom House look very miserable. Due to the problems of mass handling the convoy north of Belfast, we were anchored mid-Mersey for a full week. At least the anchor chain rattled up its rusty path and with a long siren hoot we eased out of this murky old port.

All at sea

Two days later, the shape and composition of the convoy was clear, all steaming south in the choppy winter waters of the Atlantic, under glowering rain filled clouds. One troop ship in the central area, with small cargo ships on the port and starboard. Two destroyers hunting, always near the perimeter of the formation. Over twenty ships in all. The pack changing course every hour or so to fox the German subs. Unfortunately, we were limited in progress, as the slowest freighter set the pace.

Our ship's compliment was about one hundred RAF and four hundred army types en route to help the N.African War. The mess deck had long trestle tables where we were served with lukewarm basic food.

My mess table 'crew' was making heavy weather, trying to make a neat exercise when getting in or out of their hammocks. When I was fourteen I sailed on a school sponsored cruised in the Baltic. The ship was almost identical to our troopship, so I had fifteen days to perfect a stylish gymnastic movement to master the hammock problem!

After passing the Canaries, the weather improved with spells of warm sunshine. We were settling into a routine and coping with saltwater shaving and monotonous seascapes – and the food. When we gradually tacked to port with an easterly heading, it was obvious that Freetown would be a change of scenery.

We dropped anchor in Freetown bay. Dead calm, with heavy cloud. The air was stifling, seemed like 100% humidity. Many decided to try and sleep on the deck. The second day was a huge success! A black cloud shrouded the area and around 16:00 hours an almighty tropical thunderstorm crashed into action. Raindrops like we had never seen, and almost to a man we stripped off and lathered our bodies from head to toe. The decks became a mass of white foam!

The following morning the anchor chain rattled its clarion call and a cheer went up from the motley collection of well cleaned troops! Heading south once more, we knew we had passed the half way mark (for the RAF but not the army). Four weeks from leaving the Mersey, we noticed our 'Chef' was delivering a potage of rice in every meal. We soon came to one conclusion: we had run out of palatable food! A few days later we fully understood the slang word 'grub' - most of the rice was riddled with maggots! The situation was grim as we had very little safe food for the next two weeks. Most of us were almost shrinking daily.

The safari begins

At last! Gently moving into Cape Town harbour was an amazing sight; brilliant sunshine lighting every crag and crevice of the near vertical face of Table Mountain. This three thousand foot mountain dominates the city making the city hall and prominent buildings look like scale models.

The RAF was allowed off first and a mad rush headed

for the Red Cross Service building near the docks. Bacon, eggs, fried bread was at that moment true Ambrosia! After filling our starved innards, I was approached by a lady who offered to take four of us on a tour of the Cape Peninsula. The rest of the day was a superb guided trip of over thirty miles. On day two, a few of us caught the electric train to the Indian Ocean side of the city. Here was excellent bathing in water over 70 degrees.

On day three at 15:30 hours we boarded the train. This was for all of us the longest train journey – 11,00 miles to Pretoria. The coaches were very good for a 3 feet 6 inches gauge (essential to cope with severe curves). Each compartment had two 'pull-out' beds. Our kit bags made a problem. We were glad to have thrown the stupid pith helmets in the Atlantic!

We soon steamed through Paarl and on into the Cape vineyard country. The small town of Woicester was the last 'outpost' of the cultivated areas, lying in the shadow of the massive sandstone Hex River mountains at over 6,000 feet. The two 'Pacific' type locos began their hard serpentine climb through the Hex River valley. Rock towers on each side of the track. Before nightfall we gained over 3,000 feet on to the Great Kariou, or High Veldt. The scenery was a seismic change from the lush Western Cape. The grass was a parched yellow with off rocky outcrops. This plain stretches hundreds of miles with a few very small towns and villages. Sheep farming and maize was the primary agrarian activity.

In the night we probably stopped for water and crew replacement. In the morning we realised we had passed Kimberly the giant diamond mine before dawn. We had a good breakfast with an exotic porridge! This was dark brown made from unrefined maize ('mealie') very tasty, quite different from oats. We crawled past the ghostly shanty town of Soweto on the western edge of Johannesburg. Then the strange sights of huge pyramid piles of grey waste dug from the deep gold mines drilled into the Witwatersrand granite.

We travelled non-stop through the city – another twenty miles to Pretoria. After twenty two hours we walked on 'dry land'! A few trucks carted us uphill to a bleak S.African Army barracks. This was our home for a few weeks. From here the various aircrew types, pilots, navigators, gunners and so on, would be posted to different airfields, mostly in the Transvaal State.

Afrikaanerland

In our first week we had three lectures by a RAF Officer. This was an intensive history lesson of the country and pitfalls to avoid. Although most of the wealth and infrastructure had been developed by British investors and know-how, most of the agricultural land was occupied by Afrikaner, or Boer farmers. The large retail stores and cinemas were very much a Jewish preserve. In the 1940's Johannesburg had a derogatory and racist name of 'Jewburg' (the Jewish population being over 10%). The Afrikaner population was 67% of the Whites and dominated the government. The Blacks outnumbered the Whites and 'Coloureds' by at least 3:1.

Many Afrikaners hated the British. We had erected 'concentration' camps in the Boer War, where many women and children died. Our army burnt many Boer farms. We were warned not to hitch hike, as several RAF had been abducted or run-over! Any golfers should ignore any road signs, "HOU LINKS", because this means "Keep Left"!

We were assured that all food and water was safe to drink. We also had RAF medical staff available for any serious injury or illness. Malaria had been 'tamed' and snake bites were very rare. Some of our instructors would be members of the S.African army, and were 'pro-British'!

Food

Most of our meals were similar to British fare with a few exceptions, the only potato was sweet potato. Steaks were abundant. Our bread could be rye flour or mixed. Apparently 'Lion' beer was like US 'Budweiser' and brandy was dirt cheap.

Laundry

On the airfields we would have native ('Black') families who collected each bundle and would be paid 5d plus a bar of soap!

Pretoria & Jo'burg

Pretoria is the government capital. The centre could be truly described as pretty. A fine central avenue lined with superb jacaranda trees with a profusion of lilac blossom. At one end, well elevated, is an imposing government building using pleasing red sandstone. Johannesburg is quite the opposite. It looks like a small American city; concrete apartments and office blocks, eight or ten floors. A fine park with zoo breaks up the unimposing built-up areas.

In 1940 these cities could be regarded as relatively 'new', as S Africa only became a true republican country thirty years earlier after the 1910 Act of Union. In 1939 Jan Smuts became the Prime Minister. He was a great statesman who gave Churchill his full support, especially in his 'darkest hours'. Without Smuts, there would not have been any RAF aircrew training inside S Africa.

Elementary flying school

This was on a converted meadow on the edge of a very small

mining town about twelve miles east of Johannesburg city centre. We were twenty four strong and 'rarin' to go'. The aircraft were two-seater Tiger Moths, an old trusted and tested biplane. My instructor was an English speaking S African Army flyer. His first piece of information was the fact that the field was rather bumpy and our altitude was over 5,000 feet. This required the engine to work hard for take-off and climbing. He also pointed out that landing in the thin air gave rise to floating instead of a nice comfortable 'three point' landing with wheel and tail settling down 'sans crunch'

We all found the controls very sensitive and forward view restricted. The first few hours were mostly taken up with 'circuits and bumps' and how to make accurate turns. This course was twelve weeks duration. In week three, after two take-offs and landings, my instructor taxied to the perimeter, climbing out he tapped on my helmet and shouted, "It's all yours, don't bend the b----r, on your way!" So after carefully setting the controls for take-off, I started my FIRST SOLO! Full throttle and climbing to 500 feet, turn left, then fly parallel to the field; line up and nose down for a good approach at around 85m.p.h. Ease back on the stick, lean out of cockpit and cut throttle – a fair non bumpy landing! Taxi back, soaked in sweat and ready for lunch with a steak!

Our entire course soloed after 7½ to 9 hours. Two weeks later, one of our clan tried a steep turn when solo and spun in to his death; a very sobering day. All flying was stopped for twenty four hours in respect.

The weeks rolled by which included the full repertoire of flying problems: tight turns, spins, aerobatics, cross-country routes and night flying plus ground instruction.

Advance flying school

We moved four miles further east to Nigel, another small mining community. The field was mostly bare red earth and was a large area but not level. Our number had dwindled to eighteen due to some being diverted to another station where they flew single engine planes. Our posting was to fly twin-engine Airspeed Oxfords. The change from the delicate Tiger Moths was a great shock – like moving from a Fiesta to a three ton truck.

Flying the Oxfords we soon realised we were in rarefied air. The take-off was a long, bumpy, roaring mass of striving machinery before we dare ease back the control wheel. Landing was even worse, especially after noon. The hot earth develops severe convection draughts. Gradually we learned to man handle these bucking beasts and tamed them in the air.

Except for aerobatics, the regime was very similar to the Tiger Moth syllabus, but additional skills were demanded for bombing, formation flying, long cross-country and plenty of night flying. I had persuaded the Lancashire lads of the possibility that if we obtained high marks, we could select our preferences. During the last week, we were all interviewed by the C/O. Our preferred posting was for flying boats in Coastal Command. To our amazement this was granted.

Reconnaissance navigation school

All Coastal Command pilots had to pass the special course of over-sea navigation and allied subjects. This was based on a field on the south coast edge outside a village named George (today it is a modern town with an industrial section and a motorway leading 300 miles to Cape Town!). Behind George is a 4,000 foot mountain which we soon climbed. The course was twelve weeks and quite intensive. The Lancashire lads combined resources and here we flew in pairs, taking turns at the chart table fitted in the Avro Ansons. All the instructors were RAF and very good.

Two highlights occurred. One was when we spotted the 'Queen Mary' in grey paint heading for Durban and then en route to Egypt. The second was a weekend in Oudtshoorm. This is a strange place trapped in a narrow valley between our local mountains and the edge of the Karoo. Almost desert climate, very hot and cactus like Arizona. Ostrich farms provided feathers. There is a huge cave. The train journey has lots of curves to climb above sea level and 10-15 mph is about as much as the old steam locos could manage.

We passed out with 'flying colours' and were sent to a holding camp at the foot of Table Mountain. Albeit the same latitude, we were now in the West Cape winter. This is mild weather with frequent drizzle or light rain. The 'Tablecloth' of low cloud often shrouded the summit. The climate on the George area of the coast is regarded as the most benign on the world. For twelve months there is no definite summer or winter. Rain is light and infrequent; usually sufficient to maintain a lush green environment. Much of this coast is dubbed 'The Garden Route' and is a popular resort area for tourists. However, the damp weather restricted my climbing activities and I only squeezed in one good climb with two University rock climbers.

No convoy

The Lancashire lads were informed that when a suitable ship arrived, we would be moved to Bahama to convert on to Catalinas, US built long range flying boats.

In due course we had a lift in a truck to the docks where we boarded the "Athlone Castle". This was a fine ship of about 25,000 tons and one of the fleet of Union Castle Liners. They sailed pre-war from England, round the Cape to India, and north up Africa's east coast. They carried mail – two weeks (or so we were told) UK to Cape Town. In the late afternoon we eased out of Cape Town and before nightfall we had a wonderful sight of the setting sun outlining the twenty miles of the peninsula; a truly magnificent sea and landscape.

The passengers on board gave us a shock. Just a handful of American Army personnel 'rattled' around the lower decks. They had all suffered physical or mental injuries. Our quarters were on the top deck in a large cabin with eight bunks. The ship had left Bombay, so we assumed the Americans had been bombed by the Japs, or had contracted fevers. We had no idea where we would land. After three weeks of fast sailing (occasional zigzags) we slowly steamed one morning into New York harbour! We could see the famous building 'in the flesh'. Woolworth, Chrysler and high rise apartment or office blocks in profusion.

The Americans were offloaded, but we had to wait hours, because the 'paperwork' was not working smoothly. Eventually we boarded a small launch which cruised out of the docks and sailed about ten miles to a small island between the mainland and Long Island. This was a well-built barracks used by the US Army to train young cadets who would be commissioned. Our sleeping quarters were within a dormitory. We were amazed with the weather; hellish hot and humid all day and night. Also mosquitos during the night! This was the end of August. We were told that heat waves could last weeks and everyone was eagerly waiting for a thunderstorm!

Our first day in the US of A! We decided the best action was to contact the Adjutant. He was mystified and apparently it was good luck he had four spare beds! He wisely directed us to go into the city and harangue the

British Embassy. In the meantime, he handed us a few dollars to enable us to pay our way once in the city. He also gave us rail tickets which would give us free train service to and from our 'camp' main live station.

So in the steaming heat of New York, we arrived in the famous Times Square Railway Station. Two levels of underground platforms and a vast circular concourse. The Embassy was a slow and weary experience. We were for the time being 'lost' in the USA! They were more generous with dollars than our adjutant's offer. We had to report to a specified officer three days hence and not to go beyond 48 hours' notice.

Not knowing when we would move out we decided to see the sights within a few days. We had a letter from the Embassy stating who we were etc. With this epistle we approached a Red Cross information department near Broadway. One attractive and obviously well-educated young woman took pity on us and offered to arrange a week's itinerary! After sampling a ghastly 'eat joint', we reported to our guide. So in quick succession we shot up the Empire State skyscraper and then visited the Rockefeller Centre where there was a vaudeville theatre with chorus girls. Everyone had to be at least 5ft 9ins, as the stage was so large. Then Yankee Stadium's strange baseball game, a boat tour of the bay, Wall Street and a peep inside the Stock Exchange and last of all, a party in her luxurious flat in Lexington Avenue.

We met journalists and a Native American Indian photographer for 'Life' magazine. We had to answer a barrage of questions about Britain and our travels in Africa. The 'Life' man gave us an offer to go with him on a day's 'shoot' on Long Island. The venue was to take photos of the super wealthy with their yachts and where possible their mansions. The Native American was a very dynamic and imposing man. He had 'done' the Pacific War with a mass of shots in the thick of island invasions. Hoping to get to England before the allies invaded France; he picked our brains until we were mentally exhausted.

At last our American experience came to an end when we were directed to the docks. Here was a huge ex Italian liner gutted for troop carrying. Zillions of US Army troops squeezed in. We were on the top deck which contained US Officers and twenty four attractive Red Cross girls. Our 'entente cordiale' was very!

Within six days we crawled into Liverpool. Just like when we left: grey, wet and dirty. Everything seemed strange after our long safari. I never did fly Catalinas and after further navigational specialisation if found myself at RAF Cark!

Cark airfield

Considering the urgency and strict budget, the Cark airfield was cleverly 'slotted' into the available land area. On the north perimeter is the fishing village of Flookburgh and the railway line. To the east is Humphrey Head, and of course on the south rim is the coastal edge of the Kent estuary. Similar airfields were made in a ring around the Irish Sea. Walney, Millom, Dumfries, Jurby I of M, N Ireland and a few more specialised airfields such as Silloth, Campbeltown, Blackpool and Valley in Anglesey.

These sites were very valuable due to their position on the north-west coasts of England. Further away form 'easy' targets in the south. In addition, training routes could easily be planned over the sea to avoid high ground and flying over large towns. Most of these airfields were used by Training Command. The trainees would in most cases be posted to Bomber Command as Pilots, Navigators, Bomb Aimers, Wireless Operators and Gunners.

The Cark runways were level, with No 1 set for heading into the prevailing SW winds. The No 2 runway was not often used due to its N-S direction. All the runways were fitted with the standard night lighting which was a clever design.

On the western edge of the field was a dead straight lane leading from Flookburgh village square right into the beach; essential for the horse drawn carts going out into the sea for shrimps, or flat fish. This lane became an integral part of the field, giving personnel easy access to the aircraft, lecture rooms and hangers. Most of the living quarters and communal buildings were in the N W sector close to Flookburgh. The WAAF quarters were rather isolated! Some of the amenities included a gym, cinema and squash courts. The main line, Barrow to Carnforth, was a fifteen minute hike, or a few minutes by bike. Unusually, the War Department planners had squeezed into the south west corner between the fishermen's lane and perimeter track, a small army artillery detachment camp.

By luck and certainly not by design, the small town of Grange-over-Sands was within a fifteen minute bike ride. For a period during the War, The Grand Hotel 100 rooms) was home to training courses for RAF clerical duties. The Grange Village Hall and the Grand Hotel ballroom held regular dances. Another lucky twist of topography is the proximity of Kendal - about twelve miles. Bus services were available and the town's amenities included good pubs, cinema and library. For the more adventurous, further afield were Lancaster and Morecambe.

The popularity rating of the station will never be known; the pupils had a different viewpoint from the permanent Staff. They were 'passing birds' and most of these airmen had only a fleeting interest in the nearby countryside or towns. The few in the Staff who were southerners usually regarded Cark as a "God forsaken dump soaked in rain!"

Cark's 'job description'

In the second half of the War, RAF Cark developed a very good intensive six week navigation course. The trainees were newly qualified pilots, who had been trained mostly in Canada, or other Empire countries.

The concept was two-fold. Firstly, the weather and flying conditions in W Europe are very different from the stable weather conditions prevailing in their areas of training. Secondly, most of these pilots would be posted to heavy bombers and would be the crew's captain. The close association between the navigator and pilot was essential. Prior to the Cark courses, pilots had very limited knowledge about navigation problems.

The huge expansion of the 'Empire Training' Scheme assessed a substantial flow of qualified pilots arriving in the UK. Very different from the desperate years of 1939/42 when shortages of trained crews and planes was a grave problem.

The course gave the pilots a rudimentary knowledge of practical dead reckoning navigation, together with basic meteorological/weather problems. In winter months, most courses had a fair share of bad weather. Our Staff pilots and maintenance crews played a big part in the success of the operations. In my 'watch' we had no mechanical or structural failures and to my knowledge, no staff pilot was 'fired'.

The aircraft used was the great Avro Anson with two engines and room for four crew members. A very reliable and safe aircraft used across the Empire and Training Command was well equipped with these faithful 'workhorses'. At least six airfields on the Irish Sea coasts had fleets of these planes for many long years.

Where We Flew

From Cark we had the options of several routes and these were varied during each course. The forecast weather often had to be considered before a route could be selected.

Typical routes were:
Cark – Mull of Galloway – Mts of Mourne – Calf of Man.
Cark – Blackpool Tower – Holyhead – Calf of Man
Cark – Carlisle – Mull of Galloway – Walney – Cark

Each day we flew, the instructors had to confer with the duty Met Officer (we had two full time WAAF Officers). If a flight was leaving am we had limited meteorological readings as only a handful of stations were West of Cark. A rough isobar map was drawn and our 'conference' had to use a lot of guess work. Our score for forecasting time of rain was very good. We also had to use care and cancel flying if the signs were poor. Low cloud and strong gusty winds were usually cause for cancellation.

The planned routes were designed for durations of three to four hours. Safety was the key factor. One advantage of the geographical position of Cark was the short distance from Walney Island. You could always see the white sea and beach edge of the island, even on a dark night. Once the island edge is seen, an easy run up the estuary to Cark was available and bacon and eggs ready for the crews if coming home from a night flight! If the weather turned really nasty we could land at Walney rather than risk hitting Hampsfell near Cark.

Gibb's airforce

The C/O of RAF Cark was a larger than life bod, named W/C Gibb. A peace time RAF Officer, who was on reserve list and living in Jamaica 1939. He was a tall handsome man of about 45 years and developed an amazing style and flair, which gave him almost carte blanche access to running Cark in a unique manner. So much so, some of the 'old lags' of Cark christened the initials GAF to stand for "Gibbs Air Force!"

I was an experienced rock climber. 'Gibby' asked me if I would like to add Mountain Rescue to my duties. This was agreed and within a week we received two near new Jeeps courtesy of Burtonwood US base! You will see from my notes that we never had to perform many rescues, but we had to have trials, so a group of ex climbers had rapid transport to Langdale, Coniston and other craggy meccas! We became better climbers than navigators.

'Gibby' had wangled somehow, a two-seater Miles Magister trainer. On a fine Sunday morning he would often 'beat up' the airfield and try some aerobatics over the bay! He would organise parties in the Officers' Mess and local young ladies could be invited. The Jeeps were useful taxis and one evening we collected several WAAF Officers who were trainees in the Old England Hotel, Bowness.

The best 'wangle' was in mid-Summer, when he authorised an exchange food barter system. The scheme was classic. During one of our training flights, the pilot was instructed to have 'engine trouble' and land at Jurby, Isle of Man. On board would be several large fresh salmon from the River Kent and estuary. We swapped this load for fresh hand- picked strawberries! Of course the C/O of Jurby was happy to oblige.

One week in 1944 we suddenly had about 60 Italian POW dumped on us. The head WAAF Officer at this time was a well-educated, tall fine looking woman about 30 years and disciplined her flock very well and made a lot of effort to keep unwanted pregnancies to a very low figure.

About 48 hours after the Prisoners Of War arrived, our "Queen Bee" (WAAF C/O) came into the Mess about 6 pm white with rage and generally not happy. Apparently 'Gibby' had ordered her to muster all the WAFF's into No 1 Hanger. He gave them a lecture on the sexual appetite of the Italians and how they should avoid these men at all costs. Our enraged 'Queen Bee' was certain that many of her girls would succumb to the Latin lovers!

On a more serious plane, when we were notified an airman had been killed and was to be buried in any of the local areas, 'Gibby' promptly laid on a full funeral party. It was appreciated by the next of kin and friends of the deceased.

On one occasion he gave me a very delicate mission. One of the Cark mechanics had developed a relationship with the wife of a wealthy Army Officer serving in the Middle East. When this Officer returned he found the tools for his Aston Martin sports car were missing. I had to smooth out this Officer and gave him regards from 'Gibby', that we would consult the police to retrieve these tools as soon as possible – not a pleasant visit.

When the atom bomb was dropped, we knew that RAF Cark would soon be redundant. 'Gibby' wasted no time in designing several items of furniture to be made by the joiners in the maintenance crews. The wood was pine, used in the construction of massive planks forming huge crates holding spare engines and other parts for the 'Flying Fortress' bombers. His useful contacts within the giant Burtonwood US base provided a great source of free wood! The joiner lads were happy to show their skills in cabinet making – an attractive change from 'messing about' with Ansons.

'Gibby' went too far when he fancied extracting a large section of carpet from the Officers' Mess. We believe the

Adjutant claimed there was an inventory of buildings and fittings, this curbed his excesses.

Some historians believe he emigrated to Rhodesia and was killed in an accident. In conclusion, he was a great 'character' and basically a true gentleman with the efficiency of the station and well-being of his hundreds of crew uppermost in his mind.

The Ansons – 'workhorses'

The Avro Anson was designed and made by the famous company who made the great Lancaster bombers. This aircraft was an old design and initially in the 1930's was a small bomber. At the outbreak of War the Wellington twin engine bomber was much larger and powerful. The Anson was soon established as a superb training aircraft. It was reliable, safe, easy to fly, capacious body, room for four or five crew and an air cooled engine, easier to maintain than liquid cooled (as for R R Merlins).

Training Command used the Ansons for training, navigators, wireless operators, bomb-aimers, gunners and of course, all the Ansons used for these functions required safe and accurate pilots. Many were shipped out to Canada and Africa as part of the huge Empire training scheme.

The operating speeds were relatively slow, which was a great safety factor. Typical cruising speed was 120 mph; the take-off speed is usually about 90 mph. This speed is reduced for gentle climbs. For landing, a typical speed on the final approach with wheels down is about 70 mph. At touch down the engine is throttled back in an attempt to make a three-point landing.

On twin engine aircraft, a vital part of the performance is the ability to fly level safely on one engine in emergencies. The Anson (if not overloaded) will fly at 90 mph. If an engine fails on take-off, the situation is very different and demands on the pilot increase dramatically. If the undercarriage has not been wound up, the pilot will not be able to climb. When the undercarriage is up, a slow climb may be possible. Fortunately, the Cheetah engines were very reliable.

An aircraft, is it like driving a car?

NO! There is one common factor. Keep alert to keep alive. Some people latch on to the idea of steering. In a car you simply turn the wheel to the left and the car obeys and also turns. In flying, the control 'wheel' or stick is also moved to the left for a left (port) turn. However, we can now compare the extreme. If the car travels too fast into a bend, the result will be a skid, or at worst will turn over, or hit a roadside obstacle. Let us assume the pilot is in his Spitfire flying at 20,000 feet above the English Channel. No trees or walls up here! The period is 1940, and to his horror our pilot hears some 'pings' as bullets from a ME109 ricocheting off his Merlin engine!

In a panic he lunges his stick to the left to avoid further target practice for his German foe. Forgetting all the instruction he has recently received from a seasoned flyer, due to a sudden severe 'G' force, he has a black-out; two seconds later he is recovering sight, when even more horror - the Spitfire is now in a spin heading down at considerable speed. An easier target for the ME109!

Unlike the car, the plane is not on wheels gripping the road due to friction between tyre and road surface. The aircraft has to support itself in air, not on air. The essential structural components are the wing, tail plane and rudder. The engine(s) provide the thrust, the power to propel the aircraft in a forward direction. The section of the wing (shape and size) and the tail plane are designed by highly skilled engineers. The air flowing past the wing and tail generates a 'lift' force keeping the plane airborne. Modern jet fighters have so much power they can execute vertical climbs. In the days of propeller driven planes, no such configuration was possible.

Reverting back to our disastrous tight turn to port, the pilot had not had sufficient experience to develop reflex actions whereby he would move his control smoothly and apply left rudder (left foot) and at the same time increase his power (throttle lever forward). All these three actions conducted at the same time and in harmony. Not quite as simple as turning a car steering wheel a couple of turns!

So far, we have been flying in the horizontal mode, with the airflow nicely balanced between wing and tail plane. By easing the control forward we create a dive and pull back to climb. These movements actuate the ailerons on the tail plane altering the original airflow. Usually when setting a descent, the power is reduced and vice versa for climbing. In highly manoeuvrable aircraft such as Spitfires, the control stick can be moved in a huge variety of positions, for example, forward and to left which is essential for a diving turn. In effect the aircraft is in a three dimensional environment, quite different from a car which is two dimensional as it is always in horizontal mode.

Now we should consider two key elements to our control of the aircraft; namely, the take-off and landing. These elements are basic for all aircraft but the handling and speeds vary considerably.

Take-off

To assist this action, the runway is selected to give the nearest position to flying directly into the wind. For modern giant beasts, this is not of vital importance, but most WWII planes would behave better for what assistance a head wind could give the pilot. A strong cross-wind is not pleasant for our pilot; hence most UK airfields were built with three runways which usually avoided any wind blowing at say 90 degrees to the runway.

We are now at the end of the correct runway, so we now push throttle(s) fully forward to give maximum power. We then gather speed and with most wartime RAF planes the third wheel is to the rear (some US models had nose wheels). In the case of our Cark Ansons we have rumbled over half the runway and will be over 70 mph. Then we feel the rear end lift off the runway and with experience we feel the right moment to ease back control and start climbing to say 1,000 feet. We can then reduce power and fly horizontally, or climb gradually to operating height. We have also operated the undercarriage to raise wheels.

The Anson has no vices and there is nothing dramatic in our take-offs, however this is not the case for all types. Some can swerve off the runway or require huge distance before a climb can be commenced. If, however, the engine or one engine in our Anson fails, we have a very hasty situation - usually a disastrous crash. Most twin engine aircraft will fly level on one engine, albeit hard work for the pilot on wartime models. Four engine types can cope easily on three motors.

Landing

This is in most cases more difficult than take-off. The War's single engine machines force the pilot to look 'over the side' when approaching the runway, whereas multi-engine models usually have good visibility over the nose. As remarked before, the lack of a nose wheel requires the pilot to attempt a three-point landing (two landing wheels plus tail wheel). The word "attempt" is quite apt as it is extremely difficult to arrive at such perfection.

The reverse of our take-off procedures is fairly obvious, wheels are lowered, the locking is checked and then turn to line-up with the selected runway. Throttle reduced and approach speed adjusted, approximately 80 mph for our Anson (much faster for most fighters). With experience the pilot will aim to touch-down in the one third runway area nearest to the perimeter. This gave plenty of room to slow and avoid excessive braking, or worse, to crash off the end of the runway.

Our Anson is a delight to land. With a little power the final action is akin to a 'lift' and a final ease back on the control and hey presto, a perfect (or near enough) 'three pointer' is accomplished! It's nothing like as easy in a Spitfire, Hurricane or heavy bombers, especially a Wellington. The Spitfire has a narrow undercarriage, so if wings are not steady and parallel with the field, the landing could result in a violent lurch with a possible wing tip hitting the ground.

Heavy landing with any aircraft can be disastrous, or at least result in a burst tyre or damaged undercarriage. Night landings are several degrees more difficult than daylight. Heavy rain is trying especially for the single engine types.

Instruments

Four instruments were vital: air speed indicator, artificial horizon, altimeter and compass. The artificial horizon was a brilliant piece of innovation, the sensitive diagram shows every movement of the wings in relation to the ground (you know instantly if you are flying level, diving or climbing). Night flying, or flying in clouds would be impossible without this device. The altimeter is a barometer; the thinner higher air with differing air pressure is converted into feet (or metres). The compass was a standard, approximately six inches in diameter;

very clear and reliable. Further instruments were mostly concerned with engine performance: Revs Per Minute, boost, oil pressure and of course the fuel gauge. As the aircraft models became larger and more refined, such as a Lancaster bomber with four engines, the array of dials became quite a collection for one pilot to assimilate.

Link trainer

This was a wartime boon; a very clever aid to flying 'blind'. The pupil sat in a mock-up cockpit and a hood covered the seat area to produce total darkness. A simulated instrument panel was in front of the 'pilot' plus compass and control stick. The supervisor outside gave instructions as to course and speed etc. The simulated controls were very sensitive and not easy. The result of maybe 30 minutes was shown to the instructor as a graph. Every error was clearly visible! Many pupils hated the *@?*!* Link. A common expression was "Stuff the *@?*!* missing link!"

Maintenance

The system of maintenance for aircraft is based on hours flown. The crew specialise on engines, airframe, instruments and son on. Bear in mind thousands of young men and women had to be trained very quickly in a field, which in most cases was completely foreign to their civilian occupations. At Cark the quality of maintenance was very good. The C/O W/C Gibb was keen to have a reliable team and very often he would have a brief chat with the Service Officer during the midday lunch break in the Officers' Mess.

In many theatres of the war the RAF ground staff performed miracles: in Malta; in the N African desert conditions; in tropical rain in Burma and on flying boat bases ground crews were required to work from the harbour or water base. Huge numbers of the RR Merlin

315

engines were fitted to fighters and four engine bombers. These engines were very complicated pieces of rather delicate machinery, but had to be checked and often removed and replaced by a new motor - and quickly. Too little praise has been allotted to these gallant hard working airmen and airwomen, who all helped to keep thousands of hard used aircraft flying all over the world.

Survival

One military historian graphically outlined the possibilities of a RAF Spitfire pilot surviving in a squadron engaged with interception fighting in 1940. The factors involved include: an above average flying ability, preferably exceptional ability; excellent eyesight; many hours of training on Spitfires; having a good seasoned Squadron Commander and a 'good shooting eye' to operate the fighters' guns to the most lethal. Then we have factors beyond the choice or ability of the pilot. These imply the need for an aircraft superior to the enemy: the squadron(s) to be superior in numbers to that of the enemy; excellent radar ground force information; a wide undercarriage to assist landing on a bumpy field (in case of no runways); good meteorological information; first class maintenance crews to avoid engine or structural failure and above all LUCK and more LUCK! Considering this very thorough analysis, it is amazing that any of our heroic 'few' survived at all!

Aircraft survival

Very little analysis has been exposed for public reading concerning the 'lost' aircraft. By this we can ponder over the fact that far more aircraft were produced than the number lost in front-line operations. One example is the total production of Hurricanes was about 15,000; this is far beyond the number destroyed in action. This shows the huge number damaged beyond repair in accidents:

lost in transit; damage from storms, fire and so on. Even in 1940 our production of Spitfires and Hurricanes was more than replacing operational losses. Of course our aircrew, especially pilots, were injured or died in many accidents not connected with combat duties. On this rather sombre note we can safely say there is more to handling and maintaining aircraft than driving a Ford Fiesta up the M6!

Elementary theory of dead reckoning navigation

The navigation in the air is virtually the same principle as for the mariners. The big difference however, is the relative slow speed of the ship. This infers that the calculations in the air have to be as quick as possible. Even the modest speeds of WWII bombers could be near to five miles per minute – ten times faster than a ship.

If we could fly in a wind-free atmosphere, we would not require any navigation refinements. Like sea currents and tides, the wind can blow us well off course. In the early days of the war, the Luftwaffe arrived over our cities without any unit navigation. They flew from France, a short distance to London or the south coast airfields or ports following a radio beam. A young British scientist interested Churchill in his theories. He was granted research funds and fortunately, the RAF technicians neutered the beam. So much so, on one raid a German landed near Dover assuming he was over France. This scientist saved thousands of British lives. The RAF copied this system which would reach Rhineland with great effect. Of course the Germans learned our frequencies and like the Germans, we had to disband the concept.

Astro-navigation was used extensively on ships. Bearings on stars and the sun could often be taken fairly accurately if sea was not rough and in up to maybe fifteen minutes, a good fix (position) could be achieved.

Although tuition was given in advanced RAF navigation courses, it was rarely used and exceedingly difficult.

Hence the 'Dead Reckoning' system was used. We have to find fixes by any means possible. The ideal method is to note a landmark very close to our track, or underneath it. By noting exact time, we then have the ideal situation – we know where we are at 'x' hours. To add to an accurate fix, if we know the precise wind speed and direction, we can calculate by trigonometry a good estimate of where we will be in say, the next hour's duration.

Unfortunately navigation needs some intuition and 'guessology'. For example, we always know our ground wind speed and direction very accurately at the site of our initial take-off (by anemometer etc). At say 8,000 feet the speed will increase by at least 10%. Also due to friction at ground level, the direction will be at least 10% different because of earth's rotational speed. So before we leave the runway, we have to adjust details of the ground wind. Next, if our destination is say 200 miles in W Europe, the wind details will certainly be different from our guessed initial wind. By studying meteorological information (if we have them) we can use this knowledge to improve our future guess. Additionally, en route we will probably have to alter course and adjust our estimated time of arrival (ETA).

Let me use a simple example. The wind is west 270 degrees; point A to point B is 150 miles. With the information of track direction, wind speed and direction, we can find the angle to give us the correct course. This calculation is obtained in a minute from a vital circular calculator (about four inches in diameter). About 100 miles en route we plot a landmark for an accurate fix. This gives us a revised track, course and ETA.

This process is repeated for the final journey. This shows

the ability to obtain fixes is essential for very accurate navigation. So the reader can understand the extreme difficulties in navigating at night over Germany. Hence the squadrons of the highly skilled and brave Pathfinders group were formed.

Our views from the cockpit

The best view from almost every aircraft is from the cockpit with a good arc in front and below. Most of our pilots were trained in Canada or Africa; areas which are featureless for hundreds of miles. The Prairie winter offers the pilots with (mostly) sunshine and a sea of white to the horizon. Africa delivers most of the year, a yellowish or brown plain and masses of sunshine.

The early days at Cark must have been quite a shock for any Staff Pilot, with hills almost on the end of two runways and another above Grange-over-Sands. The routes, although traversing over a lot of sea, passed over and near coastal landmarks. We had green on the hillsides and fields for twelve months of the year. Despite this variety and vastly more 'intimate' landscapes, most of the pilots became bored with the view and some never accepted the job as essential for safety and accuracy for our pupils.

It is probably a true saying, "That beauty is in the eyes of the beholder". Nevertheless, the range of landscapes when flying from Cark is distinct and very attractive. The most contrasting would be a flawless, calm, frosty day in January, flying at maybe 6,000 feet above The Lakes; snow-capped mountains and Skiddaw to Ingleborough all in view and reflections off all the major lakes, a sight never to be forgotten. Compare this with low cloud pushing the Ansons down to about 3,000 feet, gusty rain causing the plane to buck and shudder, straight ahead the yellow sand of Walney Island and the white streak of the surf crashing home!

The immediate area close to the airfield has a maze of detail: Flookburgh village on the perimeter; Grange a spit away; Holder Hall estate with superb trees and lush meadows; the complex estuary of the Kent (plus viaduct); the River Leven and Arnside Knott.

Flying north from Walney, we have the Cumbrian west coast on our starboard. No Sellafield scar had been inscribed in the landscape at this time. The most westerly point is St Bees Head with red sandstone cliffs. The Whitehaven harbour is also a good landmark. Across the Solway estuary are green fields, farms and a few villages. Flying west we come to the Mull of Galloway, a granite finger with savage looking cliffs pushing into the north Irish Sea. On the Mull itself are sub-tropical gardens, almost (but not quite!) rivalling Tresco the Prince of Wales' garden de luxe in the Scillies.

Some routes took us across the Irish side of the sea. The mountains of Munroe do come down to the sea. They have their own character, not craggy like Scafell or the Langdale Pikes, but dark and forbidding with sculptured smooth flowing lines to the beaches below. A very different view is flying toward and along the north shore of Anglesey. Form 5,000 feet the size and shape of the island is plain to grasp. The most scenic spot are the massive granite sea cliffs in the Holyhead area. Usually there's plenty of white surf with the crashing waves. In a few minutes we'd pass parallel with the superb curving beach of Llandudno.

A huge W-E runway was built near Valley. This was to assist US bombers (Flying Fortresses) to land safely after crossing the Atlantic. Today it is home to fighter-bombers flying at over 1,000 mph.

We usually turned northerly at this point and a route could pick up the sand dunes at Birkdale; then across the Ribble estuary to pin point over Blackpool Tower. It looks like a rusty piece of Meccano from our flying height. Another few minutes and Heysham to Morcambe is in sight. A good pin point could be the open air Baths, especially if it had water to reflect any sunshine.

The Isle of Man was our favourite spot to give the pupils opportunity to use either the north (Point of Ayre) or the southerly extremity (Calf of Man) for a precise fix. From about fifteen miles the whole outline of the Island could easily be recognised. There was a good sized airfield at Jurby in the NW. Another RAF Training Command Station with Ansons in use. The Calf of Man was our favourite due to its small complex cliffs and separation from the SE corner of the mainland. There were always white splurges of surf, easily visible even in poor conditions.

Then home across the last leg to our well-loved Walney Island! The sandy stretch of N-S beach was as good as a radio beacon or lit lighthouse. A few minutes of descending flying east up the narrowing estuary readied us to join the Cark circuit at 1,000 feet. About seven times out of ten we then flew over Humphrey to land on one of the runways pointing to the west. No one can say we did not have endless variety of views and weather – a long way from the Prairies of Veld!

Mountain frolics and fatalities

A very unusual duty assigned to RAF Cark was the maintenance of two valuable safety devices. On the summit of Skiddaw and Helvellyn were radio signal transmitters. They were powered by old fashioned batteries which were very heavy and bulky. They fitted on to fairly crude wooden frames. We had volunteers to carry these loads, with a usual three or four man crew. In winter we tried to use a four man system to give more relief to the 'Sherpas' and extra safety in case of any accident.

We had no disasters, but many winter ascents had snow, mist and gales etc to hamper their progress. We used a three ton truck with a WAAF driver to transport this crew to suitable bases. The RAF had no rule system to kit them out with adequate clothing. Most of the volunteers were fell walkers or rock climbers so they used their togs of choice. This practice seems typical with the reports we have seen regarding our army troops in Iraq and Afghanistan! We tried to improve frames but we could not alter the rectangular shape or size. Before the days of urethane foam, we tried various padding systems to fit under the shoulder straps.

In 1942 with momentum and two Jeeps 'organised' by W/C Gibb (C/O), we soon had a nucleus of four rock climbers including 'Scotty' Dwyer with his experience on Scottish mountains. A colourful volunteer was a burly (ex rugger) Sgt Staff Pilot. His nickname was 'Tiger', partly due to his handling the left hand drive Jeeps and his appearance. He had a mop of curly red hair matched with a bushy moustache. He was hailed as a hero and plied with free beer when he worked out a tortuous route up the lower slopes of Skiddaw and one day he reached the 1,000 foot level! There was little scope for adventure in the lower reaches of Helvellyn to the chagrin of the climbers! Fortunately he failed to overturn a Jeep to our relief.

We set up regular training sessions, which usually developed into two pairs tackling rock routes on Dow Crags, Gimmer Crag, Langdale, Bowfell Buttress, Castle Rock, Thirlmere and a few smaller ones near the valley bottom in Langdale. Our personal successes involved the second ascent of a hard climb on Castle Rock. This route had been made a few weeks previously by Jim Birkett of

Langdale. He was at the time the number one rock climber since 1938. Later we made our own first ascent on the steep shapely South Buttress of Dow Crags. We had no fancy gear in those days; hemp rope and F W Woolworth plimsolls!

The term 'rescue' was unfortunately never factual. Any crashes on the rocky hill areas involved massive destruction of the aircraft and a sudden end for the crew. In some areas of the Pennine and the periphery of the lakes, peaty, boggy conditions prevailed. An aircraft could bury deeply in such places. For most of the war years the farms had limited labour and very few ramblers walked over strange routes. In some accidents the remains were traced years after the initial tragedy.

We experienced one ghastly call-out. It was a Saturday in winter. We had a call about mid-afternoon and we had difficulty in mustering a crew. I hijacked my good friend F/Lt Dean and 'Tiger' volunteered to drive one Jeep. It was raining hard, so with canvas roofs in the 'up' position we set off with a small amount of food and rubber capes.

The destination was a remote farm some miles into the hills in the Kirkby Stephen area. We had no one inch Ordnance Survey map, so we had to find the farm by asking the nearest habitation. By the time we found the farm, it was dark, and we only had four torches between our motley gang. The farmer gave us his version of position.

He ignored the fact that we had never seen his sheep farm in daylight. After an hour in the now increasing gale, we saw a glint in our feeble torch beam. As we approached this object it was clear that we were looking at part of a tail fin of a Halifax Bomber. We struggled round the area for another hour and could find only small parts of a wing or fuselage. We came to the conclusion it had crashed some years previously and nine tenths of it was buried in the hill bog.

The Jeep headlamps were masked with just narrow slits giving a modicum of light. The trip back was a nightmare, due to visibility reducing us to about 15 mph and various stops to check a junction en route. We were very thankful that our Jeeps were left hand drive as this enabled us to follow hedges and side fences as they were often only inches away!

The massive crash on the fells above Little Langdale was a horrible sight. A large bomber pulverised into the gully and mountain outcrops of granite. The Air Force sent a Corporal mechanic and his assistant. They stayed in the local pub and eventually informed their station that any worthwhile salvage was well beyond their miniscule efforts.

Many years after the War's end, a historian author published a thin book listing air accidents in Cumbria. He had traced over one hundred accidents. Most of this horrific number was not surprisingly, in the ten year period from 1938 to 1948.

The northern sector of the county seemed to have been the worst sector. One airfield in Silloth was used to train Coastal Command pilots on twin engine Hudsons. This aircraft was a US plane and difficult to fly. The maintenance may also be involved, being a non-British made model. A macabre nickname emanated from Silloth. The Solway Firth was a graveyard for a number of crashes, so the Solway was re-christened as 'Hudson Bay'. The weirdest of crashes was when <u>three</u> Ansons in loose formation leaving an airfield outside Cumbria crashed into the northern fells.

Some local characters or "up the khyber"!

Many readers may not realise the social mix was rather extreme in the swathe of territory from Grange to Ambleside in 1939. Pre WWI the situation was almost 'rich or poor'.

Our C/O (W/C Gibb) was welcomed by some of the 'gentry' where he enjoyed shooting and salmon fishing. He received a variety of invitations, especially for afternoon tea on Sundays. He passed these on to our Medical Officer ('Doc') who would be socially accepted by most of these locals. The 'Doc' accepted a few and for reinforcement persuaded two or three officers to join him for the experience.

I enjoyed four of these strange jaunts. They were good representatives of the strands of wealth and social class at that time. Most of the wealth emanated from mill owning families from West Yorkshire or Lancashire textiles, colonial offices, or retired mid to high ranking officers from the Services. My section covers this analysis.

The most 'normal' and very engaging was an ex Attorney General of Uganda, Sir Thomas Tomlinson who had a fine old house a few miles north of Grange. His house was like an African museum! He had a great sense of humour and gave us a very good insight into the tribal labyrinth of the East African colonies. He expected most of the area would make efforts (or warfare) to extract independence from Britain after the War's end. He also expected massive upheaval and poor government. How true he was!

A very different 'local' had a nickname of 'Sinbad'! He lived near Cartmel in a Victorian house. The sizeable front garden had an uncut lawn lined with untrimmed shrubs. Half buried in the deep grass was a large dinghy, keel uppermost. Almost out of sight were oars, lanterns, coils of rope, poles and lobster posts!

This mariner was a retired Sales Director of a family woollen mill near Bradford. The mill was flat out, producing the low grade Battledress fabrics in three colours. He liked the Cartmel valley as he could catch a train heading for Yorkshire. He went to board meetings four to six times a year.

He had a huge lounge with a massive bay window. In one corner was a large steel safe. As soon as we arrived he produced malt whisky and the 'correct' style of glasses. Apparently he travelled widely from about 1910 to 1935 and displayed his old passports. A very impressive list of countries showed their stamps. The collection included Russia, Japan, most of Europe and some British colonies in Africa.

After he downed a few 'refreshers', he waxed in full spate and told us about his two boys ensconced in Sedbergh School and how he visited Harrods four times a year, to buy presents and a stock of hats for his wife. He added that she only wore some once, so they burned these on November 5th! The weirdest piece of legerdemain was when he produced a mass of bank pass books. Some were in his name and many in his wife's name. It seems he did not trust the banks overmuch, so if one or two folded he had a dozen or so left intact! The deposits varied from £2,000 to £20,000.

His nickname was earned when he first moved to Cumbria and hired some of the Flookburgh fishermen to assist him to collect yachts when he made purchases. Some were bought in the Isle of Wight and had to be sailed to Arnside. His sailings also included shipping the boats to buyers. His favourite trip was from Oban to Dublin in a heavy gale.

The 'Doc' was very enthusiastic about another of 'Gibbo's' cast offs. We had an invite to visit a retired Indian

Army Surgeon. This man lived singly, an elderly bachelor who had a superb house on the hillside above Grasmere. He had a massive window with panoramic views across the lake. In this room he had a massive library.

The books were mostly leather bound, with a fine collection of Indian history. He was in his element discussing medical matters with 'Doc' who was about thirty-five years his junior. The old army survivor had served at least thirty years in the service and had visited many areas and army stations including the notorious 'NW Frontier'. The enemy were Pushtoons or Afghans.

He expected India to seek independence very soon and could not see how a unified government would cope with the castes, tribes and schism between Muslims and Hindus. He had a live-in gardener cum chauffer and his cook. He enjoyed our company and was almost 'fluent' in navigation before we left!

Another fascinating 'local' lived in an old solid looking stone house near Newby Bridge. A very large garden had two large glasshouses. They were used for intensive tomato growing and a smaller number of beans and peppers. Another Empire servant, he had obtained a language degree from Cambridge. After some European posting in the Foreign Office service, he was promoted to a District Officer in Burma and subsequently served nearly twenty years in Malay. He often made two or three week 'tours' by boat and horse to legislate against disputes in the more remote areas. He usually had a Malay NCO and six or eight armed native troops for protection. He was awarded an OBE for this work.

His father was a very wealthy lawyer and landowner based in Barrow and West Cumbria. He had two brothers and a sister. They all had public school and university education. One brother was an architect and civil engineering adviser to the Colonial Office; he was involved in harbour building in Singapore. His other brother was a medical officer in Burma, stationed with his wife, also a qualified medical doctor. His sister had a literature degree from Cambridge, never married and 'kept home' for her parents.

Our local ex administrator's pride and joy was his large dining room. This had oak panels on the walls, a massive oak table and eight chairs to match. He claimed the panels had been removed from one of Oliver Cromwell's houses. His second indulgence was his glasshouses and products! Our host urged us to return any weekend. He estimated a load of tomatoes would be ready for picking in less than three weeks, when we were welcome to take them for the Officers' Mess!

Three years previous to our meeting his wife had died. He was very bitter with the British Army as he knew his only son had been taken prisoner by the Japanese in the debacle and surrender of Singapore. Like him, his son was also a Colonial Officer in Malay and had 'escaped' to Singapore. He also hoped the RAF could develop bases and equipment to bomb mainland Japan as soon as possible.

I believe most or all of the family died off prior to 1960; a truly fine family who were the best types of Empire builders. A pity the Empire critics could not have met many of the educated Brits. Those who spent most of their lives developing a veneer of civilisation in numerous territories and may never have lived sufficiently long enough to enjoy any retirement back 'home'.

Due to 'Gibbo's' PR expertise, we surprisingly had two very interesting visitors to the Mess. Firstly, we had more than one evening with W Heaton Cooper, the famous Grasmere watercolour artist. He showed some of his work and gave us a short talk. The other visit was also an artist, but very different. He was a retired cartoonist for one of the Manchester newspapers. He made a couple of pencil portraits and gave an insight into his work and deadlines.

Anecdotes from cark

A night flight had on board two navigational trainers and a navigation instructor. The pilot was a new Staff Pilot. On the completion of an accurate tour of the Irish Sea area, the pilot was using a green light signal to guide him on to the W-E runway. The instructor suddenly realised the Anson was heading for Carnforth Railway Station! Full throttle and a rapid climb saved the situation!

A US Liberator bomber asked for an urgent landing. The crew had flown from Canada and missed Anglesey. We advised them to proceed to Walney RAF. The pilot said he was worried about fuel shortage. After a trial circuit, the pilot made a superb approach and landing. With red hot brakes he came to a juddering stop on the Flookburgh shrimp fisherman's road, with the nose hovering over the adjacent drain ditch! After a good night's rest and food the take-off was almost as nerve shredding as the landing. An hour later he landed in one piece at the huge US base at Burtonwood near Warrington.

Not as fortunate as the American crew, a RAF Wellington two engine bomber landed wheels up on the sands at low tide. He missed anti-invasion poles but the aircraft had to be dismantled - a long and weary job!

The following event occurred before my 'watch' but was told by a reliable Cark Officer: A night flight was on the last leg from N Ireland to Cark. The route was planned to fly to the Calf of Man, an islet on the south tip at 5,000 feet. On board were a Staff Pilot and two Australian trainees. For some reason or gross error, the plane was well below the safe height and grazed the top peaty slopes of Snaefell, the highest point of the Isle of Man. By a miracle the crew survived serious injury and using the axe cut out from the fuselage into inky darkness! After a struggle and mishaps they spotted a small light, which eventually proved to be a farmer's cottage. The occupant had no phone, so it was daybreak before the farmer could cycle to the nearest police station. From this, they were collected by RAF Jurby, a training air station. The following day they were ferried back to Cark!

Dating and mating

As the War progressed it is widely accepted that the social and sexual norm of pre 1940 rapidly changed or many people believed, were eroded. The eventual promiscuity was quite understandable with the huge upheaval of family life and the concentration of young men and women on airfields and army camps.

The worst by-product of this social breakdown was unwanted pregnancies. Possibly due to the high quality of our WAAF officers, we had no epidemic among the Cark WAAFs.

The ground staff, although mostly male had a fair opportunity of making friends with the WAAF contingency, which may have limited the need to mix with the local young women. Outside the camp dances in the village halls were common place and usually crowded. The RAF had an advantage over the Army on the dance floor; the RAF wore shoes, whereas the army lads had to crunch round in boots!

A modest number of the local girls were forced out of circulation. This was the development of a small factory in Ulverston where aircraft components had to be cleaned down with paraffin baths. The girls worked shifts and most detested the job. Some were sorry they had not joined the services! There was one lonesome Land Army girl who worked hard on a farm near Cartmel. She sometimes had a break at weekends. We felt sorry for her and urged her to try for a transfer to the RAF.

Not many relationships matured into marriage. Two couples were notable. We have mentioned previously the sad outcome of our 'Queen Bee' who married a Polish Staff Pilot who was sadly killed during bombing. Another happier case was one of our Staff Pilots nicknamed 'Timber'; his surname was probably Wood! He was a quiet unassuming man and possibly slightly introspective. He was no 'oil painting' and looked older than his true age. He was however always well groomed and his shoes could advertise Cherry Blossom!

We had from time to time visitors' day and on such occasion 'Timber' brought his new girl-friend. We were bowled over. His companion looked not more than twenty, tall, slender and very pretty. She had the unusual combination of dense black wavy hair and vivid intense blue eyes. 'Timber' was bombarded with questions: How had he 'pulled' the prettiest girl in Kendal? They soon married and set up home soon after the War in S Lancashire where 'Timber' could really earn his nickname and became a woodwork teacher!

A Cartmel clanger

The King's Arms, Cartmel was packed with Cark personnel and a few locals like most Saturday nights. In the smoke screen melee was a Wing Commander who was visiting the airfield. Sitting in one corner were two WAAFs. A F/O standing next to the 'Winco' leaned over towards the girls and pointing to his three rings on his sleeve asked if they could move to make sitting room. One of the girls had imbibed in 'one too many' and in a loud voice exclaimed,

"I don't care if he has rings from his arse to his elbow, I'm not budging!" The 'Winco' thought this was the highlight of the evening!

The 'ard 'ard 'ammer of the 'orses 'ooves on the 'ard 'ard road

Some of the sleeping quarters were set parallel to the straight, narrow, paved road leading from Flookburgh Square to the shore. The shrimp fishermen used horse and carts. They worked in all weathers and had to harmonise with the tides. Unfortunately the clop, clop of the heavy horses gait often woke us. Some nights we had to suffer a convoy of three carts in succession. However, we accepted they were helping to feed the country and it was a very arduous job and not without danger. Also, some of their young men had joined the Royal Navy.

Completely squashed

One of the many virtues of life at RAF Cark was the available squash courts. This was my first opportunity to play regularly. My roommate Ray Dean was like me, a tyro, so we could easily fit in three or four sessions per week.

One day after lunch the 'Queen Bee' approached me and exclaimed, "I say Parky old boy, can you fit in a squash game around four o'clock?" I could not refuse the lady and duly reported at the court at 16:00 hours prompt.

We now draw a veil over the session. In five games I failed to extract one point! I had not been warned that her ladyship had played at her public school from eleven to eighteen. Then at university she played in the varsity team and had fairly often played near her home! Being a man I was sweating profusely, but my opponent, a true lady, was merely flushed!

A Cark of a day

The RAF more so than either the Army or Navy, concocted many colourful slang phrases. One which has lasted is 'Gremlin'. Probably the most zany is 'Wizard Prang'. This was most apt in the grim days of 1940 when many young pilots had to make belly landings on the grassy airfields due to a shot-up undercarriage.

At RAF Cark we did our bit in this area of linguistic innovation. Around 08:00 hours struggling against a gusty wind and rain, cycling to the Control Tower (all of twenty feet away), we would eventually climb the steps to be greeted by a ginning meteorological girl. She would show the Navigation Officer on duty a horrible mass of isobars and a thick pencil line denoting the depression front pushing east over the Irish Sea,

"All seagulls grounded!"

The Navigation Officer would reply, "Another Cark of a day!"

Nothing but a hound dog

One perfect early summer evening, our Mountain Rescue jeep with four on board came to a full stop on the top of the steep road leading to Lindale village. We had a married officer in our crew and were to drop him off at his rented cottage to be welcomed by his wife. A few vehicles were stopped in front, so we ambled down the hill to expect an accident.

To our amazement we found one of the locals holding up the traffic. Then we heard the howls of fell hounds. They were following an aniseed trail on the nearby hills. The route was to take them over the road and a further three miles to Cartmel Racecourse field!

The whip hand

The railways during the War were a lifeline carrying passengers, many of which were armed services and also vital freight. Delays of one to several hours were common due to breakdowns, labour shortage and minor accidents. In the Cark saga, the most famous train was the last evening train from Carnforth to Barrow. This was given the bizarre nickname of 'The Whip'. It was said to ship in the stragglers getting back to Cark from leave, or at weekends from Morecambe or Blackpool.

One Saturday when our Navigation Department was four strong, we decided for some barmy reason to train it across the bay to Arnside for a dance. This trip was on time and we soon found the crowded small village hall. Around 22:30 hours we decided to head for the station in case 'The Whip' was on time. Two hours later we all agreed 'The Whip' was NOT on time! Now the foursome had two choices: one, to sit it out and wait, or two, hike across the railway bridge to Cark perimeter!

Yes, you guessed right! Four weary navigators started plodding from 'sleeper' to 'sleeper', cursing and stumbling. The night was pitch black and we did not rise with Cark on the Sunday morning – so the railway had 'The Whip Hand'.

"The hypocritic oath!"

Our Cark Medical Officer was a great guy; quite young and dedicated to every aspect of his varied responsibilities. Although he used the Officer's Mess, he did not booze or mix much with the younger pilot mob. He made use of his limited spare time studying hard for his aspiration to become a member of the College of Surgeons. He found the examination very difficult, especially as 'Doc' had no experienced hospital medicos to confer with on a daily basis.

One week we urged him to have a leisure day, when we would introduce him to a Lakeland mountain and if he trusted us, we would steer him up a crag. We picked a perfect summer's day and selected Langdale. Bowfell Buttress looked tempting. About six of us sweated up the Band, a track up from the head of the valley towards the top ridges. 'Doc' was not over enthusiastic when he looked up the three hundred feet or so to the Buttress. After a rest and a good gulp of water, 'Scotty' Dwyer roped up and had 'Doc' as number two in a three up team. An 'easy' route was used and the Doctor, who was tall, lean and fit, did well for the first fifty feet.

He then came up to a fairly steep wall of twenty feet and a lovely stream of invectives streamed across the mountain air, "How the *@?*!* hell do I get up this, you b******s?"

The number three climber shouted up to 'Doc', "Is that what you call a hypocritical oath?"

He enjoyed his day's exertions and agreed it was a real change from pouring over anatomy, or the mysteries of pharmacology!

"The Mull of bloody Galloway"

In one of the rare weeks in summer when we had 'wall to wall' sunshine and light winds we tried to cram in four daytime flights. On the Friday we decided to give the pupils some overland delights, so the first leg was Cark to Carlisle. We flew at 6,000 feet, so if a single engine failed the Staff Pilot could turn back and re-trim the Anson. This allowed for a loss of 1,000 feet, giving 2,000 feet of spare over the highest Lakes peaks..

The second leg was turning westerly, descending to 5,000 feet and then set a course arriving to pass the south tip of the Mull of Galloway about two miles offshore.

Trust the Irish Sea microclimate to spoil our plans. The crews found that a sheet of low stratus was covering a fair area of the Solway Firth.

One crew ordered their pilot to descend and break through the cloud. The pilot followed their instruction and was around 500 or 600 feet over the open sea when breaking cloud. Up to one mile ahead were the granite cliffs of the Mull. One of the pupils was wide awake and slapped the pilot on his head and shouted, "Left hand down, full throttle, that's the bloody Mull of Galloway!"

The Staff Pilot was probably at fault, two or three degrees off his correct course and should have descended more steeply to break cover at least five miles from the Mull. The other crews had no problems.

And finally a real 'cough drop'!

To understand this aptus verbum we should explain that all services in the War years had in their surgeries a large bottle on a shelf. The label on this bottle had the intriguing inscription, "MISTIC.SPEC". Non Latin scholars guessed this may have been an abbreviation for something like 'misticus specialis' or special mixture. In fact, this concoction was a typical cough medicine of the time.

Some of the airmen's sleeping huts had a flat roof porch over the entrance. During off duty hours, one of the mechanics had a weird whim to sit cross-legged on a cushion on top of his porch. He was a great reader and with his jet black hair and thick black rimmed spectacles he always looked studious. Apparently on some days he had a well-worn tome, which was a biography of Saint Thomas Aquias, the BC religious philosopher!

A few of us were having some 'crack' in the Officers' Mess and one officer mentioned this odd bod and asked if anyone else had noticed his very bizarre appearance and leisure time occupation.

"Oh Yes," said one of the group, "he's a real cough drop!"

"No" exclaimed another officer, "I am sure he is the original MISTIC SPEC!"

G F Parkinson – 2011

JACK PATTERSON,
Millom & Auschwitz

Two things stand out in my memory of my time at Millom.

1. The Botha aircraft was used for our bombing and navigation training along with the Anson the Botha as stated above was designed as a torpedo bomber but we heard the story that it had proved unsatisfactory for this task as it could not fly on one engine and was difficult to evacuate the pilots, some of whom were Polish did not like flying this aircraft and we trainees were apprehensive of flights in the Botha I believe that not too long after my time at the millom the Botha was taken out of service.

2. I remember the last flight in my log book with pilot p/o Baird crew of pilot three trainee navigators and a wireless operator on a night navigation with about four turning points. Some way or other we found ourselves flying in a ballon barrage over Liverpool harbour and of course, we did 180 degree course change and then sometime later the pilot reported the fuel was running low and as well the w70 told us the radio was not operating.

The pilot did several low passes to see if he could see a field where we might set down but this did look very promising. Then a searchlight crew below realised we were in trouble turned on their beam pointing the direction to fly and this was followed by several other searchlights and then landing were suddenly turned on ahead of us and we came down on an airfield in wales near holyhead with very little fuel left. Next morning the cloud ceiling was very low but we took off on a dr course and flew just above the water coming our near the Millom airbase and landed ok.

Jack Patterson's Story

To begin, let me say that all members of Pop's crew knew we were most fortunate to have Geoffrey Porter as our Skipper. He was a highly skilled and experienced pilot, as well as having the best of leadership qualities as an RAF Officer and Captain of our Halifax aircraft.

Our Skipper gave the order to bail out. I followed Don Hall, our bomb aimer, out the front hatch and Ken Wilman, our rear gunner, went out from his position at the same time. I could see his parachute in the moonlight and we were able to get together soon after coming down in a Dutch farm field. Ken and I were to evade capture for the next ten days, during which time we made right calls on farmhouses for food and water

There was no question on whose side these Dutch people were on, but the penalty for helping escaped prisoners was very severe so we kept our visits short Ken, being from Rhodesia spoke some Afrikaans which was similar to Dutch, and this helped us communicate. However, the Dutch Underground was not too well organized at this stage of the war, so we did not come upon any help of this type.

In the end, while taking cover in a farm shed, our presence was detected by a dog and before we could move we found ourselves looking into revolvers held by the local police, and had to surrender We were taken first to a large German airbase near Eindhoven, where we met a German pilot who said he had shot our aircraft down. After interrogation by Gestapo in an Amsterdam prison and at a Luftwaffe transit camp near Frankfurt, we were taken across Germany in a railway boxcar to a large POW camp near Breslau (now part of Poland). I might mention here that prisoners taken during the Dieppe raid were also brought to this camp soon after my arrival. I was at this camp, known as Stalag 8B, Lamsdorf, from August

42 until September '43. Then, in company with two other airforce chaps, one of which was Frank Linklater from my old crew, I did what was called a swop-over, or exchange of identity, with a British Army chap who has been taken prisoner at Dunkirk in 1940 and who was scheduled to be taken out of the camp on a working party to a place that we later found was called Auschwitz.

Many years later, at the time of the Gulf War, I finally decided to record the story of "My Remembrance"

telling of the balance of the time I spent as a Kriegsgefangene, and in particular of Franz Irving who was one of the many prisoners in the Auschwitz concentration camp.

My Remembrance

Watching Herman Wouk's "War and Remembrance" and the T.V. pictures of the P.O.Ws captured during our war with Saddam Hussein have motivated me to recall some of my memories of an incarcerated young man w with whom I had the opportunity to meet and talk with over war with Adolf Hitler. Franz a period of almost a year back in the days of our Irving never had his name mentioned in a newspaper or a TV newscast, but just feel that his story needs to be told so that some record of his ordeal in this world will exist. Perhaps in writing about my time with Franz will help me feel that I have done something in his memory

This story begins on a day in late September 1943, as Buck, Link and I scrambled out of a railway boxcar to find ourselves at a small station called Auschwitz, or Oswiecim if you were Polish. We were members of a group of some 300 British soldiers, most of whom had been taken prisoner at the time of Dunkirk. We were a working party sent out from a large POW.camp in Eastern Germany, Buck was an English fighter pilot who flew an early wartime twin engine Whirlwind aircraft, ink and I were Canadian crew members of a downed RAF Halifax bomber. We were planning to try and escape and, as our first move, had exchanged identities (unknown to our captors) with some British soldiers who were slated to go out on the working party. I now called myself Sammy Crichton, a Scot from the Isle of Bute in the Firth of Clyde. Little did we know that we had arrived at a place, the name of which would become as well known and remembered as any battle in the war. Franz Irving was already a prisoner at Auschwitz, but in very different circumstances to our group Let me now set the scene of my view of this infamous location:

From the railway station, our group marched several miles to a fenced-in compound of barracks, which we could see was on the perimeter of a large industrial area surrounded by a high fence that was being patrolled by German SS soldiers. On the way, we passed a large number of barrack type buildings without any containment fence. About a mile to the south of our compound we could see the guard towers and fence of a large prison camp of some type. We were soon to learn that the large industrial area was an IG Farben chemical complex under construction, designed to utilize the soft coal of this Polish region of Upper Silesia, to make lubricating materials and other products supporting the German war effort. Following arrival at our barracks, we were given a long list of work trades with instructions to indicate our preference. Sammy Crichton chose the trade of blacksmith, believing that being a former bank clerk, he would not prove to be of too much use in this capacity

Early in the morning our group, attracting considerable attention in our British uniforms from the many civilians walking enroute, marched through the gate of the Farben plant. It was then that the true nature of this workplace started to become apparent. A sign on the gate spelled out "NO SMOKING in some ten languages

The workers were forced labourers recruited from all the areas occupied by the German military consisting of 3.000 or more Frenchmen; a large group of Czechs and Slovaks, along with Belgians, Dutch and Ukrainians.

The Ukrainians included several thousand women, most of whom were strong, stocky, peasant types and whom were seen digging trenches and moving heavy materials. However, the largest contingent of this multinational workforce came from the concentration camp we could see from our barrack compound. Some 5,000 or more obviously undernourished and mostly Jewish men came each day, struggling to keep up in long marching columns escorted by the SS guards and urged on by some of their own comrades wearing armbands, signifying Kapo (or group leader). Franz Irving was among these Hafiflingers, is they were called. They were highly visible in their fragile white and blue striped prison garb, with matching beret caps and shaved heads.

Our fellows often referred to them as Stripes" (or the "Dead End Kids") In this large work force there were also many Polish men and women from the surrounding villages and towns, as well as some German civilians (mostly skilled tradesmen such as welders and pipe fitters, engineers and management types) The area of this workplace was about a mile square, with various large and small buildings, mostly in the early stages of construction and connected by overhead steam and gas pipes.

"Sammy Crichton" soon found himself working in a small blacksmith shop as a helper to a short stocky Czech blacksmith called Jan, from near Prague. Jan had been a blacksmith all his working life, and it did not take him long to decide that the newest addition to his helpers knew very little about healing and hammering metal!

Several Frenchmen and Poles were also in this shop and Jan allowed me to put my time in almost as I wished.

As I found my way around the work area, I found that it was possible to move about without too much danger of being challenged. I also found that the British uniform carried a certain amount of respect from civilians and the German army guards. Shortly after the first of two Christmases at this location over half of my group including my comrades Link and Buck, were moved to another location in Poland. At this particular location we were receiving regular deliveries of Red Cross food parcels and cigarettes from home, so we did not have to depend on the daily ration of thin turnip soup that was ladled out to Haflingers, such as Franz Irving (who I would soon come to know very well).

In the spring of 1944, Auschwitz and the surrounding industrial area became almost a daily target for U.S. heavy bombers based in Italy, Bombs fell only seven times on the Farben camp, but on the first bombing eighteen of my English comrades were killed when several bombs fell on our compound one Sunday at noon.

The air-raid siren would sound just before noon almost every day until late in the fall, although on most occasions the bombers would fly on to other targets. It was fairly early after the air-raid alarms became part of our daily life that, while taking shelter among the support pillars of one of the largest I.G. Farben structures, I came into contact with Franz He was a tall, very thin, Jewish chap wearing the striped ersatz material prison garb, a matching beret on his shaven head and a prison identification number tattoo on his arm. His group was working nearby in this building and he had been able to move a little way from his guards without being missed. He said "Hello Englander, and I replied telling him that I was Canadian. I was pleased to find out that Franz spoke English quite fluently. We didn't have a great deal of time during this first encounter, but it was long enough for me to find out that Franz had been a school teacher in Berlin before the war. Anxious to improve my ability to understand and speak the German language, I suggested that we try and meet at this location as often as possible at noontime. Franz could tutor me in German and, for my part, I would try to bring him some bread and other food that I could do without It turned out that this was the first of many times that we were able to meet and talk - sometimes for only a few minutes and at other times for most of the half-hour noon break. Franz was a capable teacher and helped me considerably with my German. More importantly, I was able to bring him some bread and biscuits. I had managed to acquire a thermos flask in barter, so I also had hot tea and coffee to share with him. I like to think that, perhaps these meetings helped to make his hard struggle to exist a little more bearable.

Franz's story, as he related to me over the period of our meetings, was very sad. However, he said it was in many ways typical to that which thousands of other Jewish men in the camp would tell, if they had the opportunity. There were many more however who would never get to tell their story, as they were no longer alive.

Franz said "I was so happy in earlier days and still can not believe what has happened to my family. I was born in Berlin and, after graduating as a teacher from college in the city. I was able to obtain a teaching position at a primary school in the city. Juli, a classmate in my secondary school days, and I were married and, in a few years, we had a family of a son and a daughter, who would be nine and seven years old now. My father was a watchmaker and also ran a small jewellery store with the help of my mother. For a time, life was very happy and fulfilling for our family......."

As the world knows now, life changed dramatically after Hitler and the Nazi party gained control of the German nation. The day came when Franz was called into the school principal's office and told that being Jewish, he could no longer continue teaching Meanwhile, his father was forced to close his business because of vandalism and lack of customers. Some of his father's business friends had been ordered to join labour battalions and his father also expected soon to get a similar summons.

Franz continued, Nor too long after I was dismissed as a teacher two government men came to our flat. I was told that I must work to help the war effort and given an order to go with these men and register with a labour unit near Berlin. After registering, I was also told I could come home for a few days, and would have leave to visit my family each month. Although I had some misgivings. I had no choice but to go with these Nazi officials and that night I found myself being herded into a railway boxcar along with about fifty other Jewish men from the Berlin area, some of whom I had known. We were sent to this Auschwitz concentration camp and I have not had any word about my wife and children since I have been here. I have very little hope that they are still 'alive."

Franz went on, have little reason to continue to exist in this world. Once you become too weak to work, you are transferred to a special barrack called a hospital. However, in reality this is the first stage of going up in smoke at the nearby crematorium. Many of my fellow prisoners, usually the older men first, have been moved to this hospital and none have returned. Soon I may just give up and let them take me."

Hopefully, as we continued our talks, I was able in some degree to encourage Franz to continue the struggle.

As Christmas 1945 approached, tension in the area steadily increased with the Russian army reported to be coming closer each day. My meetings with Franz became less frequent. Sometimes Franz would not come and would think that he had been moved to another job, or was ill: then he would be there the next day.

When we did manage to meet, we just talked about our hopes for the future rather than continue with the language lessons - as this seemed rather pointless now.

It was a few days before Christmas that we had our last meeting I had promised to bring him some extra food and a special surprise for Christmas. However, there were many rumours that the Germans were soon to evacuate the area and, like my English comrades, I was trying to accumulate additional supplies in case of a sudden move. Although we had not been receiving the Red Cross parcels for some time, I did have a few extra biscuits hidden in my bunk. I guess that, when it finally comes down to our own survival, most of us tend to look after ourselves first. So I held back on my gift to Franz and brought him something less than I might have done. In his desperation, Franz admonished me for not being more generous - and rightly so! This will always be in my memory. To Franz and the others in his circumstances, the English soldiers (including this Canadian amongst them) had it all, including the hope of survival and going back to our families. Theirs would most likely not be there if they made it out. At our last meeting, we discussed the possibility of Franz coming into our compound. I would try and locate a spare British uniform and bring it to him at our next meeting. Looking back at all the confusion that developed at that time, I think now that this could have been done. If so, then Franz might have been here now to tell his own story.

During the first week in January 1945, the evacuation of the Auschwitz area began with the sound of Russian artillery not far distant with some shells even bursting over the Farben plant. German civilians with Volkssturm armbands indicating that they were now members of a peoples defence group) were marching to the East to help hold up the advancing Russian army. At least our group was marching to the West on the first leg of a long trek in the dead of winter. As we marched into the open country we came upon bodies dressed in the familiar stripe uniform, frozen in the ditches. It's possible that Franz Irving was among them. Although he had given me the address of one of his uncles living in Australia, when I wrote to him after arriving back home in Canada I never received a reply.

Mr J Patterson - 1998

W. MURRAY REID

Shortly after my wings parade, I was promoted to Sgt. and the next day to a P/O. The letters AOS stands for Air Observer School. We were taught Navigation. My regimental number R188785 is correct for an airman, but was changed to J40935 when was commissioned.

After WWII was assigned a permanent force number 24307. Incidentally the RCAF did not wish to show its low strength so numbering began at 20.000.

When the number 30.000 was reached, numbers were backtracked to 10,000 and used up to 20,000. The original 10,000 were reserved for pre-WWII members of which there were still a few. So we played games with the USSR.

I was stationed at Millom from 21 Jun 44 until 26 Jul 44. I do not recall the number of our course nor many members. Two names though were P/O's Bounds "Dad". Paul Douglas both from Vancouver. Paul was later lost while doing a night exercise over Land's End in a Wellington. Our course Instructor was a RAF F/L. The majority of our course were NCO's RAAF and RCAF.

We were transferred to 22 OTU, Wellesbourne Warwickshire and I in turn was detached to Gaydon satellite for flying training with my crew. A delightful station! I have no photos as you know taking pictures was forbidden, so I have to rely on a deteriorating memory nowadays. I wish that the policy had been different.

When we first reported in at the base we were taken on a parade around the station. When we passed the hospital there were seven coffins sitting in a row. Evidently a Wellington had crashed into a hill at the end of the runway and all the crew were killed. As a result we all paid that hill a great deal of respect when we were at or near the drome.

It might seem strange that I know so little about other members on my course. When I was at Fingal, most of my course were RAF. On graduation, most Canadians were sent to Western Canada, most of the RAF and a few RCAF were sent to London. On graduation the RAF were sent home so when I got to England I was virtually alone. On transfer to Millom almost all RCAF were from the West, predominantly Vancouver. After OTU we went our separate ways so I have scanty knowledge of the careers of the Millom group.

Our course instructor insisted on calling us "Colonials" which did not bother us to any great degree, however, the tone of voice was extremely unpleasant. The issue came to a head one day when he threatened to alter some facial features. As a result we were detailed to do some drill after 1800 hrs for the next seven days. The poor Cpl DI had a thick accent, we were not familiar with all the movements and we were certainly not interested in doing a good job. The net result was chaos so drill was cancelled after one evening. At the time we considered we had gained a victory.

We had an influx of Air Cadets for the summer. We used to take two of them on each day flight, which they seemed to enjoy. We were also detailed to act as the pilot in the AMBT and teach them how to bomb. It got rather boring to sit there for three or four hours, again they seemed to enjoy the exercise.

Most of our flying was restricted to a large extent because of so much cloud cover. A great deal of our navigation was of the Dead Reckon type so we were not challenged to any great extent. In fact, our training in Canada was much tougher. As a result, we concluded that the tour was strictly a holding exercise and since none of us had joined to just sit around, we became thoroughly disgruntled. There was one unfortunate fallout from this mood. Some RAAF and RCAF NCO'S went into Millom and got inebriated. While returning to base (walking) they were very rowdy and the police locked them in the local gaol. Normally English Bobbies were very lenient and they would have been released in the morning with an admonishment to behave themselves in the future. Word quickly got back to camp that a RAAF member was in trouble so a posse was formed to rescue him. The posse quickly determined the cell wherein the prisoner was held, tied a rope around the bars and pulled them out of the wall. The prisoners quickly escaped out of the gaol and returned to camp, the police now had a serious offence to deal with so called the CO of the camp. He in turn placed the offenders under close arrest and decided a court-martial was the next appropriate action. The next day a RAAF G/C showed up from London and escorted all the involved NCOs (RAAF) off the base never to be seen again. To this day I have no idea what transpired with these people. Interestingly no Senior RAF officer intervened on behalf of our NCO, who was sent to Sheffield as punishment. I never heard of him again.

To say the least we RCAF personnel were dismayed at this lack of support. I might add that I was not surprised when no Senior officials spoke up when Trudeau integrated us with the Army and Navy. Senior officers from both those services had plenty to say, to the extent that the navy retained Its rank structure.

The next closest big town was Barrow-in-Furness but I think I only went there one time as it was not an easy journey, despite the fact that you could almost see the downtown activities on a clear day. We used to say if we only had a rowboat we could have gone there very easily.

We did eventually became proficient at navigating, easily meeting PFF standards (H hour 30 secs So maybe Millom deserves some of the credit.

W. Murray, DASHWOOD, ONT. 1998.

WILLIAM A. (BILL) ROBERTSON

My Sojourn in Belgium

Just after completing our bombing raid on the marshalling yards of Hasselt, Belgium on 13 May 1944, we were shot down and all the crew safely bailed out. Through contact with two children of school age, their uncle supplied me with farm overalls. I was interrogated by a resistance member (Jaak Cardineals of Bree) who arranged to hide me in a barn (Bruntix's farm at Bokrijk - now Diana's Restaurant) and where I met my pilot Taffy. We then hid in the woods of Zondhoven for 7 days with escaped Russian POWS.

In that time period, we were joined by our W/Op. Nav, and F/Eng. Both gunners were POWS. My civvies were supplied by Baron De Fille Fang and most of the food supplied by Julien ?, Louis ?, and Rene Jaspers of Zondhoven. Taken by bike to Biernaux's home in Hasselt for 2 days. A young lady guided Taffy and me by train to clearance centre in Liege. Dr. Boulanger of Liege led me to Pierre Rademakers' home Dieu Donne Avenue, Liege. Spent the rest of the time there until liberation, except for a period when Dr. Boulanger was jailed by the Germans.

I was taken to the home of Mme Trokay, Quai D'orsay, Liege by Arthur Molle of Herstal and Pierre Rademaker until it was safe to return to the Rademakers'. Liberated by the U.S. Third Army early September. Hitchhiked with downed U.S. pilot Ron Moores to Brussels. Returned home in October 1944 by Queen Mary. Discharged as F/O on 22 March 1945.

William A. (Bill) Robertson 1998

DR. HERBERT J. VEAR

Low level flying at AFU

One of the highlights at Advanced Flying Unit (AFU) at Millom, Cumberland was the required low-level exercise to gain some experience in low-level navigation, in contrast to air plot dead reckoning navigation used on heavy bombers. This was the kind of map reading navigation used by navigators on Mosquitos where en route accuracy was not as critical. The major difference for this exercise was that we were flying Avro Ansons with a top speed of 150k and not to fly lower than 1000 feet, which is not really very exciting.

We were briefed on the course to fly, weather and observations to be noted in the log. As usual at AFU, the pilots were Sergeant pilots with a number of reasons for being at AFU rather than on operations. It was rare to have the same pilot and Wireless Operator (WAG) two flights in a row.

After take-off, we headed east over the Irish Sea and almost immediately the pilot dropped down to 300-500 feet. On these trips the navigator sits beside the pilot and makes airspeed, altitude and compass notes in the log and any other sightings of importance, for example ships, etc. The first landfall was Chicken Rock, a small island at the south end of the Isle of Man. We scrapped across the top with less than a hundred feet to spare. The pilots enjoyed these rare opportunities to really enjoy flying, However, accidents were not common, at least not as common as night flying.

We changed course for Northern Ireland since to fly over the Republic of Ireland was to invite anti-aircraft fire. Ireland was not at war and pretended neutrality, which was an open question for many. The Irish were accused of supporting the Germans, because of centuries of hate for the British and their policy of separation. Regardless we avoided their territory, but not everyone did. Some allied aircrew spent the rest of the war as internees. About 20 miles of the coast we spotted two small fishing boats. The fishermen were completely oblivious to our approach and startled as we climbed enough to clear their masts. We made a wide circle around them and dropped down to fly past at very low level. We wagged the wings they threatened with clenched fists. We had a good laugh and I am sure they did as well, after the shock was over, needless to say, none of this appeared in the log or did the less than 1000 feet we were flying.

The next landfall was British Ireland not far from Belfast. We were not to fly over Belfast, although a classmate, "Paddy Doyle did, he was born there and had hopes of visiting relatives before we left AFU (He did get that opportunity). We flew low over farmland and low enough to scare the hell out of the people on the ground and farm animals that scattered as we went over. I am sure there was a mixture of excitement and anger on the ground, but fortunately no reports of low flying. It would be next to impossible for people on the ground to read our station call letters since the aircraft were camouflaged.

We left land on a northerly course, as in our flight plan, and headed northeast towards the coast of Scotland. Again the trip was very low and we did pass over several small ships, who probably assumed we were part of Coastal Command, and a welcome sight. We made Ailsa Craig our turning point before heading back to base. Ailsa Craig is the historical source of granite for curling stones. It is a very small rock island with no habitation, but a convenient pinpoint for navigation. I flew over this rock so many times that I could give an accurate course to anywhere.

We flew just off the coast of England and climbed to regulation height when opposite Whitehaven. The rest of the trip was uneventful The trip took about 3 hours and was an exciting time, full of fond memories. We never did this again until OTU and HCU.

Landing on mountains

It was late fall 1944 and I was stationed at RAF AFU, Advanced Flying Unit, near Millom, Cumberland. This was a dreadful place for weather and dangerous for flying. We flew Avro Ansons, the same beasts we flew at Navigation School in Canada. The custom was to go to school all day (8am to 5pm) and fly all night and sleep from 7am to noon, back to school and more flying that night. This routine went on for several days in a row or until weather stood us down.

The flights were of 3 to 4 hours duration and wandered over the Irish Sea, Northern Ireland and much of Scotland. Since 90% of flying was at night we saw very little of the land other than the mountains reaching to 5000ft.

We were briefed to stay above the 5000ft level and were convinced by the high accident rate at this station. The CO, a Group Captain, believed that aircraft should be in the air and not on the ground. The more hours the station flew, the better chance of promotion and an operational station transfer. Let's face it, RAF Training Command was not the real war. In fact, almost all pilots were dropouts for one or more reasons from operations. The majority resented being "jockeys" for training navigators and wanted back into action. The result, all too frequently, was pilots a bit drunk or under the influence, Some were known to drop off to sleep.

The night in question was the usual routine of the first trip leaving at 9pm, returning at midnight and then followed by another briefing for take-off at 1 am and return about 4-5 am. The first trip went well, it was the second trip that lives in memory for a classmate Fred Lepage from New Brunswick. The flight plan called for a height of 5000ft across the Isle of Man to Ireland, north to Scotland and back to base, following the coast. We had an uneventful trip and welcomed the usual bacon and egg breakfast on return.

When we gathered in the briefing room, the rumor was that Fred's aircraft had come down in the mountains of the Isle of Man. Apparently, radio contact had been lost and their IFF (identification friend or foe) was no longer transmitting. Naturally we were upset and fearful for our friends safety. Most of us remained in the area for news.

Finally a hard to receive morse message was received by a WAF radio operator, who could not believe her translation. Apparently the aircraft had struck the ground and came to a sudden stop. The crew was safe, but could only guess where they were. Fred Lepage confirmed that they were on top of a mountain on the Isle of Man, according to his airplot. It took two days to guide them down the mountain using mountain climbers from the local population. It took another two days to return them to our base.

The story finally surfaced. They followed the same route as the rest of us, but either had a defective altimeter or the pilot did not maintain the 5000ft altitude briefing called for. They struck the mountain near its top and on a slight incline. It was their opinion that 10 feet higher and they would have cleared, whereas, 10-20 feet lower they would have been killed. In order to radio back to base, they had to find a way to raise the long trailing aerial high enough for a signal to be sent. After several tries, they succeeded. They spent the rest of the night trying to get comfortable in the damaged aircraft. I am certain that aircraft remained on top of Mount Douglas until well after the war ended. As expected there were hundreds of wrecked aircraft spread over isolated areas of the UK, with some only being located today. I never learned what action was taken against the pilot or crew.

Herb Vear - 1998

WILLIAM WEIGHTON

I was posted to RAF millom around June the 10th 1944. I cannot be sure of the exact date as my flying log is no longer in my possession.

It was at Millom that myself and my fellows were to be taught advanced navigation. We flew in Avro Anson aircraft and our training comprised map reading, cross-country flights and wind vector determination by the 3-drift method using a bomb-sight. On occasion we would undertake bombing practice out over the sea where the targets were moored.

My flying from RAF millom was without incident though after the lapse of 50 years my memories from the short 6 weeks or so I spent there are scant. I do distinctly recall two minor episodes. One of experiencing a severe nosebleed whilst lying prone on the nose of an Anson whilst working out a 3-drift wind and secondly of sunbathing on the dunes next to the airfield and then swimming in the Irish sea in lovely warm summer weather conditions.

William Weighton

MR L WHITE – RAF CARK 1943

I arrived late in 1943 to take a radio operators course before going on to an Operational Training Unit prior to joining my bomber squadron down in Lincolnshire. By the end of the War I simply wanted to forget about my experiences and so when I was offered the chance to apply for my flying log book I declined the opportunity. Because of this my course date at Cark is only a guess but I believe it began in November and lasted about three or four weeks. We trained in a special 'wireless room' and in the air. I was not a natural airman to begin with and suffered a great deal with airsickness but by the time I arrived at Cark I was almost over that which was as well because the routes we took on the several flights I endured as part of my course involved a rough ride in the turbulent air above the Lakeland hills.

Of the area, I recall the local fishermen; their horses pulling cars piled with nets as they made their way to the sands and the village pubs that always offered a warm welcome and good beer.

Mr L White - 1996

THE STORY OF GRIFF AND MAY

BY BARBARA HUXLEY

This is the story of Flying Officer Oscar Griffiths and May Chatten. I am Barbara Huxley, daughter of May, and the story that I wish to tell has emerged over a period of several years. It is a story of World War II, 100 Squadron and the effects of war on two young people back in 1944 and, indeed others including myself, in recent years. The generosity of many people who have helped me to unearth the story of my mother and her wartime love for Oscar Griffiths has truly astounded me. I wish to thank all those who have given me, and May, their time and memories.

One evening in April 1943, LACW May Ledson was on duty in the control tower at Number 10 Air Gunnery School, RAF Walney Island. On the floor above was a young pilot Flt Sgt Oscar Griffiths (also known as Griff) who hailed from Swansea in South Wales. Griff came down the stairs and, spotting May at work, introduced himself. May had not previously met him, but had typed his name onto Pilot Duty Lists many times. They chatted to each other and Griff asked May if he could walk her back to WAAF quarters at the end of their duty shift. The spark was ignited, and what follows is, quite literally, history. During what remained of Griff's tour at Walney Island, they spent much of their free time together. Romance blossomed as Griff and May walked around the island coastline together singing as they crossed the Barrow bridge to the Imperial Hotel for crumpets with jam (no butter, there was a war on!) Griff, who had completed pilot training in Canada, was awaiting posting to Bomber Command and gained further experience by flying aircraft at Walney as part of the Air Gunners training programme. Griff's expected posting was soon ordered, and he and May were sad at their parting but like many young couples of that era, they made plans to marry at the end of the war. Griff was posted to RAF Hemswell Heavy Conversion Unit (HCU) to convert to the Lancaster, and then on to RAF Waltham (Grimsby) and 100 Squadron in 1944. Whilst at HCU Griff was commissioned as a Pilot Officer and he telephoned May asking her how she would like to go out with an officer. May was thrilled and Griff made the long journey back to Walney to see her again. Then it was operational duty with 'The Ton'. May had sewn his 'wings' onto his tunic and had included the words "Happy Landings" on the reverse side of the brevet - the aircrew toast! Griff and May wrote regularly to each other and met whenever they managed to obtain a 48 hour pass. May loved receiving his letters – poetic and beautifully written. In one he told May that he "would always return to her and bloom again like a rose after the winter". Waltham was a happy base and Griff loved the crew that he had formed when joining 'The Ton'. In October 1944, May travelled to Waltham but Griff was detailed to fly an operation at short notice. So it was in the early hours of the morning when he returned that they were able to walk the lanes around Waltham and Holton-le-Clay in the wind and the rain. Griff's crew, also out walking after their return, spotted them and made the comment that it was a "...terrible night Skip" to which Griff's reply was "...it's a lovely way to spend an evening!" Griff and his crew went on to fly 29 'ops' and were due to be rested at 'tour-ex' after the next mission.

On Christmas Eve 1944, Griff and his crew took off for Cologne, on what should have been their final 'op' in their usual aircraft ND388 HW-G. The bombing run was good. The target of Nippes railway yard was hit, and Griff turned for home. Tragedy then struck and the aircraft, after being hit by flak, was destroyed with all crew members lost. They are all at rest in the beautifully kept War Cemetery at Rheinberg in Germany. May had lost her Griff, and it would seem that this should be the end of our story but there is more to come.

May was de-mobbed in 1946, and the pain of losing Griff eased with time. May married Harry and had two children, myself and brother Ian. Subsequently five grandchildren were followed by a great grandchild with another on the way. May was happy, but she didn't forget Griff. When May was in her seventies, she visited Walney Island again taking me along. She found that the control tower, where she had met Griff all those years ago, was still standing. She went in and the memories came flooding back. May walked around the Nissen huts and what remained of the other wartime buildings, half expecting Griff to appear out of the mists of time. It was in 2011, some 67 years after May had first met Griff, that she received a letter from Michael Gill. Michael's mother, who died when he was just five years old, was also a WAAF based at Walney and he was searching for people who might have known her. May had known her, and subsequently met Michael to tell him what she knew of his mother. Michael was a mine of information about Walney and this kindled a desire in May to find out more about the loss of HW-G and whether Griff had any relations still living. May told me much more about her time with Griff, and this spurred me to become involved with May's search. I began the search via Jim Stewart of BBMF and also made contact with two members (Brian Hulme and Dr Keith Ellis) of 100 Squadron Association. The help and assistance from the Association has been unstinting and so generous. I then made contact with The Swansea Evening News and their reporter, Geraint Thomas, ran a full page spread on the story of May and Griff. The very next day I received a phone call from a school friend of Griffs, Gordon Dennis, and he in turn helped me to make contact with Wynne

– a nephew of Griffs. A letter then arrived from Howell Evans, a mid-upper gunner from 100 Squadron (and later 550 Squadron at North Killingholme), who had also flown on the Cologne raid that fateful Christmas Eve of 1944. He provided crystal clear details of the events of that night. Both Gordon and Howell, now in their late 80's, regularly write to and phone May. Surprisingly, the three people who made the initial contact with us were Howell, Wynne and Gordon - HW-G! Other people who have got in touch include the sister of Griff's mid-upper gunner [James Islwyn Morgan] and the secretary of the chapel in Gowerton attended by the Griffiths family (who also sent us a photograph of a memorial plaque to Griff in the chapel). It would really complete the circle of fate if May were able to find someone who actually knew, and can remember, Griff during his time with 100 Squadron at Waltham*.

WAAF E.G. OWEN 2102560
BY HER SON, MIKE GILL

In October 1942, my mother Edith Owen (nee Gill) enlisted into the WAAF. She was posted to 10 AGS at Walney Isle in November that year. Her role at 10 AGS was that of 'Flight Mechanic Airframes', repairing Ansons.

I don't know much about my mother's service life, as sadly she passed away when I was 5 years old, but do I remember my father telling me she lied about her age in order to enlist. This was confirmed when I applied to the RAF records office in Gloucester for a copy of her service record. This confirmed what my father had told me, as it stated her DOB as 1924, whereas she was born in 1927!

Over the years, I have managed to contact a few WAAFs that served at Walney who knew my mother. One such WAAF was a good friend called May Ledson. May worked in the control tower so didn't see my mother on a work basis, but she saw her often when they rehearsed for one of the many shows that were put on at Barrow. May sang and performed on stage and my mother was involved in the costumes and scenery. One such show was called 'Bang On' and was performed at His Majesty's Theatre at Barrow, commencing in May 1945. May told me they had a great time at these shows and they had many a laugh backstage with the cast and crew. This show must have meant a lot to my mother as she kept a lot of photos, cuttings and tickets (signed by her friends) relating to it. My mother, stayed at 10 AGS until December 1944 when she was then posted to 11 AGS and was de-mobbed in September 1946.